Shakespeare and Digital Pedagogy

RELATED TITLES

Teaching Shakespeare with Purpose: A Student-Centred Approach
Ayanna Thompson and Laura Turchi
978-1-4725-9961-2

Shakesfear and How to Cure It: The Complete Handbook for Teaching Shakespeare
Ralph Alan Cohen
978-1-4742-2871-8

Studying Shakespeare Adaptation: From Restoration Theatre to YouTube
Pamela Bickley and Jenny Stevens
978-1-3500-6864-3

Shakespeare and Digital Pedagogy
Case Studies and Strategies

*Edited by Diana E. Henderson
and Kyle Sebastian Vitale*

THE ARDEN SHAKESPEARE
LONDON • NEW YORK • OXFORD • NEW DELHI • SYDNEY

THE ARDEN SHAKESPEARE
Bloomsbury Publishing Plc
50 Bedford Square, London, WC1B 3DP, UK
1385 Broadway, New York, NY 10018, USA
29 Earlsfort Terrace, Dublin 2, Ireland

BLOOMSBURY, THE ARDEN SHAKESPEARE and the Arden Shakespeare logo are trademarks of Bloomsbury Publishing Plc

First published in Great Britain 2022

Copyright © Diana E. Henderson, Kyle Sebastian Vitale and contributors, 2022

Diana E. Henderson, Kyle Sebastian Vitale and contributors have asserted their right under the Copyright, Designs and Patents Act, 1988, to be identified as the authors of this work.

Cover image: William Shakespeare collage by Oscar Vila Nieto
(© Lebrecht Music & Arts / Alamy Stock Photo)

All rights reserved. No part of this publication may be reproduced or transmitted in any form or by any means, electronic or mechanical, including photocopying, recording, or any information storage or retrieval system, without prior permission in writing from the publishers.

Bloomsbury Publishing Plc does not have any control over, or responsibility for, any third-party websites referred to or in this book. All internet addresses given in this book were correct at the time of going to press. The author and publisher regret any inconvenience caused if addresses have changed or sites have ceased to exist, but can accept no responsibility for any such changes.

A catalogue record for this book is available from the British Library.

A catalog record for this book is available from the Library of Congress.

ISBN: HB: 978-1-3501-0971-1
PB: 978-1-3501-0971-1
ePDF: 978-1-3501-0973-5
eBook: 978-1-3501-0974-2

Typeset by RefineCatch Limited, Bungay, Suffolk
Printed and bound in Great Britain

To find out more about our authors and books visit www.bloomsbury.com and sign up for our newsletters.

CONTENTS

List of Figures *viii*
Notes on Contributors *ix*
Foreword Michael Witmore *xiv*

Introduction 1
  Diana E. Henderson and Kyle Sebastian Vitale

Part One Teaching Academic and Digital Literacy

1 Shakespeare Students as Scribes: Documenting the Classroom through Collaborative Digital Note-taking 13
   Cyrus Mulready

2 The *Shakespeare CoLab*: A Digital Learning Environment for Shakespeare Studies 25
   Rachael Deagman Simonetta, with Melanie Lo

3 'Read[ing] Strange Matters': Digital Approaches to Early Modern Transnational Intertextuality 38
   Kathryn Vomero Santos

Part Two Teaching Diversity, Equity and Inclusion

4 (Early) Modern Literature: Crossing the 'Sonic Color Line' 51
   David Sterling Brown

5 Diversifying Shakespeare: Intersections of Technology and Identity   63
   Meg Lota Brown and Kyle DiRoberto

6 The British Black and Asian Shakespeare Performance Database: Reclaiming Theatre History   78
   Jami Rogers

7 Reading Interculturality in Class: Contextualizing Global Shakespeares in and through A|S|I|A   89
   Eleine Ng-Gagneux

Part Three Teaching with Traditional and Modern Archives

8 Shakespeare at Basecamp   107
   Kristen Poole, with Jake Cohen

9 The *Victorian Illustrated Shakespeare Archive*: Art to Enchant   120
   Michael John Goodman

10 Student-Curated Archives and the Digital Design of Shakespeare in Performance   132
   Marcia McDonald, Joel Overall and Jayme M. Yeo

Part Four Teaching in Hybrid and Online Learning Environments

11 Performance and Pedagogy: The Global Shakespeares Online *Merchant of Venice* Course   147
   Sarah Connell

12 Translating Shakespeare from Scene to Screen, and Back Again: Digital Tools for Teaching *Richard III*   159
   Loreen Giese

13 Dividing the Kingdoms: Interdisciplinary Methods for
   Teaching Shakespeare to Undergraduates   172
   Jaime Goodrich, with Sarah Noble

Part Five Teaching in Web 3.0

14 Mapping the Global Absent in Shakespeare: Lessons
   Learned from a Student–Faculty Collaboration   185
   John S. Garrison, with Ahon Gooptu

15 Shakespeare Reloaded's *Shakeserendipity* Game:
   Pedagogy at the Edge of Chaos   198
   Liam E. Semler

A Closing Note   211
   Diana E. Henderson and Kyle Sebastian Vitale

Index   213

FIGURES

1.1	'Evil Kermit' Shakespeare Meme (created by Dylan Perles).	20
4.1	Voyant word cloud: *Titus Andronicus*, Act 4, Scene 2 entire dialogue and stage directions as corpus.	55
5.1	Screenshot of TouchCast presentation.	66
7.1	Screenshot of pie-chart display page.	95
7.2	Screenshot of the Points of Reference data display and 'Shakespeare' sub-field of the Yohangza Theatre Company's *A Midsummer Night's Dream* data-map.	98
8.1	Screenshot of Basecamp site, showing discussion threads; University of Delaware, 5 May 2021.	109
8.2	Screenshot of Basecamp progress view; University of Delaware, 5 May 2021.	111
11.1	An example question from the *Merchant* course.	150
14.1	Filtering a search for absent elements in *The Merchant of Venice* on the mapping tool.	191
15.1	Screenshot of *Shakeserendipity* online game page for *Richard III* with four flipped cards.	205

NOTES ON CONTRIBUTORS

Meg Lota Brown is Professor of English and Director of the Graduate Center at the University of Arizona. She is the author or editor of four books on early modern women, Donne, the global Middle Ages and Renaissance, and early modern discourses of conscience. She has published articles on Renaissance science, art and theology; Reformation politics; and authors from Christine de Pizan to Shakespeare. She has won nearly every major teaching award at the university.

David Sterling Brown – a Shakespeare and premodern critical race studies scholar – is Assistant Professor of English at Binghamton University. His anti-racist research, which centres on how racial ideologies develop and circulate in and beyond the early modern period, is published or forthcoming in *White People in Shakespeare*, *Literature Compass*, *Shakespeare Studies*, *Hamlet: The State of Play*, *Shakespeare Bulletin* and other venues. His forthcoming book project examines how whiteness and anti-blackness operate in Shakespearean drama.

Jake Cohen is a student at the University of Delaware, where he majors in Spanish Studies and Art. He plans to enter the field of graphic design.

Sarah Connell is the Assistant Director of the Women Writers Project and the NULab for Texts, Maps, and Networks at Northeastern University. Her research focuses on text encoding and computational text analysis, medieval and early modern historiography, and pedagogies of digital scholarship. Her current projects include a text encoding and analysis project on early modern narratives of national identity and an NEH-funded seminar series on research and teaching with word embedding models.

Kyle DiRoberto is Associate Professor and Program Director of English at the University of Arizona, Sierra Vista. She has received funding from the NEH and the Folger Shakespeare Library and has published articles and chapters on early modern literature, sacred parody, social media and pedagogy, gender studies and, most recently, 'Corrupting the Curriculum: The Abject in J-Horror, Shakespeare, and Digital Games'. She is completing a book entitled *The Rhetoric of Reformation: Robert Greene in Context*.

John S. Garrison is Professor of English at Grinnell College. He is co-editor of three essay collections, *Sexuality and Memory in Early Modern England: Literature and the Erotics of Recollection*, *Ovid and Masculinity in English Renaissance Literature* and *Making Milton*. His books include *Shakespeare at Peace*, *Shakespeare and the Afterlife* and *Performing Gods in Classical Antiquity and the Age of Shakespeare*.

Loreen L. Giese is a Professor of English at Ohio University, where she teaches in-person, hybrid and online courses in Shakespeare, early modern English drama, and composition. The author of books and articles on Shakespeare, teaching Shakespeare and early modern English courtship and marriage, she is working on a monograph that examines practices of and attitudes toward marital cruelty in late sixteenth- and early seventeenth-century London court cases.

Michael John Goodman is a postdoctoral researcher based at Cardiff University's Centre of Editorial and Intertextual Research. He is the director of the Victorian Illustrated Shakespeare Archive, an online open-access resource that contains over 3,000 illustrations taken from Victorian editions of Shakespeare's plays. Michael is currently writing his first monograph, *Shakespeare in Bits and Bytes*, which explores how the digital can help students and the public engage meaningfully with Shakespeare.

Jaime Goodrich is Professor of English at Wayne State University and Principal Investigator for 'Dividing the Kingdoms: Interdisciplinary Methods for Teaching Shakespeare to Undergraduates'. Her favourite pedagogical approaches involve the public humanities (e.g., service-learning projects, student-generated digital editions). She has published two monographs: *Faithful Translators: Authorship, Gender, and Religion in Early Modern England* (2014) and *Writing Habits: Historicism, Philosophy, and English Benedictine Convents, 1600–1800* (forthcoming, autumn 2021).

Ahon Gooptu is an undergraduate student at Grinnell College, majoring in English and theatre and dance, with a concentration on technology studies. Originally from Kolkata, India, he identifies as a theatre artist, writer and educator. Gooptu's intersecting identities as a queer immigrant artist of colour inform his work, including his approach to interpreting plays and sonnets in the Shakespeare canon.

Diana E. Henderson (co-editor), Arthur J. Conner Professor of Literature at MIT, is author of *Collaborations with the Past: Reshaping Shakespeare Across Time and Media*, *Passion Made Public: Elizabethan Lyric, Gender, and Performance* and many scholarly essays. She edited *Alternative Shakespeares 3* and the *Concise Companion to Shakespeare on Screen*, and (with James R. Siemon) co-edits the annual *Shakespeare Studies*. She works as a dramaturg and served as PI for the edX course 'Global Shakespeares: Re-creating *The Merchant in Venice*'.

Melanie Lo teaches in the Division of Continuing Education and the departments of English and Women and Gender Studies at the University of Colorado, Boulder. Her research focuses on early modern emotion and digital humanities pedagogy.

Marcia McDonald is Professor of English at Belmont University. Areas of research and publication include Shakespeare's plays of the 1590s, comic theory and cultural materialist and ecocritical approaches. She has served in university administrative roles and writes on issues in English studies and higher education.

Cyrus Mulready is Associate Professor of English at the State University of New York at New Paltz. He is the author of *Romance on the Early Modern Stage: English Expansion before and after Shakespeare* (2013) as well as essays on Shakespeare, book history and literary genre. His teaching has been recognized with awards at SUNY New Paltz and the University of Pennsylvania, including a statewide SUNY Chancellor's Award for Excellence in Teaching (2017).

Eleine Ng-Gagneux is a Research Fellow at the National University of Singapore. Her research interests are in intercultural Shakespeare performance and translation, and digital archiving. She is an editor (English) of the Asian Shakespeare Intercultural Archive. Her publications include 'Beyond words: performing translation in Ong Keng Sen's intercultural *Lear Dreaming*', in *Shakespeare Jahrbuch* (2020), and 'Rojak Shakespeare: devouring the self and digesting otherness on the Singapore stage', in *Eating Shakespeare: Cultural Anthropophagy as Global Methodology* (2019).

Sarah Noble currently teaches choir in the Berkley School District in Berkley, Michigan. She earned a MM in Choral Conducting from Yale University and a BM in Music Education from Wayne State University. While at Wayne State, Noble developed an interest in interdisciplinary studies, partly due to her involvement in 'Dividing the Kingdoms'. She was a member of the student focus group and then went on to develop the service-learning assignments for each of the *King Lear* modules.

Joel Overall is Associate Professor of English at Belmont University in Nashville, Tennessee, where he teaches courses in writing, digital rhetoric and sound and persuasion. His work has appeared in *Rhetoric Society Quarterly* and *Rhetoric Review*.

Kristen Poole is the Ned B. Allen Professor of English at the University of Delaware. She is the author of numerous books and articles on early modern literature, including *Supernatural Environments in Shakespeare's England: Spaces of Demonism, Divinity, and Drama* (2011), and is co-editor (with Thomas Fulton) of *The Bible on the Shakespearean Stage: Cultures of Interpretation in Reformation England* (2018). She is the General Editor of the digital Routledge Encyclopedia of the Renaissance World.

Jami Rogers trained at the London Academy of Music and Dramatic Art (LAMDA) and holds an MA and a PhD from the University of Birmingham. Previously she worked for PBS and at WGBH-TV/Boston on PBS's *Masterpiece Theatre*. She is an Honorary Fellow at the University of Warwick. Rogers was Principal Investigator on a research project into diversity in television drama for Equity. Her monograph *British Black and Asian Shakespeareans: Integrating Shakespeare, 1966–2018* will be published by Arden Shakespeare in 2022.

Kathryn Vomero Santos is Assistant Professor of English and co-director of the Humanities Collective at Trinity University in San Antonio, Texas. Her cross-historical research explores the intersections of theatrical performance with the politics of language, empire and racial formation in the early modern period and in our contemporary moment. She is currently writing a book about embodied practices of live translation and co-editing an anthology of Borderlands Shakespeare plays.

Liam E. Semler is Professor of Early Modern Literature in the Department of English at the University of Sydney. He is editor of *Coriolanus: A Critical Reader* (2021) and *The Early Modern Grotesque: English Sources and Documents 1500–1700* (2019). He is author of *Teaching Shakespeare and Marlowe: Learning versus the System* (2013) and co-editor (with Gillian Woods) of the *Cambridge Elements 'Shakespeare and Pedagogy'* series.

Rachael Deagman Simonetta teaches in the English Department and the Division of Continuing Education at the University of Colorado, Boulder. She studies early British literature and specializes in designing elegant learning solutions for the twenty-first century.

Kyle Sebastian Vitale (co-editor) is Associate Director of Temple University's Center for the Advancement of Teaching, where he supports student learning and faculty professional development. His work on literature, theology and teaching is published or forthcoming in *Religion and Literature*, *Christianity and Literature*, *Pedagogy*, the *Edinburgh History of Reading* and the *Palgrave Handbook of Academic Professional Development Centers*. He loves teaching about writing, literature and learning. Soli Deo gloria.

Michael Witmore was appointed the seventh director of the Folger Shakespeare Library in July 2011. He was formerly Professor of English at the University of Wisconsin-Madison, and before that he served as Associate Professor of English and Assistant Professor of English at Carnegie Mellon University. Dr Witmore earned a BA in English at Vassar College, and an MA and PhD in rhetoric at the University of California, Berkeley.

Jayme M. Yeo is Associate Professor of English at Belmont University in Nashville, Tennessee, where she researches emotional communities and political theology in early modern literature. She also writes on politically engaged pedagogy. Her work appears in *Literature and Theology*, *Exemplaria*, *Teaching Social Justice through Shakespeare* and elsewhere.

FOREWORD

Michael Witmore

This collection speaks to the current state of pedagogy in the digitally engaged classroom. Its subject is a particular domain area – the various works, adaptations and reformulations of Shakespeare. As such, this volume serves as a snapshot of current and past work, but also – as in so many things digital – as a placeholder in a field that is developing within and alongside the humanities.

It would be an understatement to say that both the humanities and the digital are in flux. Each is operating in a changed world, changed most obviously both by a global pandemic and a long overdue reckoning with racial inequity and injustice. Within higher education and in research libraries, we are witnessing a series of new pressures building on the humanities. What kind of life, community and culture is served by humanistic education? Who benefits and who pays? As institutions and educators move into this changed world, they see both challenges and opportunities. I hope that readers of this volume get a view of both. While no survey of digital pedagogy can be comprehensive, this collection provides insights into a series of valuable case studies, but also gives readers a sense of what is on the minds of students and practitioners. Now more than ever, it is at the level of practice that the humanities must find its way in a changed world. The focus on practitioners and pedagogy, then, is a welcome complement to more theoretical work that has been done in this space over the past five years.

My own perspective on the overlapping circles of 'Shakespeare' and 'digital' began to take shape in the early 2000s as a faculty member, and has developed yet further during my time as Director of the Folger Shakespeare Library. In the latter role, I have been struck by how quickly digital media and computational thinking have found their footing in a research library and cultural institution. We had the good fortune to recognize early on that digital media would be a key area in which experts, students and the public encountered Shakespeare and then engaged with the staggeringly complex legacy that his works represent. The transformation of the texts of the Folger Shakespeare Editions into a piece of software – deeply encoded, massively addressable, queryable through an API – felt like a step down a path that would involve people with the texts in new ways. But it also felt as though we needed better questions to pose with our students and the public: what happens when users can interact with the texts of these plays and poems in new and largely self-directed ways? What are the relevant paths that learners will take as they find new ways of accessing textual and collections materials? What do we owe students who must still learn the basics of humanistic inquiry – contextualizing their own experience of words, patterns and objects – in an informed and meaningful way?

Think of this collection as a partial view of the horizon as it is visible now. The work here shows a range of practitioners using Shakespeare as a test case for larger pedagogical problems – problems and opportunities that we regularly negotiate in classrooms. And as many great teachers will tell you, the challenges we face in classrooms are precisely the ones we face in life. How do we make sense of history, memory and experience when none of these comes fitted out with ready explanations? How, day after day, do we rise to the challenge of living in community in a diverse and democratic society? For its emphasis on *practice* and its commitment to further engagement, I look to this work as a harbinger of things to come. We can be grateful that so many talented thinkers and teachers put their minds to the question of pedagogy and have asked us to view it in manifestly new ways.

Introduction

Diana E. Henderson and Kyle Sebastian Vitale

Overview

When we first discussed this book idea in 2017, we had no idea how drastically its mission would transform. Then, we were looking to remedy a perceived gap in the literature: the absence of a substantial volume dedicated to gathering, theorizing and sharing the state of digital approaches to teaching Shakespeare. Isolated teaching essays existed in a scattershot manner across journals and volumes devoted more generally to the digital humanities or 'Digital Shakespeare', but few addressed patterns, coherence and gaps amongst our teaching approaches, nor did they add up to a truly inspiring 'user's guide' for instructors.[1] As a Shakespeare specialist (by chance and necessity turned digital humanist) and an educational developer, both with ample teaching experience, we felt that the field was behind in its self-reflection and potential for collaboration. With the number of texts separately devoted to teaching Shakespeare, early modern literature and digital pedagogy continuing to swell, the time was ripe to assess where 'Shakespeare digital pedagogy' had arrived, and – a question we thought would be intriguing and exciting, but relatively docile – where it was heading.[2] Our original move thus responded to Peter Kirwan's observation in *Shakespeare and the Digital World* that 'the speed at which new technologies are adopted does not always leave time for *pedagogical* reflection on how and why they are being used' (2014: 58). A well-planned volume could do just that: collectively reflect on emergent digital projects, tools and technologies in Shakespeare, defamiliarize our teaching a little so as to see it afresh and provide a kind of 'timestamp' on Shakespeare and digital pedagogy in the early twenty-first century that describes what we've been thinking and where we think we are going. And then the pandemic of 2020 happened.

Our original aims persist in this volume, which we hope can provide a kind of map of approaches and habits of mind that are developing internationally in Shakespeare classrooms. Like any map, it selectively provides a big picture while suggesting ways forward. Each chapter blends theory and reflection on Shakespeare and pedagogy with practical descriptions of digital projects or approaches (including, in many cases, the processes involved in building and sustaining those projects) and adoptable materials (assignments, syllabi, webpages and more). Our mapping metaphor extends into chapter structure itself: each chapter follows this introduction's organizational schema, offering an overview of its project, a description of its creation and component parts, an exploration of intended and resulting student learning, and useable objects and takeaways for application.

But the world has also changed, dramatically. As Hotspur observed all too pertinently, 'Diseasèd nature oftentimes breaks forth / In strange eruptions; oft the teeming Earth / Is with a kind of colic pinched and vexed / By the imprisoning of unruly wind / Within her womb' (*1H4* 3.1.26–30). SARS-CoV-2 raced around the world in the early months of 2020, shuttering our social lives, imprisoning us inside our homes, pinching and vexing our best efforts to continue semesters and develop new projects. The disease continued, as the northern hemisphere's summer of 2020 saw fatal spikes in COVID-19 and autumn saw countless colleges and universities close down after the briefest of reopenings. Across the world, instructors were forced to engage students through computers alone: 'emergency remote teaching', we rightly insisted on calling it, in contradistinction to the types of deliberately developed online learning projects captured here. Teachers worked frantically to maintain quality of content and assessment, learn (or learn more about) new digital tools such as Zoom and Canvas and incorporate those tools into existing curricula. An already difficult academic job market stalled with the economy, and prospects for early career scholars grew even more precarious. In the United States, continued social unrest resulting from the deaths of George Floyd, Breonna Taylor, Ahmaud Arbery and others burgeoned into a global anti-racist movement underscoring the need for more fundamental, systematic reforms in support of Black lives and other marginalized groups; and furore over the handling of the pandemic and the November 2020 presidential election only exacerbated existing tensions in and beyond the classroom. In what felt like both years and a single night, our volume was no longer simply documenting a new history of digital tools. Instead, we were now crafting a users' guide for the desperate, a paradoxically urgent reflection, maybe even a vision for how to keep doing our work in a CAT 5 cultural hurricane . . . and how to rebuild after the dams burst.

Shakespeare and Digital Pedagogy thus became, like its subject, many things: another visit with Shakespeare, a fascinated exploration into what does and does not change in our understanding of the world, and a committed, even anxious, striving to find ways to practice restorative acts within a context of ruinous possibilities. The volume is divided into five sections which span traditional and emergent conversations in Shakespeare Studies, but more importantly name skills and spaces that are deeply in flux at this moment, crying out for attention and direction: Teaching Academic and Digital Literacy; Teaching Diversity, Equity and Inclusion; Teaching with Traditional and Modern Archives; Teaching in Hybrid and Online Learning Environments; and Teaching in Web 3.0. We hope that the essays in all these sections can act both as imaginative spurs and reassuring maps for you: reminders of either favourite places or places you've wanted to visit along with the vehicles to get there, invitations to move in new directions and suggested routes and bridges that can help you on your journey.

The year 2020 vexed the world, and a wide swath of the world is in our volume: we embrace writers and perspectives from across the United States and its borderlands, Wales and England, Singapore and Australia, with their topics further expanding the map to consider performances from Italy to Korea. We welcome new teachers and senior scholars, experienced digital humanists and first-time technologists, with a touch of perspective from administrators and students themselves. Many contributors drew on their experiences with the 2016 Folger Shakespeare Library initiative *Teaching Shakespeare to Undergraduates*, a grant programme and summit conference amounting to what became this book's central emphasis.[3] As a leader and innovator in digital approaches to Shakespeare, the Folger's DNA is all over this book and we are privileged to have opened with some reflections from its Director, Dr Michael Witmore.

Shakespeare wrote that 'True hope is swift, and flies with swallow's wings' (*R3* 5.2.23). As widespread vaccination began in 2021, we continued to yearn for greater understanding of one another, and trusted that education could find timely new means to provide transformative experiences for our students. To be in education is to believe that transformation for good is possible, and to choose hope every day you teach. We hope this book supports your choices in whatever season it reaches you and maintains its value beyond, perhaps even offering wings for flight.

Description

After providing an overview of a digital teaching project, tool or approach, each chapter then explores its development and central features. In designing the volume's five sections we looked to emphasize traditional strains in Shakespeare pedagogy while pointing to emergent dimensions: the first such unit, 'Teaching Academic and Digital Literacy', embodies both these impulses. Essays by Mulready, Simonetta and Lo, and Santos emphasize the classic tools of Shakespearean study including textual editing, critical print analysis and annotation, alongside newer skills such as text encoding, showcasing how digital tools can adroitly host and further age-old practices. As higher education and the digital world continue to transform, these essays point to the need to continue training students in rigorous critical awareness, responsible creative practice and effective synthesizing of ideas.

The next two sections explore new dimensions of traditional themes in Shakespeare studies. 'Teaching Diversity, Equity and Inclusion' asks how digital approaches can further student understanding of human diversity, societal hierarchies and affective experience through Shakespeare's international adoption. Essays by Brown, Brown and DiRoberto, Rogers, and Ng-Gagneux offer philosophies, databases and approaches that both celebrate and challenge current intercultural understandings of Shakespeare, helping to expand student conceptions of the works' socio-political value. Part Three, 'Teaching with Traditional and Modern Archives', likewise takes up one of the places where Shakespeare has long lived and been taught – the archive – and asks how digital approaches can deepen student understanding of the archive as cultural object and maker of meanings. Poole, Goodman, and McDonald, Overall and Yeo offer new archives and new approaches to special collections, helping students understand the relationship of structure to meaning and inviting them to become co-creators in new meanings.

The final sections look to dynamic technologies in the immediate present and future – and their more promising pedagogical uses. Part Four, 'Teaching in Hybrid and Online Learning Environments', responds most directly to the pandemic and to what for many became the new normal, as it delves into ways instructors have innovated and found effective means to deliver Shakespeare instruction over the internet. Essays by Connell, Giese and Goodrich explore practices that range from sharing digital notes to constructing fully online modules; they also demonstrate the urgent need to keep building humane, engaging and intellectually challenging dimensions into hybrid and remote teaching. Our final section, 'Teaching in Web 3.0', looks to the future. By 'Web 3.0' we designate recent chatter about the internet's long-anticipated realization of even greater openness, connectivity and user-friendliness. This coming phase relies more on semantic understanding and appears more ubiquitous across devices and platforms. For us, Web 3.0 suggests teaching and learning opportunities that place education, creation and construction more fully into the hands of students.[4] Essays by Garrison and Semler showcase student digital creation at its finest, emphasizing new forms of discovery in Shakespeare based on user decisions and serendipity. In the projects described by these chapters, students and users have an expanded relationship with the creation of knowledge, which hints at a movement toward even more project-based and interactive approaches to Shakespeare down the road.

A word on scope. On the one hand, these collected essays touch on the wide range of Shakespeare's corpus and educational legacy, working with plays from across the past century's generic subdivisions of comedies, histories, tragedies and romances/late works. They often address similar themes and tools, such as representation or online modules (sometimes even writing about intersecting projects or citing one another), and as often carve out original spaces with invitations for further inquiry. They also expand beyond higher education, discussing how tools and approaches can benefit high school settings (Semler and Goodrich particularly); in some cases, they were also co-constructed with the aid of high school student partners. Several essays address the new opportunities for independent learners afforded by digital platforms. All these elements point to valuable partnerships, public outreach and shared goals across education levels that we should take more seriously, even as they reaffirm the dominance of the plays in the study of Shakespeare.

On the other hand, several blind spots give us pause. Despite some attention to poetics and metrics embedded within the projects described, none of the non-dramatic poetry is foregrounded here. This derives in part from an alternative emphasis on the new opportunities to understand and enact multimedia performance that digital pedagogy affords, and in part from the dominant role of general and non-major education which tends to focus on well-known plays. Furthermore, 'gen ed' or core classes are often perceived as areas demanding pedagogical innovation, as well as being more likely to receive the kinds of institutional support which sustained digital projects require. Linked with these institutional conditions are the broader cultural tendencies towards multimedia and visual learning that characterize the digital era, especially post-YouTube and a discernible diminishment in many students' interest in reading per se; such changes have also offered important new opportunities to reach non-traditional and differently abled audiences. At the same time, Shakespeare's predominance in his time through the sonnets as well as his potential hand in other playwrights' works (and vice-versa) suggest that more historically situated approaches to his works may better serve some novice learners than we have yet had time to learn.

Similarly absent in an explicit way are religious topics, although some do appear embedded within historically engaged projects (such as Connell and Goodman describe). If not simply one result of having a necessarily limited set of contributions, this may speak as much to the challenging wider conditions currently facing Religious Studies within the academy as it does to Shakespeare pedagogy, especially given the renewed turn to religion in early modern studies. Additionally, this seeming lacuna may in some measure derive from particular sensitivities involving religion as an affective and personal as well as intellectual domain, considered potentially explosive when transmitted across media – albeit other aspects of identity and nation formation arguably can be just as divisive. In this regard, we are also acutely aware of the dominantly Anglophone bias of this collection, especially at a moment when new translation studies and global Shakespeares projects have paved the way for a major reimagining of the field. In an important sense, the types of projects described by Ng-Gagneux and Rogers represent the vast possibility and future promise of digital pedagogies truly transforming Shakespeare classrooms the world over. At present, the economic expense of infrastructure for sustaining digital projects means that they tend to congregate in wealthier nations; moreover, imperial legacies involving Shakespeare mean that other topics and authors may locally serve more urgent needs, politically, culturally and educationally. Nonetheless, we hope to see, and encourage, more attention to projects focusing on the global South and indigenous populations.

After 400 years of global circulation, Shakespeare is as broad a topic as humanity itself, and readers will doubtless find more omissions and more fascinating inclusions than we address here. What reading and editing these essays showed us, beyond curricular and research agendas, is how richly and graciously Shakespeare's body of work continues to invite human inquiry, development, critique, longing and modality to play out across it. As our essays in turn bless and levy heavy charges against Shakespeare the artist and cultural object, we are reminded of the values of honest engagement and frank discussions in preference to the erasure of uneasiness or of the complexities of the works' historical legacies. These chapters reveal new ways in which digital strategies enable us to help address persistent questions, in our own diverse cultures and times.

Student learning

These essays offer much by way of new information, data sets and findings that may be of value to researchers, students and Shakespeare aficionados. At the same time, we are primarily interested in showcasing the gains in actual student learning these projects afford, which is a subject each essay takes time to address vis-à-vis their digital approach. In these segments, instructors share direct student quotations, excerpts from assignments and their own observations, all indicating developments in their students' grasp of concepts, histories and most importantly their sense of themselves as learners and scholars (see Brown for a deep dive into teaching identities).

It is here that the volume acknowledges and moves past the ongoing tensions between discipline-based teaching and the movement towards supposedly evidence-based teaching practices. Where recent studies like Freeman et al. (2014) and Deslauriers et al. (2019) potentially signal deeper student learning in active, engaged classroom activities over the traditional lecture, disciplinary pushback points to the benefits of many kinds of inherited teaching practices. The co-authors, a professor and scholar of Shakespeare and a faculty developer, might be perceived to sit on either side of this aisle. Yet our experience editing this volume together proved time and again our ability to find shared ground and accept each other's perspectives. Indeed, shifts in the debate seem to indicate more commonality emerging internationally.[5] We realized while editing that all too often a different set of terms for the same goals creates gossamer barriers, easily pulled down with additional dialogue.

The volume's essays themselves bear out this observation. On the one hand, contributors such as Semler incisively call out what he calls 'SysEd':

the experience of evaluative and assessment-based teaching expectations as constraining and numbing. On the other hand, a bevy of authors including Goodrich, Poole and Giese underscore the value of project-based teaching approaches of the kind endorsed by educational developers, which actively invite students to create, problem-solve and reflect on their learning progress. Connell too writes eloquently of the benefits of immediate feedback and practice for summative assessment. In a middle territory, Mulready mounts an effective defence for the intellectual benefits of lecture (a point of tension in professional discussions of teaching effectiveness) when incorporated with engaged notetaking practices. We admire and affirm all these perspectives, and by capturing this tension we applaud all instructors who find any and every way to help their students learn.

Recognizing that student learning and its assessment come in many forms, the volume evinces several interesting patterns.

- First, the theme of serendipity arises across many essays. Some projects embrace it as a teaching practice (Semler) while others appreciate its role in developing a project (Garrison). In a year that almost drowned us in the unexpected, this theme reinforces that effective teaching cannot be an entirely planned activity, but thrives on unanticipated occasions which, if managed well, can deepen the relevance of course content and open up unplanned, and rich, discussions or discoveries.
- Second, students are hungry to create. Many chapters detail projects that invite students into 'authentic' learning, or practices that mimic those of the working world. Simonetta and Lo and also Santos's students pursue actual textual editing and encoding; McDonald et al.'s students build a functioning and culturally significant performance archive; Brown et al.'s students craft new digital objects to better visualize character arcs in the plays. These scenarios give students more control over their learning and help them understand its relevance to their present and future lives. Many of these arrangements developed far enough that students themselves became co-creators of the projects/tools, and several of those students contribute to the essays in this book (see those anchored by Poole, Goodrich and Garrison).
- Third, colleges and universities (and the schools and departments within them) benefit when they continuously and supportively scrutinize their commitments to student learning, and also sponsor more experimentation and public discussions about its improvement. All too obvious as we edited was the uneven landscape of institutional support for experimental teaching projects on university campuses. Some instructors had ample resources while others appeared to toil alone; some feel embattled by their own institutions while others are

excited to align their projects with the university's mission. Our inclusion of administrative experiences provides some perspective on organizational leadership, and emblematizes the much-needed call and response we need to practice in higher education.

Application

Shakespeare pedagogy continues to pursue its traditional conversations in new ways while remaining flexible enough to integrate incoming challenges. This book is itself what we share as our 'Application'. What practices or approaches might re-enliven a reader's teaching as we work ourselves out of the shadows of 2020 and beyond? What other patterns and assumptions run through these essays that may be worthy of development? Where could the students of our readers gain from more actively engaged or project-based learning? What educational systems, institutions or departments need support and affirmation that (now more than ever) resources invested in teaching are worth the risk?

We invite readers the world over to mine the Application sections of these chapters for ideas and sources for preparation and use in their classrooms, adapting them to local conditions. We encourage greater collaboration and coordination across institutions and projects, to promote both greater diversity and coherence amongst ourselves – an approach acknowledging yet moving beyond traditions of romanticized individualism that have sometimes hampered the humanities in larger political and institutional contexts. Contributors have shared materials intended to be adopted, adapted with permission from the creators and reflected on to spark new ideas. Some sections focus more on curricular objects; others share processes and tips for effective project management. We also acknowledge that for each single essay included here, hundreds of instructors around the world are creating comparably innovative and enriching experiences for their students. To draw on the project concept described in Garrison's chapter, their absence is but a statement of their impactful presence around the world.

Our focus on praxis and application invites us, as we invite you, to consider 'what's next?' for the teaching of Shakespeare's works. Post-pandemic, in our new era of racial strife and at the cusp of new virtual realities, how should we be helping our students learn? This volume's contributors offer some clues: more nuanced approaches to identity-based discussion, increasingly more authentic online experiences and the preservation of worthy traditional classroom practices are all great places to start. Quieter affirmations abound too: like the contributors of *Teaching Social Justice Through Shakespeare* (Eklund and Beth Hyman 2019), ours see vital connections and opportunities for students in the local community. As the pandemic lifts and we take up communal practices new and old, what does Shakespeare's corpus have to say about the interpersonal and the neighbourhood, and how can digital means expand our ability to explore these concepts with students? Intersecting with those ideas, 2020's political landscape emphasized our fracturing, polarizing polity. It reminded us how susceptible we are to our own emotions and opinions. We must learn and ever relearn how to speak with one another; how can the strife and recovery throughout Shakespeare's work, and the new collaborative means available in digital tools, help students practice and forge empathetic, reasonable and real dialogue together?

And to what are we 'applying' these digital pedagogies? To student minds, yes; to Shakespeare's oeuvre, to conceptions of the humanities, to our curricula, to ideals of justice and equity, we say yes. We also suggest that new frontiers are coming, ones we as yet do not see, but that compel us to make ready through rigorous reflective practice and sober postures toward our teaching. Resisting those persistent cries that demand we defend our field of inquiry's intrinsic worth, yet hearkening to that inner voice which reminds us we have the opportunity to enrich students' lives every day, how can we improve the ways we teach and better support the people we teach? Whose needs remain to be heard, how can we best mobilize our resources – and then, where shall we journey together?

Notes

1. L. Ellinghausen (2017) offers a diverse and helpful 'Contemporary Media' area, albeit focused on one genre and tending toward the teaching of adaptations. Recent volumes by A. Hiscock and L. Hopkins (2007), G. B. Shand (2009), R. Gibson (2016), A. Thompson and L. Turchi (2016) and H. Eklund and W. Beth Hyman (2019), while helpfully inquiring into classroom practices, do not address digital pedagogy holistically. Conversely, J. Jenstad, M. Kaethler and J. Roberts-Smith's 2016 volume addresses new media but does not address pedagogy.
2. For recent examples, see G. Dujardin, J. Lang and J. Staunton (2018); J. Stommel, C. Friend and S. Michael Morris (2020); and H. Bell and A. Borsuk (2020).
3. To learn more about the 2016 Folger programme (directed by Dr Kathleen Lynch, Folger Institute), visit https://folgerpedia.folger.edu/Teaching_Shakespeare_to_Undergraduates,_Folger_Institute_NEH_microgrant_project_(2016-2017). A central project from that programme, *DIY First Folio*, forwards Shakespeare and digital pedagogy through an interactive virtual printing house (https://www.folger.edu/shakespeare/first-folio/diy-first-folio). More about *DIY First Folio* can be found in M. Brown, R. Niles and S. Redick (forthcoming).
4. In defining Web 3.0 as a new relationship to modality and creation we are thinking along similar lines to W. B. Worthen (2008), whose concept of 'Shakespeare 3.0' traces the successive media stages through which Shakespeare's works are adapted and received.
5. See G. Dujardin, J. Lang and J. Staunton (2018).

References

Bell, H. and A. Borsuk, eds (2020), 'Teaching Shakespeare: Digital Processes', *Research in Drama Education* 25, no. 1: 1–7.

Brown, M., R. Niles and S. Redick (forthcoming), 'Implementing the Do-It-Yourself First Folio: from concept model to pedagogical tool', in A. Silva and S. Schofield (eds), *Digital Pedagogy in Early Modern Studies: Method and Praxis*, Iter Press (online).

Deslauriers, L., L. McCarty, K. Miller, K. Callaghan and G. Kestin (2019), 'Measuring Actual Learning Versus Feeling of Learning in Response to Being Actively Engaged in the Classroom', *PNAS* 116, no. 39: 19251–7.

Dujardin, G., J. Lang and J. Staunton, eds (2018), *Teaching the Literature Survey Course: New Strategies for College Faculty*, Morganton: West Virginia University.

Eklund, H. and W. Beth Hyman, eds (2019), *Teaching Social Justice Through Shakespeare: Why Renaissance Literature Matters Now*, Edinburgh: Edinburgh University Press.

Ellinghausen, L., ed. (2017), *Approaches to Teaching Shakespeare's English History Plays*, New York: Modern Language Association of America.

Freeman, S., S. Eddy, M. McDonough, M. Smith, N. Okoroafor, H. Jordt and M. Pat Wenderoth (2014), 'Active Learning Increases Student Performance in Science, Engineering, and Mathematics', *PNAS* 111, no. 23: 8410–15.

Gibson, R. (2016), *Teaching Shakespeare: A Handbook for Teachers*, Cambridge: Cambridge University Press.

Hiscock, A. and L. Hopkins, eds (2007), *Teaching Shakespeare and Early Modern Dramatists*, New York: Palgrave Macmillan.

Jenstad, J., M. Kaethler and J. Roberts-Smith, eds (2017), *Shakespeare's Language in Digital Media: Old Words, New Tools*, New York: Routledge.

Kirwan, P. (2014), Part II Introduction, in C. Carson and P. Kirwan (eds), *Shakespeare and the Digital World: Redefining Scholarship and Practice*, 58–63, Cambridge: Cambridge University Press.

Shakespeare, W. (2002), *Henry IV, Part 1*, B Mowat and P. Werstine, eds, New York: Simon and Schuster.

Shakespeare, W. (2009), *Richard III*, eds B Mowat and P. Werstine, eds, New York: Simon and Schuster.

Shand, G. B. (2009), *Teaching Shakespeare: Passing It On*, Malden, MA: Wiley-Blackwell.

Stommel, J., C. Friend and S. Michael Morris, eds (2020), *Critical Digital Pedagogy: A Collection*, Washington, DC: Hybrid Pedagogy, Inc.

Thompson, A. and L. Turchi (2016), *Teaching Shakespeare with Purpose: A Student-Centred Approach*, New York: Bloomsbury Arden Shakespeare.

Vitale, K. (forthcoming), 'The Virtual Printing House: Exploring Early Modern Book Construction', in M. Pangallo and E. Todd (eds), *Options for Teaching the History of the Book*, New York: Modern Language Association of America.

Worthen, W. B. (2008), 'Shakespeare 3.0: Or Text versus Performance, the Remix', in D. Henderson (ed.), *Alternative Shakespeares 3*, 54–77, London: Routledge.

PART ONE

Teaching Academic and Digital Literacy

1

Shakespeare Students as Scribes

Documenting the Classroom through Collaborative Digital Note-taking

Cyrus Mulready

Overview

In the courses I teach I think carefully about the 'digital capital', as I imagine it, spent with my students each term: the limited resources of time, patience and buy-in for working with digital projects that students bring to my classes. Each technology introduced comes with both a benefit and a cost. While having had great experiences using language datamining tools such as the indispensable Voyant, for instance, I know that the learning curve in implementing it with my students (both conceptually and technologically) will be steep. It will take a full period to introduce the tool, perhaps more if we have any connectivity problems in class that day. If I use the tool for an assignment, I will have to commit hands-on time either in class or, more likely, outside of class to help them troubleshoot issues that arise. I may have students without the proper computing equipment or who have poor internet access that will make using the tool outside of class a challenge. I may have to devise an alternative assignment for them.

Especially in my Shakespeare I and II classes, upper-division undergraduate courses where the material already introduces significant challenges for many of my students, I have learned to measure and maximize the opportunities any technology can afford against those costs. I choose tools that will be somewhat familiar to my students, that emphasize collaboration (one of my learning objectives) and that focus more on the outcome of the assignment than the medium of its completion. That is not to say that the technologies themselves are unimportant – I still think of them as key to the successes in my classroom – it's just that they play a supporting role in the coursework I assign.

The 'Digital Scribes' project detailed here is just such an example. First, working in groups of three to four, students compile a synthesized record of lecture and discussion topics of the day (or days) they are assigned. They collaborate in a wiki or shared document (using a platform like Google Docs) and post their notes to a central place where they can be shared (or linked on my class's digital syllabus). Second, the students take the original notes and 'remix' them into something new: a video, a multimedia webpage, a podcast, a collection of memes, an alternative lesson plan, a series of tweets, or other social media expressions. Finally, the students submit a brief reflection and group evaluation of the project through a brief questionnaire I set up in Google Forms. Through this project, students engage in meaningful collaboration with one another toward a larger collective class project (documenting the lectures and discussions of our semester). Students also exercise their own creativity and vision in shaping the notes, and in this way the notes serve as an outlet for students to make and remake the course. All of this is carried out in a fairly 'low cost' technological format. The assignment could be done in analog or by using simple word processing software, but making the project digital enhances both the collaborative and creative dimensions of the assignment.

The Digital Scribes assignment also serves to support more traditional pedagogical approaches and outcomes in the Shakespeare classroom. Note-taking may be the least considered student activity in the college English classroom. But research demonstrates that it is a form of writing worthy of attention; students, even some of the best, struggle when it comes to synthesizing the materials we want them to learn. Students typically capture only 20–40 per cent of main ideas in a lecture, according to the research of Kenneth Kiewra, a scholar who has written extensively on college student note-taking (2002: 72). He concludes there is 'strong evidence that recording lecture notes leads to higher achievement than not recording notes', and that 'higher quantities of note taking are associated with higher achievement (and vice versa)'. His solution is simple: 'students must record more notes and instructors should take steps to increase lecture note taking' (Kiewra 2002: 72). Some of the most basic tools of digital pedagogy (wikis, collaboratively authored online documents) allow for an easy way to bring more focus to note-taking. Further, the Digital Scribes assignment incorporates a dimension of active learning into the lecture-based classroom.

The lecture may be a maligned classroom teaching strategy, yet it remains a popular format for Shakespeare courses. There are good reasons for this: budget restrictions make higher enrolments the reality for many institutions around the world, and since Shakespeare is often a course (as it is at my institution) that Education as well as English majors must take, larger lecture-format courses are necessary to accommodate student demand. Moreover, Shakespeare is a topic that can attract students from outside these majors and, especially at larger universities, may be taught in lecture format to accommodate those students. Indeed, even at some institutions where large class sizes are not the norm, Shakespeare remains a popular enough author that the course can be offered as a general elective. Such was the case at the University of Pennsylvania, where the Shakespeare courses I served as a Teaching Assistant typically enrolled well over 100 students.

My inspiration for this assignment came from a blog post Mark Sample wrote in response to rising class enrolments due to budgetary cuts at his institution. He posed a set of questions that I suspect many ask in the face of ongoing financial pressures in the academy: 'How do I continue to engage students on a dialogic plane when they, my department, and institutional momentum all expect me to lecture as the most efficient means of delivering content?' (Sample 2009). The solution Sample proposed was to 'exploit technology that my students are already familiar with, but in different contexts' (Sample 2009). Thus, in thinking how to adapt the collaborative note-taking assignments I learned about from Sample (as well as others in the Digital Humanities [DH] community; see Croxall 2010), I wanted the process and project of note-taking to reflect the various forms of work that my students and I undertake in the classroom. I also wanted to allow students the opportunity to make their own contributions, either during class or in reflecting on the class session, as a means of opening the course to their interests in the material. Further, as a practical outcome, I wanted the notes to be useful documents that could serve as a record of what we had covered. They would provide material that other students could review if they missed class, or to assist them in preparing for essays and exams.

In recent years, my Shakespeare courses have also become 'hybrid': three credit hours of instructional time is dedicated to the traditional, seated classroom, and one additional credit hour involves virtual or online education. Hybrid listings have gained wide acceptance on our campus as they transform courses previously taught on a three-days-per-week schedule into two-day courses, freeing limited classroom space and giving faculty more freedom to shape their courses through work done outside the classroom. Hybrid courses also had the unintended effect in the spring and fall semesters of 2020 of facilitating easier transitions to remote teaching, as seated class time nearly disappeared on our campus due to the pandemic. When I began teaching Shakespeare in the hybrid format, I wanted to develop assignments and activities for my students that truly (and non-trivially) integrated the work they were doing in the classroom with that done for the online portion of the class. Furthermore, I sought to devise clear ways to make technology in the classroom an asset. Although aware of the research on the disruptive influence of laptops, tablets and other digital tools in the classroom (Mueller and Oppenheimer 2014), I also know that these tools, when used properly, can indeed help our students learn.

I saw the notes assignment contributing towards a central goal I set for the term: to 'build a community of Shakespeare scholarship that enhances our understanding of his work', as I say in my learning outcomes. Even in my relatively small class (thirty to forty students), building that community can be a challenge because Shakespeare coursework captures the full range of students we find in our upper-division offerings at New Paltz: Education majors, commuters, first-semester transfer students, creative writing concentrators, theatre students, as well as English Literature majors with advanced critical reading skills. Early in my teaching career, I found this course especially difficult to teach precisely for this reason; it also seemed Shakespeare brought to the surface many students' insecurities about their position in the major or institution. But as I integrated this notes assignment as well as collaborative blogging (where students exchange written responses with one another in small groups), they became more forthright with me and their classmates through their shared struggles. These collaborative assignments provided a structure for the students to learn the material, as well as to find a foothold in the department and institution.

Description

From set-up to completion, the Digital Scribes project involves a high level of student autonomy and little labour from me as instructor. I have two main digital projects, as mentioned: a collaborative blogging space for my students, and the Digital Scribes assignment. With the blogs, I assign groups based mainly on major affiliation (I have found that grouping together students in our Elementary Education programme, Creative Writing, Adolescence Education, etc. helps create productive writing groups). The Digital Scribes groups, however, are self-selected: I send around a sign-up sheet at the start of term after introducing the assignment and allow students to create their own groups or sign up for a play that interests them most. Working within these groups, students collaborate in class (oftentimes helpfully disrupting the seating arrangements students fall into). I ask for a week's turnaround for the notes themselves, but allow a longer period for the remix that they construct after completing the notes. I encourage students to use Google Docs for its simple collaboration functions and will sometimes look at drafts of notes before they are submitted for posting. When I receive their work, I simply create a link to the document in our Wordpress-based syllabus. While students will occasionally consult with me on their remixes, usually with this portion of the project they are excited to reveal their ideas to me at the end – their submissions are often accompanied by proud emails saying that they hope I enjoy their work.

I have experimented with other versions of these activities over the years, including having students live-tweet class discussions, assigning them single days, weeks of class or entire plays and instructing groups to create 'enhanced' notes for the class that include video clips, links to scholarly articles, or other secondary resources. Despite some variations in approach, important underlying steps have remained: having students first document and synthesize the class and then, in some way determined by their group, recreate and develop the work of the day.

The main challenges presented by this project have always been with collaboration, especially as my classes typically have a mixture of on-campus students and commuters. It can be difficult for these students to find the time to meet together and discuss the various project components. In recent years, however, as our campus has adopted Google Suite applications for our students and they have become more adept at using collaborative functions within Google Docs (as well as other social media and video chat), these problems have largely subsided. The last time I used the assignment, I heard no complaints and saw no evident issues with students' ability to work together. As detailed below, the potential for seamless collaboration is one of the advantages of carrying out this project in a digital framework.

Nevertheless, the highly volatile landscape of technological tools can create more daunting challenges (as shared elsewhere in this volume). Over the years, commercial applications on which I have built various iterations of the assignment have gone from free to pay-only, radically altered their features or went out of existence entirely. I once used Storify, a wonderful platform for building digital 'stories' through a wide range of social media tools. My students created interactive class maps that integrated video, images, tweets and other related content. Storify then ceased operations in 2018, and no similar tool has replaced it. Likewise, I used an application called 'GroupTweet' that allowed my students to contribute through a centralized web domain tweets that were then routed through a single account (@NPShakespeare), which others could follow. When the number of accounts for the course exceeded their user limit, however, they required me to shift from the free to educational (paid) model, which ended my ability to use that technology. I have learned from these experiences that it is best to adapt tools that are supplied and supported by my campus (for us, Google, Blackboard, Office365, CampusPress), even if these options do not fit my or my students' needs as well as I would like.

In my years using this assignment I have found some delightfully unintended consequences. For example, it offers students an opportunity to reimagine the class work we do more creatively than I could have anticipated. They find valuable resources on the internet or through other research. It has inspired, for instance, students to include a host of Shakespeare-inspired memes and to create their own based on our class discussions. A more personal example was my discovery of *She's the Man,* a film based loosely on *Twelfth Night* that our students adore but which passed my notice when released in 2006. Through this notes project, I first became aware of the film and have since integrated it into discussions of social constructions of gender when teaching *Twelfth Night*. I have learned of several other innovative productions through this project as well, including some web series and other small-scale productions; my favourite of these is the brilliant New Zealand adaptation of *Much Ado* shot as a confessional vlog (*Nothing Much To Do*). Bringing these materials into my classes as starter points for discussion – a clip from the recent *Twincidents*, a YouTube-based adaptation of *Comedy of Errors*, for instance – marvellously sets up discussion of the identity issues raised in that play. In other words, the assignment allows my students to collaborate with me as I continue to develop my teaching.

Student learning

Generally in my classes I try to present various kinds of writing opportunities as a way to expose students to a range of possibilities for engaging with Shakespeare's works (analytic, creative, synthetic). Thus, the first outcome for Digital Scribes is for students to synthesize clear, well-organized notes from the contributions made by different members of the note-taking group. Humanities students sometimes underestimate the value their writing skills hold outside the academy. I suspect this derives from the emphasis we place on academic essay writing, a genre that does not have clear corollaries beyond the classroom. Many of our students are exceptional writers, and an assignment like this one allows them to demonstrate and hone skills that they discover are more transferrable. As several career studies and humanities advocacy groups have noted, humanities students show great aptitudes for 'organizing information from multiple sources' and 'manipulating information and data, using technology where appropriate' (British Academy 2017: 10); they are able 'to feel at home with mountains of incomplete, haphazardly organized information ...[and] distill everything into a few powerful insights' (Anders 2017: 37). My assignment taps into an underutilized opportunity for further developing these aptitudes. It also demonstrates to students who do it well that they have a valuable set of analytic writing skills.

The assignment cultivates other valuable skills sets as well. The use of digital pedagogical tools can fit more broadly within educational practices of 'Problem Based Learning' or 'Authentic Learning', activities that engage students in work more closely mirroring what they might find in 'real world' contexts. This body of knowledge teaches us that collaboration, on its own, is not enough to guarantee high levels of learning (Bozalek et al. 2013: 630–1). Any teacher knows this – give students a meaningless group task and they will produce lacklustre results. But combining 'authentic' work with a collaborative process is much more effective. Therefore, I work to frame the notes as having a practical outcome: they are shared with the class through our digital syllabus and are understood, at some level, as an official record of what we accomplished that day. Further, the element of implicit collaboration between the lecturer and student creates another layer of responsibility: students understand that they are trying to convey and document their expertise developed through the course back to the professor.

For these reasons, the Digital Scribes assignment tends to engage students in effective forms of collaboration. This outcome also, importantly, gives a degree of freedom to the students as they define and negotiate the roles that the group undertakes. I insert an important piece of accountability for them, a final reflection and group assessment that each student completes through a Google Form that only I see. I ask each student to describe how the work was distributed within the group and whether they believe it was divided fairly. I also ask students to reflect on whether the project helped them take better notes or changed the way they thought about their class notes.

Although the rudiments of this assignment could be carried out using just pen and paper, I believe that it is the digital collaborative dimensions of the assignment that enable the 'Writing' and 'Creating' outcomes of my course. I have come to think of my classes (to borrow a concept from digital studies) as a multi-use platform rather than an individual application. I give brief lectures on textual history and social context, engage in close readings, discuss bigger issues involving gender roles, politics, sexuality, economic stratification and so on; we view and analyse performance adaptations and discuss the implications of various interpretive possibilities for the plays and poems. To me, the Digital Scribes assignment should ideally reflect and advance the collaboration happening in the classroom. And whether my students ultimately record a podcast, create a multimedia presentation, write a poem or develop a lesson plan for middle schoolers, my sense is that these ideas grow most fertilely in the collaborative interactions that digital tools allow.

This 'remix' part of the project has produced some of my favourite student work to evaluate, as it swerves from the expectations that bog down the argument-driven essay into higher-order operations like creation. Digital responses offer an outlet for aptitudes in certain students that might not otherwise be able to flourish. I recall, for instance, a student who mastered a note-taking app on her digital tablet that allowed her to make illustrations, reformat text and even insert media. A student-produced podcast is possibly my favourite example as it formally captures the conversations I hope students have about Shakespeare outside the classroom. Three students in the fall 2019 course recorded a rich discussion about gender power and politics, following our study of *Twelfth Night* into their considerations of the #MeToo movement and campus sexual consent policies. Technologically speaking, the podcast *Shake it Up Shakespeare* was simply produced (a musical fade-in was as adventurous as it got) but I imagine in future semesters, as students' technological capabilities increase, we will see more elaborate features in these small-scale productions.

Some students have impressive expertise using digital presentation software (PowerPoint, Slides, Keynote), which I choose not to use in my classroom. It is a fascinating (and instructive) exercise to read an account of a class recycled back through this format, and I receive subtle clues about what is working in class through what my students reproduce in their notes. Thus, most of all I appreciate the opportunity to learn something new about my students, myself and even Shakespeare from the feedback loops set up in these assignments.

Students can also recast our discussions through a series of memes and images, some of which they gather from the internet, others of which they create. In recent years, memes have been an especially popular choice for this assignment, perhaps because they allow for a mingling of Shakespeare with a form of visual communication that has become such an indelible part of their culture. In the example below, for instance, the students took the famous 'Evil Kermit' meme and adapted it to the opening of *Henry V* to represent the duplicitous Archbishop of Canterbury.

Student groups for this project almost universally produce notes that are detailed, thorough and well crafted. The remix portion also gives me insights into the ways in which they are developing their understanding of Shakespeare through personal connections to other courses they are taking, elements of popular culture and their own creative pursuits. Many students report that they find the assignment helped them improve their note-taking skills: 'This assignment definitely helped me take better lecture notes. Having the assignment in mind while in class disciplined me to take notes that not only I understand, but my peers understand as well,' wrote one student. Students who consider themselves to be good note-takers often share similar

Act 1, Scene 1, Lines 73-81

FIGURE 1.1 *'Evil Kermit' Shakespeare meme (created by Dylan Perles).*

comments: 'I have a personal style of notes that works very well for me, but rewriting the notes so that they would make sense to everyone gave me a few new ideas to help me take my own notes'. Revising and editing the notes seems to be a key part of the learning process, as students synthesize their work for others in the class.

There are some students, however, who find bearing the responsibility of note-taking a distraction: 'I feel as if my notes were messy and very unorganized because I was worried that I was going to miss something, which ended up making me miss some valuable discussion we had in class'. Especially for students who are conscientious note-takers, the assignment can bog them down in details – something that I see in notes that are almost a transcript of our class (rather than a synthesis): 'I was more focused on writing down every word you said than listening to the discussion . . .'

The way to address this last issue is to encourage students to find other roles and methods for note-taking that allow for more shared work. Some students might excel at synthesizing central points of a discussion into a neat outline, while others can go into more depth in elaborating the details of a close reading. In semesters when I incorporated Twitter in this assignment, I have found that there are certain students who prefer the format live-tweeting to note-taking. I have learned from this assignment that 'notes' can take various forms and remain effective. It may be that there are possibilities with live-capture and voice recognition technologies that could help this assignment evolve in new directions. I can imagine what are now two disparate portions of the assignment fusing into a single multi-media form – a new digital script – that integrates with our syllabus to produce a permanent record of a course each term.

Application

Here is the most recent iteration of the assignment as I present it to my students:

Digital Scribes Collaborative Assignment
Overview:
A 'scribe', in Shakespeare's time and before, was a professional copyist: someone whose job it was to write out (by hand) various documents and to record transactions. In the theater, scribes were an important part of the business. Indeed, it is because of scribes that we have Shakespeare's plays with us today, for it was their job to take the transitory words of the theater and make them permanent.

In this course, the 'Digital Scribes' will do similar work, recording the proceedings of our lectures and discussions and posting them for all to read. Each group will be responsible for documenting a day of our class. The goal of the collaborative notes assignment is to create a record of the work we do over the course of the semester. I anticipate that you will find these notes useful for your assignments, exam, but also, I hope, for your future study and, perhaps, teaching of Shakespeare.

1. Collaborative Notes:

The first goal of this assignment is to produce a detailed synthesis of our discussions and notes from class for the day you are assigned. How you choose to do this is up to your group, but give some careful thought to how you want to present the material. My expectation is that the final document will not be a random collection of notes and bullet points, but a well-edited and thoughtfully structured document of summaries, resources, and notes that brings together our explorations of the day.

2. Class Remix:

In addition to providing a record for the class you took notes in, your group will also be responsible for creatively using the materials from our discussion to produce something that enhances, develops, or even twists our work in class that day. The goal of this portion of the assignment is help you and your classmates think both creatively and in more depth about our class material and expand our understanding of Shakespeare. I encourage your group to have some fun in coming up with your own ideas, but to get you started, here are some possibilities for this portion of the assignment:

- A CrashCourse-style video that summarizes the play and topics we covered in class.
- A podcast discussion of the material that gives further background into the issues that interest you ('Queer Shakespeare', 'Shakespeare and Education') . . . you might even invite guest interviews (Prof. Mulready is available for this!).
- A series of memes that humorously explore the topics of our class.
- A remixed lesson plan that revisits the material we covered and reimagines how it could be taught differently for other age groups (or even for our class!).
- A collaboratively authored essay or story inspired by the topics we have covered in class.
- Create an entry on Genius.com for one of the passages we discussed in class and add commentary based on our discussion (and your further ideas about it).

You may divide the work for this project in any way you choose, but I expect the work for this project to be shared equally by the members of your group. Please complete the Statement of Collaborative Work **once** you have finished with your Class Remix.

Due Dates: Your Collaborative notes are due within a week of your class; your Remix is due one week later (two weeks after the date of your class).

PLEASE NOTE: If you are absent the day you are assigned to take notes, it is very difficult to make up the work. Please make every effort you can to be in class on your assigned days. If there is an emergency and you are unable to come to class, it is your responsibility to talk to me about making up for your missed work.

Below is the rubric I use for evaluating the assignment:

Requirement	Description of an Excellent Assignment
Collaborative Notes	– Notes offer a detailed synthesis of our discussions and main points from class lectures. – Collaborative notes present an organized, well-edited and thoughtfully structured document of summaries and resources for study.
Remix	– The remix demonstrates true *creativity* – the materials from our discussion should be used to produce something that enhances, develops, or even twists our work in class. – The remix should also help the reader engage with more depth about our class material and expand our understanding of Shakespeare. – Although the remix can explore new directions, it should also be clear that the project is rooted in the issues and topics that were part of our class discussion.
Collaboration	– The work of the project should be distributed fairly as determined by the members of the group.
Grammar, Spell-Checking, and Proof-Reading	– Though not necessarily perfect, notes and written materials in the remix are written with correct grammar and usage, are properly punctuated, and are carefully proofread and spell-checked.

Acknowledgements

I am immensely grateful to my SUNY New Paltz students who generously allowed me to share or reference their work in this essay. In addition to those cited in the text, I thankfully acknowledge Hannah Bauer, Zach Percy, Catherine Incledon, Tori Kalberer, Gracie Mackin and Bonnie Simmons.

References

Anders, G. (2017), *You Can Do Anything: The Surprising Power of a 'Useless' Liberal Arts Education*, New York: Little, Brown, and Company.

Bozalek, V., D. Gachago, L. Alexander, K. Watters, D. Wood, E. Ivala and J. Herrington (2013), 'The Use of Emerging Technologies for Authentic Learning: A South African Study in Higher Education', *British Journal of Educational Technology* 44, no. 4: 629–38.

British Academy for the Humanities and Social Sciences (2017), 'The Right Skills – Celebrating Skills in the Arts, Humanities and Social Sciences', London: British Academy.

Croxall, B. (2010), 'Whither Technology in the Graduate English Seminar?', Brian Croxall.net, https://briancroxall.net/2010/07/06/whither-technology-in-the-graduate-english-seminar/.

Kiewra, K. A. (2002), 'How Classroom Teachers Can Help Students Learn and Teach Them How to Learn', *Theory Into Practice* 41, no. 2: 71–80, https://doi.org/10.1207/s15430421tip4102_3

Mueller, P. A. and D. M. Oppenheimer (2014), 'The Pen Is Mightier Than the Keyboard: Advantages of Longhand Over Laptop Note Taking', *Psychological Science* 25, no. 6: 1159–68, https://doi.org/10.1177/0956797614524581

Sample, M. (2009), 'Teaching Technologies for Large Classes', @samplereality, https://www.samplereality.com/2009/05/13/teaching-technologies-for-large-classes/.

2

The *Shakespeare CoLab*

A Digital Learning Environment for Shakespeare Studies

Rachael Deagman Simonetta, with Melanie Lo

Overview

> I am not tall enough to become the function well, nor lean enough to be thought a good student, but to be said an honest man and a good housekeeper goes as fairly as to say a careful man and a great scholar.
>
> *Twelfth Night*, 4.2.6–10

While donning the gown of a mischievous dissembler in *Twelfth Night*, Feste pokes fun at the starving student and interrogates the work of the great scholar. Yet all joking aside, the problems Feste's words suggest – how we might both nourish the good student and make visible the work of the great scholar – undergird the *Shakespeare CoLab* (www.shakespearecolab.org). Housed at the University of Colorado, Boulder, the *CoLab* aims to create digital assignments for Shakespeare courses; develop a digital tool for use in the classroom; and teach students how to make digital editions.

The *Shakespeare CoLab* was built for in-person and online classes, and thus highlights both synchronous and asynchronous pedagogy. Faculty and graduate student teachers use *CoLab* materials in English Department courses; concurrently, instructors and post-doctoral teachers leverage the assignments in online classes offered by the Division of Continuing

Education. Students in our courses learn to annotate William Shakespeare's plays and to publish those annotations on a public-facing website so that they can see the immediate impact of their academic research. Our hope is that the project will generate a digital repository of student data across time that might support future scholarly analysis.

While the *Shakespeare CoLab* is one among countless digital humanities (DH) tools and student annotation projects, our project possesses particular pedagogical value because it is teachable across modalities – that is, the project's pedagogy is equally effective in the traditional, in-person classroom and in an online, asynchronous environment. Instructors teaching online classes in the humanities grapple with how to create well-designed courses that provide rich learning experiences for students without holding in-person conversations. Often, the online discussion board fails to capture the depth and breadth of a face-to-face discussion because open-ended prompts allow students to repeat the observations posted by the first few students. Pedagogical shifts to remote learning in the wake of COVID-19 only exacerbated these issues. With these challenges in mind, we developed a series of sequenced, scaffolded assignments for use as online discussion prompts. The prompts ask students to begin with low-stakes, time-tested exercises such as tracing etymologies and identifying key terms in a close-reading assignment. Once students master these lower-order tasks, the assignments grow in complexity so that by the end of term, the class engages in complex scholarly research to achieve higher-order learning. At the end of term, the sequential posts become public-facing annotations on the *CoLab* website, which is itself a digital edition. The site highlights keywords, and when a user clicks on that highlighted word, a student generated annotation pops up. By participating in these exercises, our undergraduates learn to read and interpret complicated texts; encounter and grapple with the unfamiliar to better understand different perspectives; improve verbal and written communication; undertake original research; increase digital literacy; and participate in active knowledge production.

Description

One affordance of the online digital edition is the free, open access it provides to otherwise inaccessible materials. Teachers at various schools are doing text-editing with their students, often addressing less canonical works that need to be shared. Similarly, the *Women Writers Project*, a long-term archival project devoted to early modern women's writing and electronic text encoding, provides important access to texts that might not otherwise be available. This archival, primarily scholar-oriented project does in fact also show pedagogical potential in its commitment to accessibility, which is a focal point in our pedagogy project as well.

We acknowledge that there is no shortage of digital Shakespeare editions, scholarly or otherwise, available to readers. With that said, the design of this particular project aligns productively with larger initiatives at our institution aimed at leveraging twenty-first-century learning platforms to explore future applications of humanities education. First, a cross-disciplinary team of scholars in English and Theatre are partnering with the Colorado Shakespeare Festival to produce Massive Open Online Courses that are public-facing educational experiences. Second, the College of Arts and Sciences and the *Arts & Sciences Support of Education Through Technology* initiative are sponsoring an 'Innovation Incubator' to promote the use of learning technologies. The *CoLab* is part of this cross-disciplinary collective whose members produce digital, print and multimodal publishing projects that meet academic standards and are accessible to the community.

Our institutional commitments to creating active learning and research opportunities also cross institutional boundaries. One exciting DH endeavour was to integrate *The Merchant Module*, the first residentially-focused iteration of the MITx course appearing in this volume, into an asynchronous class that ran entirely on an LMS. We partnered with Diana Henderson and Sarah Connell to import this experimental, immersive environment of resources for *The Merchant of Venice* into our English Department course available exclusively to online learners. The *CoLab* online class first focused on etymology and close-reading skills and then pivoted to consider how Shakespeare's plays transform from page to stage. We incorporated MIT's 'Director's Chair Annotation' assignment for discussion posts on staging Act 4, Scene 1 of *Merchant of Venice*, in which our students read, analysed and annotated the play while also flexing their creative muscles to imagine designing a performance. We hope that this type of collaborative, cross-institutional annotation creation paves the way for future study of interoperable annotations across digital platforms.

Student learning

Above all, we want our students to learn digital literacy skills so that they have the ability to complete an online course successfully, to use online databases to facilitate research and to engage in the work done by digital humanists. To be sure, many open, accessible texts already facilitate digital learning. The Folger Shakespeare Library provides digital versions of Shakespeare's plays that are available in a free, downloadable format. However, these texts are difficult to use in the classroom because they lack textual apparatuses that provide, for example, important historical or cultural context. Borrowing digital texts from the Folger, the *CoLab* expands the accessibility of Shakespeare's plays by providing explanatory notes generated from original student scholarship.

The project thus contributes to field-wide conversations about the role of the scholarly edition in the digital age. The 2015 MLA Committee on Scholarly Editions describes several possible affordances of the digital format:

> First, [scholarly editions] allow the data in an edition to be used as the basis for other editions, as transcriptions that can be compared using collation tools, as a contribution to a digital repository, and as part of a text corpus that might support quite different types of analysis. Second, digital modalities make it possible to support features such as user annotation, commentary, citation, and the creation of additional layers of editorial information. Third, digital modalities allow edition interfaces to serve as environments for manipulation and exploration of the edition's textual space, so that the user can occupy the role of a contingent editor.
>
> Modern Language Association of America 2015: 1

Along this model, the Folger's scholarly digital editions serve as the basis for the *CoLab* student editions. Our undergraduates then extend the Folger's textual spaces by composing annotations, commentary and additional layers of editorial information; this practice allows undergraduates to occupy the role of an editorial apprentice. *CoLab* undergraduate contributors serve as the scholar-editors who craft each play's textual apparatus through their emendations, glosses and annotations.

Importantly, our mission to foster digital literacy skills connects to our larger belief that, as citizens, students need opportunities to take ownership of the digital spaces and texts with which they interact and from which we ask them to learn. While the *CoLab* provides students with practical skills such as research, writing, editing and web design, we also want students to engage more deeply with questions concerning digital identities and ethics. The *CoLab* draws upon and shares in the ethos of Domain of One's Own initiatives happening across various institutions of higher education; these initiatives strive to give learners and educators tools and spaces to exercise agency over their digital identity. Amy Collier, Middlebury College's Associate Provost for Digital Learning and Domain of One's Own advocate, asks, 'What does it mean to no longer be a passive consumer of the web, but a creator of the web?' (Collier 2016). The *CoLab* transforms students into active editors and creators rather than leaving them to be passive consumers of a web-based text.

Applications

The *CoLab*'s digital pedagogy, born from teaching in online learning environments, connects the practices of textual editing with the digital humanities to transform Shakespeare's text into a student-built and student-edited Open Educational Resource. Students produce written work in areas foundational to Shakespeare Studies, such as etymology, close reading, visual and performance studies, interacting with archives, and analysis of secondary scholarship. The skills and knowledge attained in these assignments enable students to create the textual, intertextual, contextual, dramatic and critical annotations inherent to a traditional scholarly edition of Shakespeare's works (Wilcox 2003: 199). At the same time, the *CoLab* trains students in the principles of textual encoding and web design to create the digital space where those annotations live and where they will be read by other students.

While the *CoLab* has assignments for creating and encoding every annotation subtype mentioned above, here we provide descriptions for the creation of etymological and contextual annotations. These assignments illustrate the *CoLab*'s intensive process of scaffolding – of moving students from small tasks to complex research – to enable digital humanities research in the undergraduate classroom. We conclude by showing how our pedagogy culminates in the process of TEI mark-up that converts student scholarship into student-produced pop-up annotations on the *CoLab* website.

Most aspects of the *CoLab*'s pedagogy take place in digital learning environments, using digital tools and research databases. Students therefore require preparation and training to conduct research using online databases, just as they need training to successfully navigate an LMS in online classes. This training can take place either through online video tutorials or through a classroom workshop for in-person modalities. Prior to assigning the etymology assignment, for example, the residential or online instructor can demonstrate how to search for words and read an *Oxford English Dictionary* (*OED*) entry using the classroom's projector system. Students then execute guided searches that familiarize them with crafting an etymology. In online or hybrid courses, the instructor flips the classroom by recording a video to walk students through the search process, which students watch on their own prior to completing the assignment.

Etymology: single keyword as a digital research foundation

The etymology assignment introduces students to the ways language changes over time while asking them to employ that knowledge in an analysis of how language creates meaning. Students first identify and unpack the meaning of an individual word, and then progress to using that knowledge to produce close readings. By the end of the assignment, students are prepared to create 'textual' and 'etymological' annotations for digital editions.

The first assignment addresses one impediment to teaching Shakespeare in any learning environment: the difficulty of Shakespeare's language. Etymology research facilitates students' basic comprehension of Shakespeare's word choice and serves as the foundation of our pedagogy. Students begin by selecting a word, say from one of Hamlet's soliloquies, that is either new to them or used in a new way. They navigate to the *OED* site, search for their word, and carry out the following tasks based on their findings:

- Identify the text in which the earliest entry for the word appears. After clicking through to the full dictionary entry of the word, identify the word's earliest use and note the text in which the term appears.
- Identify the definition of the word in (or close to) 1604 [the publication date of the Second Quarto: eds.]
- Decide which definition entry fits the word in the context of the speech in which the term appears.

When students complete this process, they realize that words and their meanings can function as evidence to enrich interpretation and that the history behind words adds nuance to how we understand a text today. Ultimately, the etymology assignment teaches students that Shakespeare's word choice shapes the meaning of the play and that literary interpretation depends upon an awareness of what words mean at different stages of literary history. Thus, the *CoLab*'s first assignment integrates technology and pedagogy to foster undergraduate research that stands on the foundations of literary study: knowing what words mean and have meant historically, and analysing a text's content based upon that formal knowledge. The etymology assignment also serves as the first stage for teaching students to 'think like a textual editor'. When students identify moments when they are confused or do not recognize a word's meaning and then excavate that meaning through etymology, they are practising a form of textual engagement geared toward creating a readable and usable text for others.

EEBO: keyword search, contextual exploration and textual comparison

Once students complete the etymology assignment, they become attuned to how a single word creates meaning in the context of its textual moment. From here, students progress from the singular to the multiple, employing several keywords in a research assignment that explores the multiplicity of texts and contexts surrounding Shakespeare's works. The *Early English Books Online* (*EEBO*) assignment introduces students to archival research, techniques in digital liberal arts scholarship, and higher-order connections between Shakespeare's plays and the larger context of the early modern world. Students' success with the *EEBO* assignment is facilitated by the skills developed through an exploration of etymology, a nuanced understanding of close reading and a broader contextual analysis of multimedia culture in relation to Shakespearean performance.

In the *EEBO* assignment, individual students or groups first identify an interesting theme or issue in the play. They then investigate this theme in the *EEBO* archive to better understand how ideas that appear in Shakespeare's plays are dealt with in contemporaneous (and earlier) texts from the period. The instructor might consider specifying the themes, texts or even acts/scenes to investigate. Perhaps students focus on the theme of plants in *A Midsummer Night's Dream* and explore early modern herbals; or students could identify a theme of their choosing that appears in the first act of *Hamlet*. We recommend providing instruction in as many forms as possible to make sure that students have a clear understanding of expectations. Creating written instructions, a video tutorial and going over how to conduct successful searches in-person are all good options to ensure students produce the desired results of detailed contextual knowledge that serves as the basis for a scholarly annotation.

Students begin by learning how to search for texts in the *EEBO* digital archive. Because the archive has moved to Proquest, which may limit accessibility, we guide students to the University of Michigan's Early English Books Online Text Creation Partnership site, which allows access to the open-source version of the archive. From the home page, the site offers five search options: Basic, Boolean, Proximity, Bibliographic and Word Index Search. We recommend beginning with the basic search.

Students choose a theme and brainstorm a series of keywords they believe capture that theme: for example, on the theme of witchcraft in *Macbeth*, 'witchcraft', 'witch', 'magic', 'sorcery' and 'familiar' might all guide their exploration. Students then navigate to the 'Basic Search' tab on the site and enter their keywords in succession into the 'Find' field. We recommend directing students to amend the 'Restrict By Date Range' fields to range from 1473 to 1620 to produce results that most plausibly could have influenced Shakespeare during the period when he was actively writing. Once students become more comfortable with *EEBO*, they can adjust these dates to further refine search results.

When students have entered their keyword and changed the date range, they click 'Search'. Students will see a list of texts in which their given keyword appears. At the top of the page, a 'Sort By' dropdown menu will appear, and we recommend that students choose either the 'Date Ascending' or 'Date Descending' option and click 'Sort Results' in order to have a chronological view of the results. Students can explore keyword results in a specific text by clicking on the 'Results Details' link below each result. The keyword will be displayed in the context of the sentence in which the term appears in the text. A breadcrumb trail will be visible above the contextual snippet that allows the student to click on the specific chapter or section in which the first instance of the text appears. The keyword will be highlighted and an option appears at the top of the page to 'Go to the first matched term'. Once the students select a text, they answer these prompts to connect their chosen keywords to a larger theme in the play:

Please answer the following questions to provide information about your theme and keywords:

- What is your chosen theme? Why did you choose this theme?
- Which five keywords did you derive from your theme?
- Which keyword produced the most results? Which keyword produced the fewest results? If there was variation, why do you think this was the case?
- Which keyword did you choose to explore further? Why?
- How does this keyword connect to the specific play, act, scene, passage?
- Is there a particular type of book that you can identify in which your chosen keyword appears most? If so, what is it? If not, why do you think this is?

Finally, students make connections between the keyword that they chose and the context in which the term appears in their chosen secondary text. Students also analyse how the *EEBO* text's treatment of the keyword connects to the larger theme of the chosen Shakespeare text:

Please answer the following questions to provide information about your keyword as it appears in your chosen secondary text:

- What information about your keyword does your chosen secondary text provide? Provide at least three specific examples.
- How does this information change your understanding of your chosen larger theme? Provide at least three specific examples.
- How does this information change or support your reading of the particular play, act, scene, passage?
- How does this information change your understanding of early modern English culture?

One student's *EEBO* project on Act 1, Scene 1 of *Hamlet* usefully illustrates the results of this research experience in a digital archive. The student focused on the moment when Bernardo asks Francisco how the night watch has gone, to which Francisco responds, 'Not a mouse stirring' (1.1.8). The student expressed interest in this seemingly ubiquitous turn of phrase and its connections to issues of early modern vermin control, which the student demonstrated is a recurring metaphor for political chaos throughout the play. The student searched *EEBO* for the terms 'mouse', 'trap', 'mousetrap' and 'rat'. All these terms, except for 'mousetrap', produced many results, and when she sorted them in descending order, she noticed that one text included all of these terms. The text is a manual, entitled *A Booke of fishing with Hooke & Line*, published in 1590 by Leonard Mascall, that primarily provides instruction on fishing as well as developing means for trapping and destroying animals considered vermin. Fascinatingly, the text describes various methods for catching rats and mice using traps, which the student used to assess Shakespeare's own familiarity with vermin eradication since Hamlet uses his knowledge of rodent behaviour to construct the 'Mousetrap'. This information about trap-design then led the student to analyse Hamlet's own methods for attempting to entrap Claudius by assessing the varied simplicity and complexity of Hamlet's plans in relation to the manual's practical advice concerning vermin-control. Thus, the *EEBO* assignment provides students with a richer understanding of the textual and cultural history of Shakespeare's plays, and prepares students to produce 'intertextual' and 'contextual' annotations using digital tools.

Becoming a digital editor: TEI (Text Encoding Initiative) mark-up

Importantly, the *CoLab*'s annotation creation assignments do not exist in a vacuum, with students simply creating explanatory material divorced from the Shakespearean textual apparatus. Rather, in the final assignments of *CoLab* courses, we ask students to temporarily set aside content, which they have mastered through the annotation assignments, to focus on textual structure. Through this last stage of our pedagogy, students create the text and paratext of a scholarly edition within the digital format of a webpage. As previously stated, a student-generated annotation appears when a user clicks on a highlighted word. Thus the assignments and the website itself hinge on the keywords: for example, the rich information from the *EEBO* assignment could appear when the user clicks on the word 'mousetrap' in a digital edition of *Hamlet*. But to create those highlighted, pop-up annotations, students first need to learn how to mark up a digital text.

For the purposes of this chapter, we focus on how we teach students TEI mark-up as a foundational practice of digital humanities editing. In more advanced courses, the TEI unit would be supplemented by units on CSS (Cascading Style Sheets) and web publishing. But the work of TEI mark-up allows us to introduce students to what we view as a key principle of all editing, but particularly Shakespearean editing: that every act of editing is an interpretive choice, and that any interpretive intervention has to be justified through close reading and evidence. Students already learned this through their extensive scholarly work on the annotation assignments; but we reiterate the lesson as students explore how marking up and encoding textual structures requires interpretive, analytical judgement too.

To teach students the basics of TEI and XML (Extensible Mark-up Language) more generally, we dedicate a unit to the vocabulary and key principles behind a TEI document tree and have students complete homework in learning modules provided by existing resources such as TEI by Example. Our pedagogy for teaching TEI hierarchies and tags is founded on a simple analogy: that TEI represents the structures of a physical book and that the code communicates to a computer the information one finds in the front, middle and back of a book object. This analogy allows students to quickly conceptualize TEI's various tags and to employ those tags in order to mark up Shakespeare's text as a dramatic document (i.e. identify speech prefixes, acts, scenes and lines, stage directions, etc.) and as a scholarly edition with critical emendation.

In this introductory assignment, students have a worksheet containing a TEI skeleton for encoding a dramatic cast list, and their first step is to enter the skeleton into their text editor. The instructor directs them to use their text of *Hamlet* to replicate the print cast list in TEI code. On their worksheet, next to each closed tag, we ask students to offer a short hypothesis regarding what the tags stand for. The skeleton would look like the following for one character:

```
<castList>
<head>         </head>
<castItem>
<role> Hamlet </role>
<roleDesc>          </roleDesc>
</castItem>
</castList>
```

At first glance, the assignment looks like a deceptively simple task of 'fill in the blanks'. However, success at this assignment is not measured by students simply putting Hamlet's name in the right place, but rather by their ability to correctly open and close the tags. If students do not enter their tags correctly, or if they do not observe hierarchies that dictate that a role cannot exist in TEI if a cast item has not been created first, their schema won't be validated. So in this introductory exercise, students set aside the content of the cast list – who the characters are, their relationships to one another, and how the print edition chooses to describe them – to instead focus on the cast list as a structure whose rules need to be followed to be properly represented on a webpage. Once students fully master the structural rules of the TEI document tree by working with TEI skeletons in this way, they can progress to more in-depth tagging and encoding of their annotations through segment analysis.

Our use of segment analysis in our students' digital editions draws upon the work of Kate Singer, who articulates how attributes in TEI allow for more descriptive and interpretive forms of textual mark-up. Singer states that 'TEI's broader language for poetic encoding, particularly when it comes to figurative language, may actually allow for greater creativity and ambiguity in marking poetic features, a tactic that can be quite liberating and helpful to students learning poetic vocabularies, concepts, and interpretive strategies' (Singer 2013). Segment analysis capitalizes on TEI's ability to customize tags and tagging categories, which enables students to encode their close readings and literary analysis. By asking students to revise and condense advanced scholarly research into such customized one- to two-word tags, students employ their skills as literary scholars and attentive readers in order to develop TEI language and engage in editing work that finally fuses their mastery of Shakespearean content and digital literacies.

Once students understand the structure of a tagged text, our segment analysis assignment asks them to think about how they can encode Shakespeare's text to illustrate the close readings and analysis they produced in their original annotation assignments. To start, we ask students to evaluate their previous annotation assignments using the following questions:

- For your etymology assignment: which keywords did you define? Why were they important and how did they create meaning in your chosen scene? Are any of those keywords ambiguous, or do they carry multiple meanings in their use by Shakespeare? Why should a reader be attuned to those multiple meanings?
- For your *EEBO* assignment: what concepts or theme did you choose to investigate? What *EEBO* text dealt with that concept in the most interesting or relevant way given Shakespeare's play? How does the *EEBO* text help us understand Shakespeare's text in terms of politics, science, theology, or any other big picture concept?

Students use these reflections to translate their scholarly research from annotation assignments into the short tag that highlights their chosen keyword for a pop-up annotation. Developing segment analysis tags requires a student to identify overarching concepts or features of the text that require intervention and interpretation to be fully appreciated by a reader. For example, one student noted the astonishing amount of travel in Shakespeare's *Pericles*, and completed various annotation assignments that explored movement in the play and its connections to early modern geography and geopolitics, as well as the play's concern with familial separation. The student's process of revising and translating their travel research into mark-up categories is illustrated below.

KEY TERMS, LIT FIGURES, THEMES, and CONCEPTS	TRANSLATE INTO <seg ana = ""> TAG
travail: n. 'the labour and pain of childbirth'. Interestingly, the term is also used to mean 'the straining movement of a vessel in rough seas', which equates Thaisa's pregnancy and labour with the state of the ship in the stormy sea where she gives birth.	<seg ana = 'travel'> <seg ana = 'movement'> <seg ana = 'ship'> Code example: 'The lady shrieks and, well-a-near, Does <seg ana = 'movement'>fall in travail </seg> with her fear.'
EEBO: map of the Mediterranean *Compare to modern map that shows where they are located in terms of modern geographical knowledge. *Interesting thing for readers: when Pericles is trying to return from Tarsus to Tyre, he shipwrecks at Pentapolis, which is odd because Pentapolis is very far out of the way on the route between Tarsus and Tyre.	Ex. <seg ana = 'map'> Ex. <seg ana = 'travel'> Ex. <seg ana = 'ship'> *My temple stands in* <seg ana='map'>*Ephesus* </seg>; <seg ana='travel'> hie thee thither </seg> *And do upon mine altar sacrifice.*

When the student's annotations and mark-up are encoded into a *CoLab* digital edition with an applied style sheet, 'fall in travail', 'Ephesus' and 'hie thee thither' would each be highlighted and when a user clicked on the hyperlink, a pop-up annotation would appear containing the etymological and contextual information they outline above, as well as actual images of the maps they found through *EEBO*. Even at this advanced stage of textual editing, where this student identified how the plot device of travel demands robust editorial intervention and interpretation to be fully appreciated by readers, we remain rooted to our pedagogical base unit of the keyword. Through segment analysis, students transform the thematic content and figurative meanings of their play into a single word that communicates to the computer that a pop-up annotation needs to appear. We believe that this training in editorial practice, coupled with the previous assignments that focus more explicitly on Shakespeare's plays, provides students with a deeper understanding of early modern literature by educating them in a hands-on digital learning environment.

Acknowledgements

Our essay reflects the pedagogical, research and writing contributions of Nodin DeSaillan, Melanie Lo and Rachael Deagman Simonetta. Much as William Shakespeare himself cooperated with his colleagues, we believe that teaching Shakespeare in the digital age hinges on our collective efforts.

References

Collier, A. (2016), 'What is Middcreate?' *Middlebury Digital Learning*, http://digitallearning.middcreate.net/digital-tools/whymiddcreate/.

Folger Shakespeare Library Digital Texts, https://www.folgerdigitaltexts.org/?chapter=0.

Leuner, K. (2015), 'Markup Theory and Practice with the TEI in ENGL 53.06 "Women's Literature and Technologies of Transmission"', https://kirstynleuner.wordpress.com/2015/06/11/markup-theory-and-practice-with-the-tei-in-engl-53-06-womens-literature-and-technologies-of-transmission-12-130pm-52615-baker-library-dartmouth/.

Modern Language Association of America (2015), 'Considering the Scholarly Edition in the Digital Age: A White Paper for the Modern Language Association's Committee on Scholarly Editions', Web, 2 September 2015, https://scholarlyeditions.mla.hcommons.org/cse-white-paper/.

Northeastern University's *Women Writers Project*, https://www.wwp.northeastern.edu/.

Singer, K. (2013), 'Digital Close Reading: TEI for Teaching Poetic Vocabularies', *Journal of Interactive Technology and Pedagogy* 3, https://jitp.commons.gc.cuny.edu/digital-close-reading-tei-for-teaching-poetic-vocabularies/.

TEI By Example (updated 2020), https://teibyexample.org/.

University of Mary Washington's *Domain of One's Own*, https://umw.domains/about/.

University of Michigan's *Early English Books Online Text Creation Partnership*, https://quod.lib.umich.edu/e/eebogroup/.

Wilcox, H. (2003), 'The Character of a Footnote . . . Or, Annotation Revisited', in A. Thompson and G. McMullan (eds), *In Arden: Editing Shakespeare – Essays in Honor of Richard Proudfoot* [The Arden Shakespeare], 194–208, London: Thomson Learning.

3

'Read[ing] Strange Matters'

Digital Approaches to Early Modern Transnational Intertextuality

Kathryn Vomero Santos

Overview

One of the defining features of the robust teaching editions produced for series such as the Bedford Shakespeare 'Texts and Contexts' and the Norton Critical Editions is the selection of excerpts from texts that Shakespeare seems to have drawn upon in the process of composing a given play. Such inclusion is designed to offer historical background and, ideally, to spark conversation about what the playwright and his audiences may have been reading or listening to at the time that particular play was first composed and performed. Teachers interested in presenting this kind of information to their students might also turn to transcribed and sometimes edited selections found in scattered places online or to print copies of Geoffrey Bullough's landmark 1957 multi-volume collection, *Narrative and Dramatic Sources of Shakespeare*, and revised editions thereof. With these resources, students can begin to get a sense of Shakespeare's process of creation as one that involved actively adapting and appropriating texts that were often non-dramatic and not English.

As (time-)effective as it may be to use such pre-selected passages to situate Shakespeare within a broader textual network, this approach misses an opportunity to introduce students to the early modern printed books themselves and to understand them as material objects and forms of knowledge and storytelling that existed independent of – and that were sometimes more popular than – Shakespeare's texts during his lifetime. What, in other words, are students *not* seeing when they only see the carefully selected and transcribed excerpt in an edition or anthology? How is what they see skewed by Shakespeare and the long shadow he continues to cast? How might students see Shakespeare's process as a writer differently if they have their own encounters with the books he may have been reading? How might we encourage our students to think about intertextuality as a process that is facilitated by material texts, translation and intercultural contact?

Digital tools, I want to suggest, offer several possible answers to these questions, and they provide key access to rare materials for students who would not otherwise be able to consult them. This chapter aims to open up a conversation about how teachers can integrate digital resources and tools in the classroom in order to encourage students to 'read strange matters' – the materiality and the intercultural interactions – that shaped the early modern European literary landscape in general and Shakespeare's writing process in particular.[1] In doing so, I answer Dennis Austin Britton and Melissa Walter's recent call to rethink Shakespearean source study – a field that has largely been cast aside 'based on the notion that its frequent or traditional goal was to find what material Shakespeare used so as to portray Shakespeare's unique genius' (Britton and Walter 2017: 3). In what follows, I propose several pedagogical possibilities for using digital technologies to move beyond such unproductive notions about Shakespeare's inimitable brilliance and instead towards a critical and generative understanding of the intertextual processes in which he participated. The approaches I outline involve using digital facsimiles and tools to read, transcribe and analyse Shakespeare's intertexts, and they are all directed at a shared goal: to decentre Englishness and to resituate Shakespeare's plays within the transnational textual networks that made them possible. Such approaches, I hope, will equip students to see his works as one node – albeit an important one – in a much larger intercultural history that continues to shape and speak to our present moment.[2] As Britton and Walter's collection has shown, 'scholars are exploring the intersections of early modern political, gendered, sexual, and racial subjectivities, conditions of theatrical practice, and the materials from which Shakespeare produced his plays' (2017: 1). With the help of digital tools and technologies, teachers can build on the momentum of a renewed and reframed source study to invite their students to do so as well.

Description

I draw here from the experience of working with my students at Texas A&M University–Corpus Christi, in collaboration with Drs Laura Estill and

Hilaire Kallendorf at the flagship campus of Texas A&M University in College Station, on a digital scholarly edition of Bartholomew Yong's 1598 English translation of Jorge de Montemayor's *Siete libros de la Diana*. A bestselling text in its own right, Montemayor's 1559 Spanish pastoral romance became an important intertext for Shakespeare's *The Two Gentlemen of Verona* and, later, *Twelfth Night*.[3] With the support of a 'Teaching Shakespeare to Undergraduates' microgrant from the Folger Shakespeare Library and National Endowment for the Humanities as well as a grant from the Texas A&M University Initiative for Digital Humanities, Media, and Culture, we designed our intercampus experiment to extend the resources of a flagship research university in the middle of the state to a regional university in the US–Mexico borderlands within the same system.

We chose Yong's translation of Montemayor's *Diana* with a specific goal in mind: to engage students at a Hispanic-Serving Institution in South Texas in a conversation about an earlier contact point between English and Spanish, during the period when the nations who spoke and wrote in those languages were engaged in nation-building and colonial projects that would reshape the land we occupied in present-day Corpus Christi. This was an attempt not to draw a direct line from early modern Europe to our situation in the US–Mexico Borderlands but rather to provide an occasion to interrogate terms like 'Hispanic', to discuss intersecting colonial histories and contemporary language politics and to examine the Spanish roots of the author who has become so closely tied to notions of Englishness and the hegemony of the English language both globally and locally. Although still very much a part of the Western European tradition, a popular early modern Spanish text written by a Portuguese-born author was poised to disrupt the linguistic and cultural hierarchies that we have inherited and often perpetuate in our classrooms. Indeed, as Stuart Gillespie writes, '[t]hat the name Jorge de Montemayor is unfamiliar to students of English literature is a reminder of the standard assumption about Shakespeare that his creativity characteristically takes the form of transforming the material he found in minor, provincial works into the stuff of timeless masterpieces' (Gillespie 2004: 103). The stakes of such assumptions are especially high in the case of early modern literature written in Spanish, which, as William Childers has argued, has been neglected in ways that are 'complicitous, albeit inadvertently, with the marginalization' of the Latinx population of the United States.[4]

Of Shakespeare's 'timeless masterpieces', *The Two Gentlemen of Verona* is probably not at the top of many teachers' or scholars' lists. But the fact that it is the work of a young playwright testing out some of the tropes, plot devices and turns of phrase that would recur in later plays, perhaps in more sophisticated (or indeed insidious) ways, is precisely what makes it interesting for many students and scholars alike. While Bullough aptly described the play as 'a dramatic laboratory in which Shakespeare experimented with many of the ideas and devices which were to be his stock-in-trade and delight for years to come' (Bullough 1957: 210), it is also true that it contains some of the earliest iterations of the sexist, racist and classist threads of intolerance that run throughout his body of work. This uncomfortable messiness is the reason why I invited my students to study this early play in conversation with one of the texts Shakespeare was probably reading as he started thinking about how to dramatize stories for audiences in London during the late sixteenth and early seventeenth centuries. Our digital engagement with Yong's translation of Montemayor's *Diana* occurred in four stages, which I describe below under the headings of observation, transcription, annotation and conversation.

Observation

With the help of a guest lecture by Dr Kallendorf, a scholar of early modern Spanish literature, we began by acknowledging the context and broader popularity of the *Diana* in its own time. We then turned our attention to the digital colour facsimile of Yong's translation that has been made available on Google Books by the Universidad Complutense de Madrid. We reflected briefly on the circuits of translation and transmission that made it possible for us, in South Texas, to access an English translation of a Spanish text currently held in a library in Spain. As a class, we analysed the title page, which in this case had been modified by a past reader, and we read the translator's paratexts, which prompted a discussion about the essential and difficult labour of translation that enabled a wider circulation of texts during this period. We then turned our attention to the processes and practices of early modern print. Rather than simply lecturing about how early printed books were made, however, I invited students to make observations together in small groups and to ask questions about what they could see on the screen. Based on what they noticed about early modern orthographical practices, typefaces, catchwords, signatures and *mise-en-page*, we were able to learn together about the history of printing and the labour of making and selling books.

Transcription

With questions about historical context and textual history in mind, my students were well primed for a presentation about transcription and tagging by Dr Laura Estill, who joined us the following week via Skype, itself a useful digital tool for bringing scholarly expertise into one's classroom that predates the now-ubiquitous Zoom platform. Before describing the transcription tasks ahead, Dr Estill provided a working definition of the Digital Humanities and shared several sample projects to illustrate the wide range of ways digital technologies can serve to enhance humanistic inquiry in general and the study of literature in particular.

For our purposes she introduced my students to TypeWright, a free web-based software tool that uses Optical Character Recognition (OCR) to mechanically generate a transcription from the *EEBO* digital facsimile, which human readers can correct and then encode with a mark-up language developed by the Text Encoding Initiative (TEI).[5] Widely used among digital humanists and librarians, TEI allows for the tagging of key features of printed texts, including italics, drop-caps, inverted letters and form work elements such as catchwords, page numbers and signatures. Dr Estill explained that although transcription and encoding are time-intensive and sometimes mundane practices, they encourage us as readers to slow down, read carefully and engage directly with what we see on the page. A full transcription, in turn, would allow us to use digital tools in order to start asking different questions about linguistic patterns and frequency of words. Finally, she introduced students to the collaboratively composed 'A Student Collaborator's Bill of Rights'. This document allowed her to explain how the students would receive credit for and continued access to the work they completed on this project once it was published on a freely accessible WordPress website that would be hosted by Texas A&M.[6]

While this transcription and encoding work could be done asynchronously, I chose to reserve a campus computer lab for my students so that they would have equal access to technology. Even though it resulted in some unexpected glitches and a substantially reduced speed for TypeWright, working on the same text in the same web-based platform at the same time allowed us to troubleshoot and discuss common – or anomalous – issues together.

Annotation

Once they had transcribed their assigned pages and completed their careful review of a peer's transcription, students then selected words that they thought needed further explanation and organized them into a collective glossary in a shared Google Doc throughout the following week. We worked together in class to access the *Oxford English Dictionary* online through our library's recent database subscription. In addition to sharing in the delights and frustrations of etymology as students examined the histories embedded in individual words, we engaged in conversations about how this activity and digital resource encouraged slower and deeper reading of the text.

Conversation

It was at this point that we finally focused our attention on *The Two Gentlemen of Verona* with a multifaceted familiarity with one of the texts with which it was in conversation. After reading and discussing the play in full, we returned to the scenes in which Julia disguises herself as a boy in order to follow Proteus to Milan and to serve as his page as he woos Silvia. Keeping our transcription of Montemayor's corresponding scene open on their individual devices and rereading it alongside their print copies of Shakespeare's play, students collectively made the following observations about the differences between the two: Montemayor's narrator tells readers in passing that Don Felis (Felix in Yong's translation) forgets his former – but apparently more beautiful – love Felismena when he seeks the affection of Celia after being sent away by his father. Shakespeare's Proteus, on the other hand, justifies the rejection of his betrothed Julia in favour of Silvia – the beloved of his friend Valentine – in a soliloquy that uses a blatantly racist metaphor to describe what he perceives to be a physical difference between the two women when he compares them to one another: 'And Silvia – witness heaven that made her fair – / Shows Julia but a swarthy Ethiope' (2.6.26). For many reasons, this moment gave us pause. How did Shakespeare get here? How did Montemayor's Felismena (the Julia character) go from being described as someone who 'in beautie farre excelled' that of Celia (the Silvia character; Montemayor 1598: F1r) to being described as a black or dark-skinned African in comparison to the 'fair' Silvia? Was it Shakespeare who introduced this racism?

To begin answering these questions, we turned to *EEBO* (with the access provided to me as a member of the Renaissance Society of America), where we located digital facsimiles of the story of Titus and Gisippus as told by Giovanni Boccaccio in the *Decameron* (1353; trans. William Walter, 1525, and Edward Lewicke, 1562) and by Thomas Elyot in *The Boke named the governor* (1531). Although these texts presented the additional challenge of blackletter typeface, students were able to apply their newfound curiosity about and patience with the 'strange matters' of early modern books. With some guidance and assistance from transcriptions made available through the Text Creation Partnership (TCP), they examined the versions of this tale translated and printed in English.[7]

The conclusion that we came to together was that the combination of this triangulated plot line – in which Titus falls in love with Sophronia, the woman his best friend Gisippus is supposed to marry – with that of Montemayor's Felis, Felismena and Celia seems to have complicated matters for the English playwright. Act 5 was no longer as (horrifyingly) clear-cut as one man sacrificing his beloved without her consent to another in the name of absolute friendship, nor was the central conflict as predictable as one man forgetting his beloved and pursuing another. As an amalgam of two plot lines, Shakespeare's Proteus somehow needed to justify betraying not only his friend but also his betrothed with the same set of actions. Through careful and challenging conversation, we determined that the approach the playwright chose to take in weaving these two triangles together was to use the metaphor of racial difference and white supremacist standards of beauty – standards we had seen take shape in Renaissance poetry and prose earlier in the semester – in order to elevate one white woman over the other.

My students and I went on to discuss the fact that, as Kim F. Hall has detailed in *Things of Darkness*, Shakespeare would return to this kind of racist and sexist logic that defines white beauty against blackness throughout this play and in several other plays, including *A Midsummer Night's Dream, Romeo and Juliet, Love's Labour's Lost* and *Much Ado About Nothing* (1995: 1, 22, 69–71, 181).[8] Our conversations were not limited to this moment alone, of course, but it is an example that illustrates exactly how examining Shakespeare's plays in conversation with their intertexts can open up pathways for difficult but necessary forms of close reading. And it was precisely our adoption of a range of digital technologies and literacies that made these conversations possible. By carefully reading *The Two Gentlemen of Verona* in dialogue with the 'strange matters' that Shakespeare read and reshaped in the process of writing it, we acknowledged that we cannot celebrate the play as an early iteration of the things that delight without grappling with the ways in which it also participates in interlocking systems of oppression.

Student learning

As the above description makes quite clear, this multifaceted project took us in some unexpected but ultimately productive directions. Without a doubt, doing this kind of intertextual work with the assistance of digital facsimiles and computing technologies created access to technologies of print that would not otherwise have been possible, and it allowed students to attend to the ways in which literary form shaped and was shaped by the medium of print. Having the opportunity to experience and scrutinize old technology by means of new digital tools, furthermore, also had the effect of estranging modern digital technologies. While working on this project, students reflected on a newfound realization, as well as a frustration, that the platforms that pervade their daily lives are not merely transparent conduits used to communicate and gather information; rather, they are tools designed by humans to create new forms of access while also producing new forms of exclusion and bias. One student even remarked upon the fact that this project made him reconsider the stakes of ongoing debates about net neutrality and elevated his concerns about unequal access to all content on the internet.

In the case of the specific moment from *The Two Gentlemen of Verona* that I described above, students were also able to see that a moment of racism in Shakespeare's text was not merely a single blip on the radar of the past but rather part of a process of race-making and the formation of larger epistemologies of difference whose consequences continue to play out in the present. The ultimate objective of this project was not to devote yet more uncritical attention to Western European literature but rather to use a continental text that was repeatedly translated and transformed in order to decentre England and the English language in our literary histories of the early modern period. This approach emphasized the ways in which the texts that have come to be revered as the crowning achievement of 'English genius' would not have been possible without translation and the transnational circulation of texts and ideas that print technologies enabled.

For my students, studying the mechanisms by which Shakespeare engaged with and reshaped a wide range of texts had other implications beyond the early modern period as well. Although we did this work in the context of a course on Renaissance pastoral literature, students came away from the project with a sense that reading is key to *all* acts of writing, as well as an understanding that adaptation and appropriation are not processes that merely radiate outwards from Shakespeare or other canonical authors.

Application

The version of this project outlined above is admittedly time-intensive. It worked well in a course on Renaissance literature in ways that might not succeed in a course on Shakespeare alone. But I believe it can be modified to meet the various needs of instructors and their students in order to open up fresh and urgent conversations in classrooms while expanding opportunities to engage with early printed texts as they circulated throughout Europe during the sixteenth and seventeenth centuries.

As one possible starting point, teachers could select any intertext that is relevant to a play they wish to explore in more detail with their students or to the theme of their course. Depending on their course goals and available time, teachers might first consider inviting students to read early printed books directly from digital facsimiles and with the help of existing transcriptions that may already be available through the TCP. If a transcription is not yet available or if teachers wish to devote more hands-on time to this kind of assignment, they could arrange for their students to use a familiar word processing programme such as Microsoft Word or Google Docs to create a transcription. Others may choose, as I did, to use TypeWright because it allows students to contribute to a larger crowd-sourced transcription project and gives users a head start by generating a base OCR transcription that requires correction and tagging by human readers. Once a transcription is complete, students and teachers may choose to make their transcriptions freely accessible on an open-access web platform such as WordPress. All of these approaches would achieve the goal of inviting students to 'read strange matters' and to spark conversations that will go far beyond the printed page as well as the screens through which they encounter it.

Below are the instructions I gave to my students as they prepared to use TypeWright to transcribe and encode Yong's translation of Montemayor's *Diana*.

1. Make an account at https://18thconnect.org/typewright.
2. Once you have logged in, visit http://www.18thconnect.org/typewright/documents/311469/edit.
   Note: the link above will not work if you are not logged in.
3. Navigate to your assigned pages using the drop-down menu.
   Note: the page might take a minute or two to load. Be patient.
4. Transcribe/correct existing transcription for the page.
   Do not modernise spelling. Please type exactly what you see on the page.
   Do not normalise punctuation. Please type exactly what you see on the page.
   In the case of a long 's' (which looks like an 'f'), please type an 's'.
5. Once you have finished transcribing a page, please add the basic TEI tags for that page before moving on to the next page. You may access a table of tags by clicking on the 'Optional Markup Guide' in the bottom left corner.

Regardless of the approach a teacher may take in using digital tools and techniques of transcription, response and reflection is key to student learning. I have therefore also reproduced a prompt for a reflective blog post assignment that could serve as a guide for other teachers seeking to assess learning and to engage students in further conversation.

1. How would you describe your experience of transcribing and encoding your assigned pages? What challenges or triumphs did you encounter?
2. In what ways did your experience of this process encourage you to think differently or more consciously about your practices of reading texts in print and digital media?
3. What have you observed or learned about early modern printing practices and the features of early modern books in the process of creating and encoding a transcription of your assigned pages?
4. What new questions or ideas do you now have about how books are made, how they are translated, and how they circulate in physical and digital forms?

The blog responses I received revealed that while some of my students were genuinely excited by the tasks and prompts of this project, others found them quite tedious or technologically challenging. But the range and variety of their experiences indicated that the primary value of this assignment was in its capacity to prompt several new ways of thinking about texts and students' relationship to them. As I hope to have illustrated in this chapter, using digital tools to 'read strange matters' has the potential to create important and exciting forms of access and to open up conversations that simultaneously estrange what is familiar and make the 'strange' matter.

Notes

1 I repurpose 'read strange matters' from Shakespeare's *Macbeth* to match my change of emphasis. Seeing that her husband's face might openly give away their intentions, Lady Macbeth remarks, 'Your face, my thane, is as a book, where men / May read strange matters' (1.5.62–3).

2 I prefer to use the term 'intertext' rather than 'source' here in order to avoid hierarchical or linear ways of thinking about the relationships among these texts. As John Drakakis writes, 'the closer we look at what we used to call sources, the more we identify a complexity that defies hierarchical organization, and extends well beyond the linearity that would allow us to invoke the exclusive privilege of "authority"'. Drakakis himself advocates for 'a more neutral term such as *resources*' (Drakakis 2018: 74).

3 Schneider 2002: 262. Charlotte Lennox was the first to make the connection between *The Two Gentlemen of Verona* and Montemayor's *Diana* in print (Lennox 1754: 4). While it is unclear whether or not Shakespeare read this particular translation, another translation or the Spanish original, it is quite clear that he had this text in mind when composing *The Two Gentlemen of Verona*. For a more expansive consideration of the network of texts that Shakespeare drew upon in writing this particular play, see Skura 2018: 225–37.

4 On the marginalization of early modern Spanish literature in the Anglo-American academy, see Childers 2006: 234 and Fuchs 2013: 95.

5 For more details about TEI, see https://tei-c.org/.

6 'A Student Collaborators' Bill of Rights' is available at https://humtech.ucla.edu/news/a-student-collaborators-bill-of-rights/. See also Keralis 2018: 273–94.

7 For more information about the use of digital tools in early modern literary studies in general and on *EEBO*-TCP in particular, see Estill, Jakacki and Ullyot.

8 Ambereen Dadabhoy recently illustrated how one might use digital tools in the classroom to ask questions about a racialized term such as 'Ethiope' throughout Shakespeare's corpus: 'a quick search for "Ethiope" in a Shakespeare concordance will yield nine results, almost all of which, except *Romeo and Juliet*, are in Shakespeare's comedies. What do we make of these moments when we stumble upon them in the plays? How do we explain the operations of race in texts that we have not identified as being explicitly about race?' (Dadabhoy 2020: 2).

References

Britton, D. A. and M. Walter, eds (2017), *Rethinking Shakespeare Source Study: Audiences, Authors, and Digital Technologies*, London: Routledge.
Bullough, G. (1957), *Narrative and Dramatic Sources of Shakespeare*, London: Routledge.
Childers, W. (2014), *Transnational Cervantes*, Toronto: University of Toronto Press.

Dadabhoy, A. (2020), 'Skin in the Game: Teaching Race in Early Modern Literature', *Studies in Medieval and Renaissance Teaching* 27, no. 2: 1–15.
Drakakis, J. (2018), 'Inside the Elephant's Graveyard: Revising Geoffrey Bullough's *Narrative and Dramatic Sources of Shakespeare*', in K. Halsey and A. Vine (eds), *Shakespeare and Authority*, 55–78. London: Palgrave.
Estill, L., D. K. Jakacki and M. Ullyot, eds (2016), *Early Modern Studies After the Digital Turn*, Toronto: Iter Press.
Fuchs, B. (2013), *The Poetics of Piracy: Emulating Spain in English Literature*, Philadelphia: University of Pennsylvania Press.
Gillespie, S. (2004), 'Shakespeare's Reading of Modern European Literature', in A. Hadfield and P. Hammond (eds), *Shakespeare and Renaissance Europe*, 98–122, London: Bloomsbury.
Hall, K. F. (1995), *Things of Darkness: Economies of Race and Gender in Early Modern England*, Ithaca, NY: Cornell University Press.
Kennedy, J. M., ed. (1968), *A Critical Edition of Yong's Translation of George of Montemayor's 'Diana' and Gil Polo's 'Enamoured Diana'*, Oxford: Clarendon Press.
Keralis, S. D. C. (2018), 'Disrupting Labor in the Digital Humanities; or, The Classroom is Not Your Crowd', in D. Kim and J. Stommel (eds), *Disrupting Digital Humanities*, 273–94, n.p.p.: Punctum Books.
Lennox, C. (1754), *Shakespear illustrated: or the novels and histories on which the plays of Shakespear are founded, collected and translated from the original authors, Vol. 3*, London: n.p.
Montemayor, J. de (1598), *Diana of George of Montemayor*, trans. B. Yong, London: n.p.
Schneider, R. (2002), 'Of Oaten Flutes and Magic Potions: Montemayor's "Diana" as Pastoral Romance', *Narrative* 10, no. 3: 262–76.
Shakespeare, W. (2004), *The Two Gentlemen of Verona*, William Carroll, ed., London: Arden Shakespeare.
Skura, M. (2018), 'Multiple Materials and Motives in *Two Gentlemen of Verona*', in D. A. Britton and M. Walter (eds), *Rethinking Shakespeare Source Study: Audiences, Authors, and Digital Technologies*, 225–37, London: Routledge.

PART TWO

Teaching Diversity, Equity and Inclusion

4

(Early) Modern Literature Crossing the 'Sonic Color Line'

David Sterling Brown

Overview

Some of my students cannot *hear* me because race hinders their ability to *listen*. Race colours the sound of my voice, which students process or perhaps actively do not process through willing or resistant ears because, as Jennifer Stoever introduces through her 'sonic color line' theory, race is as much an audible phenomenon as a visual one. We see race; and we hear it. Stoever asserts, 'The sonic color line describes the process of racializing sound – how and why certain bodies are expected to produce, desire, and live amongst particular sounds – and its product, the hierarchical division sounded between "whiteness" and "blackness"' (Stoever 2016: 6). The expectations surrounding my blackness, then, inform the preconceived notions students have about me, especially because many of them, I often learn, have never had a Black teacher before or even conceived of a Shakespearean as being Black. This lack of exposure can manifest for students as resistance to how they hear and respond to my scholarly authority.[1]

Further defining her theory, Stoever continues, 'The *listening ear* drives the sonic color line; it is a figure for how dominant listening practices accrue – and change – over time, as well as a descriptor for how the dominant culture exerts pressure on individual listening practices to conform to the sonic color line's norms' (Stoever 2016: 7, 13). Dominant white listening practices regulate what registers as unintelligent/smart, improper/proper and loud/quiet, distinctions conveniently corresponding with the inferior/superior dynamic perpetuated by the Black/white binary (Stoever 2016: 12).

In other words, race gets in the way, even as one hears my racialized writerly voice, which is a Black voice, because of one's individual developmental listening experiences and practices (how one was taught to listen and to whom). That I sometimes cannot be heard in my own Shakespeare classroom is a problem, a problem I contend that technology and digital pedagogy can help expose while forming avenues to address prejudice, to conscientiously activate antiracist action as a key learning outcome.[2]

As such, this chapter argues for the fundamental importance of using technology in the Shakespeare classroom to cross the 'sonic color line' and influence what the listening ear hears.[3] Specifically, this essay builds on my 2016 *Radical Teacher* article, '(Early) Modern Literature: Crossing the Color-Line', which examined my critical–personal–experiential method for constructing and teaching a hybrid early modern English drama/African American literature course at Trinity College (CT) in 2013. As the racial demographics of Shakespeare classrooms continue to shift – and do so at a much faster rate than the racial demographics of the field – I assert that instructors can adopt digital technologies to help adapt their teaching approaches and attend to equity, inclusion and diversity of thought while simultaneously shifting away from pedagogical emphases on white (male) centrality that can occur both through the literature taught and through those teaching the literature.[4]

Drawing on my original 'Crossing the Color-Line' pedagogy (the shorthand name for my course), I will reflect on several ways instructors can use 'critical digital pedagogy' – that is, 'instruction that requires an engagement with reality that is persistent and demanding, [. . .] and must result in real action' (Morris and Stommel 2017: 177) – to challenge the norms of 'white listening practices' (Stoever 2016: 5): by way of learning management systems (LMSs) such as Desire2Learn (D2L)/Brightspace and Blackboard; opportunities for marginalized scholarly voices to enter students' listening ears; and the digital corpus linguistics tool Voyant.[5]

Description

In *Radical Teacher*, I gesture toward the sound of my Black voice and body as being fundamentally important when I teach. The focus on my Black body indicates my awareness of how instructors can productively use their own race, regardless of their racial backgrounds, to challenge deliberately hegemonic values. More interesting retrospectively is the awareness of how the materiality of my racialized voice is a filter through which students receive their education (Brown 2016: 70). Yet, in this course, engagement with digital resources means my voice is not the only educational filter that prompts students to critique the world and become liberated 'critical co-investigators' and agents of social change, as Paulo Freire suggests is possible in *Pedagogy of the Oppressed* (Freire 1970: 81).

By creating textual intersections among early modern English and African American authors, my self-designed 'Crossing the Color-Line' course resists a traditional approach to Shakespeare Studies and recognizes that, as Ayanna Thompson contends, 'destabiliz[ing] Shakespeare does not mean to destroy, vilify, or denigrate' (Thompson 2011: 18). When scholars use critical digital pedagogy to teach early modern English Studies, we produce opportunities to diversify the field's overwhelming whiteness while using technology to interrogate significant inequities. As an antiracist scholar-teacher and activist, it is imperative that my teaching considers and appeals to the oppressed, those who may be left out since early modern literature – a form of 'white property', as Arthur Little has identified Shakespeare – is not seen as being for them (Little 2016: 91–2). Yet, Shakespeare, understood as being for all white people, is also mine; and he is my students', too, regardless of their racial backgrounds.

One way I illustrate this point is through Learning Management Systems (LMSs) such as Blackboard, which are not simply tools for content delivery or basic interaction. To integrate LMSs into critical digital pedagogy, I use the LMS to cross the sonic colour line by elevating all student voices through a required assignment I call the 'inroad'; students post this assignment weekly in the LMS and base their in-class presentations on it. (Brown 2016: 70–1). What does it mean for students in a racially, ethnically diverse classroom setting to use their listening ears to hear Black student voices and close-read work produced by those voices? What is the effect of contrasting the sound of those Black voices with those of students who are white, Native American, Latino and Asian, for example? And perhaps even more powerful to consider, what is the effect of *not* being able to contrast voices in a Shakespeare classroom, what is the effect of bolstering what the dominant culture already perpetuates, the notion that white people must be listened to, that white voices matter?

Reinforcing a goal of the course structure, the LMS also gets us away from centring whiteness because I purposefully use it to promote the hearing of all kinds of voices, not solely my students': I play audio clips of authors like Warsan Shire, Amiri Baraka and June Jordan reading their own work; I show videos and film clips that feature racially different bodies; I incorporate culturally diverse music into my lesson plans; and I require each student to do two technology-dependent in-class presentations so the course actively centres them and their ideas. By allowing students to build their confidence in using their own writerly voices, the LMS also assists in transferring that developing confidence into the physical classroom space where, after some weeks of trust building, course participants realize that their rhetorical and verbal contributions matter.

LMSs can also be beneficial for introducing students to other scholarly voices, particularly voices of people of colour. Centring different voices as part of one's pedagogical agenda is invaluable in the early modern classroom setting, given that students are often taught Shakespeare by white instructors (the overwhelming majority of Shakespeareans being white) (Coles, Hall and Thompson 2019: 4–5). This means that the people viewed as authorities in Shakespeare Studies are generally *imagined* as being white. This can, and has, created particular challenges for me since I am often not who students expect to see at the front of the classroom. Some of them have, in fact, articulated as much when I invite them to be candid about their thoughts on what a Shakespeare professor looks like: white and often male. So, precisely how can LMSs serve the aims of diversifying student perceptions of Shakespearean authority?

To answer this question, I turn to W. E. B. Du Bois's *The Souls of Black Folk* and the beautiful line of blank verse, 'I sit with Shakespeare and he winces not' (Du Bois 1994: 67). For Du Bois, Shakespeare was at a distance in many ways, yet somehow we find them together figuratively in the text. Following Du Bois's lead, I have students *sit* with distant intellectuals through the LMS, and not solely through readings, for the colour of racialized voices does not always register on the page. I include podcasts and YouTube interviews, for instance, so students get opportunities to sit virtually through recorded presentations with pioneering 'BlacKKKShakespearean[s]' like Kim F. Hall and Ayanna Thompson.[6] By only reading Thompson's work, one cannot see her skin tone, her hair texture, her Black features that defy the dominant perception of a Shakespeare professor. Exposure to other Shakespeareans – Black women in this case, which affirms the course's Black feminist agenda – is eye-opening for students who learn there is a BlacKKKShakespearean history that includes scholarship pre-dating the era of widespread digital tools.[7]

As a means of promoting social justice, critical digital pedagogy demands the prioritization of antiracism, inclusion and diversity. My students' repeated exposure to voices of different hues normalizes the existence and voices of BlacKKKShakespeareans, for instance; it individualizes our different research, presentation and pedagogical styles.[8] Therefore, the LMS becomes a tool to reframe students' ideas about how a Shakespearean teaches and who can speak Shakespeare's language or be a Shakespeare character. They become aware of and see practitioners like Keith Hamilton Cobb (*American Moor*), Leontyne Price (Cleopatra in Samuel Barber's 1966 opera), Denzel Washington (Kenneth Branagh's *Much Ado* film adaptation), Condola Rashad (as Juliet on Broadway in 2013) and Colombian-born actor John Leguizamo (Baz Luhrmann's *Romeo + Juliet* film adaptation). This kind of exposure has significant implications for the Shakespearean pipeline, as it enables students to grasp *who* is entitled to study Shakespeare – anybody.

Beyond utilizing LMSs strategically, I train students how to close read and reflect on inequality by using Voyant, an online textual analysis tool that can generate word clouds, and by using digital Shakespeare texts, such as those available through the Folger Shakespeare Library.[9] Before developing students' close-reading skills, however, I need to help them get accustomed

FIGURE 4.1 *Voyant word cloud*: Titus Andronicus, *Act 4, Scene 2 entire dialogue and stage directions as corpus. The following link can be used to access and manipulate online this specific word cloud in colour: https://voyant-tools.org/?corpus=56a07197289f2fd9e693d03e646d9c8e&visible=500&view=Cirrus.*

to managing the digital text. Once that is done, I can begin showing how Voyant makes close reading an interactive exercise. This process is exciting for me because I step outside my doctoral-training comfort zone, giving students a brief introduction to corpus linguistics. In Figure 4.1, I include the results of a Voyant-generated word cloud based on a corpus comprised of the dialogue from 4.2 in *Titus* (Shakespeare 2009). As Kieran O'Halloran explains, 'The use of a large corpus can assist in the evaluation of initial responses to a literary work' (O'Halloran 2014: 120).

The words appearing largest in Figure 4.1 are the most frequently used terms in this scene (the word cloud can track up to 500 words); adjusting the 'terms' dial changes what users see on screen to as few as the twenty-five most used words in the corpus, as pictured. 'Aaron' appears most frequently, uttered ten times, and 'Empress' comes second, appearing nine times. Other key words include 'child' (seven), 'nurse' (seven), 'mother' (seven) and 'black' (five). This word cloud, created through Voyant's 'cirrus' feature, is a creative way to ask students for their impressions of what is most crucial in the scene's dialogue, and to get them to see how race matters here, especially whiteness, and critique why. The word cloud reveals how the play directs our gaze towards blackness despite the fact that this scene says so much about whiteness, and white womanhood, through the words Empress, mother, nurse and midwife.

Some of what students highlight includes the centrality of Aaron, 'black[ness]' and bigotry; the interracial parental tension between Tamora and Aaron; the significant, but short-lived, role of the white Nurse; and, thinking structurally, the chaos that ensues during the play's falling action largely because the innocent infant 'child' is Black. Analysing the word cloud tends to add colour to class conversations because students see the text differently, deconstructed in a way that aids the enhancement of their critical thinking skills. When I couple the Voyant exercise with a viewing of 4.2 from Julie Taymor's 1999 *Titus* film adaptation, students build on our previous discussion. They see racism's effects through Aaron's fierce protectiveness of his child, whom the white characters want to kill, and they also *hear* it in the play's disparaging anti-Black language. When put into action with the help of digital tools, Shakespeare's words magnify the impact racism can have on one's senses.

Student learning

If digital (like much traditional) pedagogy does not consciously address structural inequalities – racism and anti-blackness, for example – then it participates in the structuring of inequality. By highlighting structural inequity, a course like 'Crossing the Color-Line' supports existing impulses toward activism in some students while encouraging others to use their discomfort productively. In so doing, they learn that their voices – regardless of their race – matter. They demonstrate their awareness of how the (sonic) colour line creates invisible boundaries they must cross to avoid being complicit in perpetuating oppression, including their own, since what we see racially can limit what we hear, and what we hear racially can limit what we think we see (Stoever 2016: 14). Regardless of where I have taught this course, a consensus among students emerges: they feel empowered to engage others, especially in the popular digital realm where they spend much of their time connecting with people. In addition to seeing that LMSs, websites and social media apps such as Twitter, Facebook, YouTube and Instagram expand the reach of my pedagogy, I have discovered fascinating ways my students champion the reach of my instruction in the digital real world (the world beyond campus and LMSs), how they intertwine my Black voice with theirs and how they build on what they learn so as to teach *me* that the act of educating knows no bounds.[10]

The practical applicability of 'Crossing the Color-Line' is what facilitated, and continues to facilitate, my traversing institutional boundaries pedagogically as a Shakespearean whose blackness is seen and heard. I modified this class for the University of Arizona (U of A) curriculum in 2017, after incorporating my course's foundation – specifically the emphasis on identity, diversity and the Shakespearean-Du Boisian framework – into another U of A digital pedagogy course. That course, 'Diversifying Shakespeare', I co-taught with two non-Black colleagues in 2017. It was also at U of A that a student assessed how the colour line works in a digital space I had not yet considered in class – the world of dating apps. For me, this was an enlightening teachable moment that afforded me an opportunity to see how this particular student applied their close-reading skills to identify and, more importantly, call out racism, fat-shaming and internalized homophobia, what Karen Lumsden and Emily Harmer outline as 'online othering' (Lumsden and Harmer 2019: 211–14).

In one of our final U of A discussions, during which students were synthesizing many of the textual intersections they had identified throughout the term, class members reflected on the many instances of rejection and exclusion, on the basis of identity, that we covered in our texts: the Romans' racism toward Aaron and his Black infant son in *Titus Andronicus*; the Maltese Christians' displays of anti-Semitism toward Barabas in Marlowe's *The Jew of Malta*; the Barons' resistance to Gaveston and the King's homosocial bond in his *Edward II*; and Negro-Sarah's hatred of her biracial self, particularly her blackness (also understood as internalized racism), in *Funnyhouse of a Negro*. Extending this conversation out into the digital real world, or rather, bringing that world into the classroom, a student critiqued the prevalence of exclusion that they observed on Grindr, an LGBTQ dating app.[11] Specifically, this student 'inscribed [their] own identity into shared learning' and homed in on offensive, dehumanizing phrasing they would often see on people's profiles: 'No Fats', 'No Femmes', 'No Blacks', 'No Asians'. Seeking my approval to take our conversation in this direction, my student asked what I thought. As is typical of my pedagogical style when students are on to something brilliantly provocative, I threw the question back at the class (Kirwan 2014: 61–2).[12]

'No Fats, No Femmes, No Blacks, No Asians' – language that generated a visible mixture of discomfort and bewilderment for everyone in this racially and ethnically diverse classroom setting – enabled an intriguing conversation that revealed how students were applying in a more digital, public fashion their knowledge acquired from the study of early modern English and African American literature. In hindsight, I realize my students had a nascent awareness of how the colour line operates socially, as they identified how reading those exclusionary phrases, especially those referencing race and ethnicity, often appeared in the profiles of gay white men whose voices seemed dominant and prescriptive. And even when the discriminatory phrases appeared in the profiles of people of colour, my students determined that such biased 'preferences', as they are masked rhetorically on the app, could be rooted in self-hatred, internalized racism and idealized beauty standards. The class concluded that such preferences are, in fact, not preferences at all but deliberate ways to harm others with racist, discriminatory discourse that centres the symbolic power of whiteness.

By seeing digital text (representing a certain subset of white male writers' messages on Grindr) and reading race, my students recognized some of the socio-political dangers of the digital world that are also class based. Their criticisms of these dangers indicate their understanding of so much that they learn during the term: that the issues we address through Shakespeare are indeed relevant now; that attention to diversity and inclusion requires action and activism; that race is a social construct; that stereotypes are not *proof* of anything about particular groups of people; that individuals believe in and use stereotypes as a means to police their own and others' actions; that phrases such as 'no fats' and 'no Blacks' reinforce superior–inferior dichotomies that keep structural inequality intact; that the digital world sometimes makes the expression of intolerance easier; that they, my students, have a social responsibility to confront injustices if they want to be effective allies and antiracist accomplices (Kendall 2020: 257); and that the reinforced centring of whiteness occurs overtly and covertly every day as a form of racist 'distraction' (Morrison 1975).

Application

Critical digital pedagogy must be implemented through intentional methods that do not perpetuate systemic inequalities such as racism. While this kind of critical pedagogical work has potential to be enjoyable on some level, it comes with psychological and emotional costs. And for Black scholars, and scholars of colour, who are often tokenized, this work becomes even more difficult when white colleagues do not assume such labour as genuine allies or partners. As Brett D. Hirsch proclaims, 'We owe it to ourselves (and indeed to our students) to pay more than lip service to pedagogy in our field[s]. Whether as a student or an educator, pedagogy should not be parenthetical to the experience in higher education' (Hirsch 2012: 6). For me, the professor, and for my students (as I learn in course evaluations), 'Crossing the Colour-Line' discussions, especially preliminary discussions that deliberately establish our comfort with one another, can leave class members feeling quite drained. Aware of this, I offer opportunities for some relief throughout the term. But perhaps most significantly, I remind students they are doing hard work and that, as a result, they will be rewarded with their own personal, intellectual growth by continuing to invest in their educations in this way.[13]

Having now taught this course at three very different higher education institutions, I have perceived some commonalities among the varied demographics of students regarding the hard work that is required in an antiracist course. Without fail, the literature and our conversations present challenging learning opportunities: for Black students who must confront anti-Black racism and racial epithets in our texts; for Jewish students, and other religious minorities, who must think about their families' roots and continued religious intolerance; for LGBTQIA students who must think about heterosexual norms and (internalized) homophobia; for women students who must repeatedly witness the power of sexism and patriarchy; for racial/ethnic minorities who must learn to resist the socio-political emphasis on white centrality that makes them feel less than; for everyone who identifies with a particular social class or marginalized group, such as low-income students with disabilities; and for white students who must confront their own complicity in upholding white supremacy. It goes without saying that this course also presents challenges for me, a gay, Black professor who studies and teaches literature thought of as white property. Based on my experience, I am convinced that this kind of antiracist digital pedagogy can (re)shape the essence of those who embrace it seriously. This kind of pedagogy, which tends to attract a self-selecting group of students (though not always), deliberately aims to bring people in from the social margins, to centre their voices; and, in the name of equity and inclusion, it inevitably decentres those members of the dominant culture who are accustomed to always being heard.

Investing in a commitment to critical digital pedagogy in the 'post-postracial' era is one way to transform traditional approaches to Shakespeare Studies, for such an investment opens up opportunities to innovate while being flexible with students' varied learning styles.[14] Even if revitalizing one's pedagogy is initially time consuming, it can make teaching more exciting for instructors in the long run; and, more importantly, it can make learning more engaging for students. Additionally, critical digital pedagogical approaches should embrace diversity of all kinds, particularly racial diversity; and instructors should try to adapt their teaching approaches so as not to address whiteness only when it is convenient, thus allowing instruction to perpetuate (consciously or unconsciously) the aims of white supremacy.

CODA: This is hard work. It is not for those who simply want to use their pedagogy for virtue signalling; in fact, such pedagogy can reinforce problematic agendas to which instructors should not subject students. Such agendas are negligent and constitute pedagogical malpractice. Without antiracism and without working to dismantle white supremacy, which continually structures inequality, instructors allow race to get in the way. This means that many people – regardless of their race – are destined never to hear a Black person like me because what sounds best to their listening ears, what sounds right, will always be what sounds white. Across the sonic colour line I ask: Do I have your listening ears? Can everybody hear *me*?

Notes

1   Stoever (2016: 22) argues 'that the sonic color line's disciplining of the senses disrupts notions of "universal listening." In certain contexts, for example, and depending on the listener, a black woman's scream is heard differently from a white woman's, even if both screams displayed similar properties of pitch, tone, timbre, and volume.'

2   Gallon (2016) proposes that 'technology [. . .] can further expose humanity as a racialized social construction' (paragraph 1). Available at: https://dhdebates.gc.cuny.edu/read/untitled/section/fa10e2e1-0c3d-4519-a958-d823aac989eb#ch04.

3   I have also taught this course at the University of Arizona (2017) and Binghamton University (2018, 2020).

4 Coles, Hall and Thompson (2019, paragraph 2). After a generative discussion with Arthur Little, I chose to refer to Kim F. Hall and Ayanna Thompson as 'BlacKKKShakespeareans' to honour their powerful co-authored piece and to acknowledge the socio-political and historical work the term 'BlacKKKShakespearean' should prompt readers to do given the spelling.

5 To learn more about Voyant, see https://voyant-tools.org/docs/#!/guide/about. I was introduced to this tool by three generous University of Arizona librarians: Niamh Wallace, Anthony Sanchez and Jennifer Nichols.

6 For examples, see Hall 2016 and Thompson 2016.

7 See especially E. D. Jones 1965 and 1971; see also Brown 2020.

8 For a reading of (de)individualization, see Brown 2018, esp. 12.

9 Such textual analysis 'exploits the digital nature of the texts by analyzing them computationally' (Hoover, Culpeper and O'Halloran 2014: 2). The Folger Shakespeare Library offers *Folger Digital Texts* via https://www.folgerdigitaltexts.org/?chapter=0.

10 Thompson 2011: 146–67 discusses race, performance and YouTube.

11 To learn more about Grindr, see https://www.grindr.com/about/.

12 This approach is inspired by Freire, who claims that 'the teacher cannot think for her students, nor can she impose her thought on them' (1970: 77).

13 The course LMS site contained a semi-extra credit online forum called Afterthoughts; I responded to every post each week to sustain student engagement.

14 Jackson, Jr (2005: 400) recognizes the challenges of dealing with race in the 'post-postracial moment'. Kyle Farmbry posits that we live in a 'post-postracial administrative state' (Farmbry 2010: 527). In her consideration of 'post-postracialism', Alison Landsberg asserts, 'We are witnessing a reemergence of race as a socially and politically significant discourse, and that this discourse is appearing largely in the arena of culture' (Landsberg 2018: 199).

References

Bloom, G. (2007), *Voice in Motion: Staging Gender, Shaping Sound in Early Modern England*, Philadelphia: University of Pennsylvania Press.

Brown, D. S. (2016), '(Early) Modern Literature: Crossing the Color-Line', *Radical Teacher* 105: 69–77.

Brown, D. S. (2018), '"Is Black so Base a Hue?": Black Life Matters in Shakespeare's *Titus Andronicus*', in C. Smith et al. (eds), *Early Modern Black Diaspora Studies*, 137–55, New York: Palgrave Macmillan.

Brown, D. S. (2020), 'Things of Darkness: "The Blueprint of a Methodology",' *The Hare: An Online Journal of Untimely Reviews in Early Modern Theater* 5, no. 1, https://thehareonline.com/NODE/74.

Coles, K., K. F. Hall and A. Thompson (2019), 'BlacKKKShakespearean', *Profession*, https://profession.mla.org/blackkkshakespearean-a-call-to-action-for-medieval-and-early-modern-studies/.

Du Bois, W. E. B. (1994), *The Souls of Black Folk*, New York: Dover Publications.
Farmbry, K. (2010), 'Introduction – Administrative Theory in a Post-Postracial America', *Administrative Theory & Praxis* 32, no. 4: 520–31.
Folger Digital Texts, Folger Shakespeare Library, https://www.folgerdigitaltexts.org/?chapter=0.
Freire, P. (1970), *Pedagogy of the Oppressed*, New York: Continuum.
Gallon, K. (2016), 'Making a Case for the Black Digital Humanities', in M. K. Gold and L. F. Klein (eds), *Debates in the Digital Humanities 2016*, 42–9, Minneapolis, University of Minnesota Press.
Grindr, https://www.grindr.com/about/.
Hall, K. F. (2016), 'Othello was my Grandfather: Shakespeare in the African Diaspora', Folger Shakespeare Library, https://soundcloud.com/folgershakespearelibrary/shakespeare-anniversary-lecture-series-kim-hall.
Hirsch, B. D. (2012), '</Parentheses>: Digital Humanities and the Place of Pedagogy', in B. D. Hirsch (ed.), *Digital Humanities Pedagogy: Practices, Principles and Politics*, 3–30, Cambridge: Open Book Publishers.
Hoover, D. L., J. Culpeper and K. O'Halloran (2014), 'Introduction', in D. L. Hoover, J. Culpeper, and K. O'Halloran (eds), *Digital Literary Studies: Corpus Approaches to Poetry, Prose, and Drama*, 1–8, New York: Routledge.
Jackson, Jr, J. L. (2005), 'A Little Black Magic', *South Atlantic Quarterly* 104, no. 3: 393–402.
Jones, E. D. (1965), *Othello's Countrymen: The African in English Renaissance Drama*, Oxford: Oxford University Press.
Jones, E. D. (1971), *The Elizabethan Image of Africa*, Charlottesville: University Press of Virginia.
Kendall, M. (2020), *Hood Feminism: Notes from the Women That a Movement Forgot*, New York: Viking.
Kirwan, P. (2014), 'Introduction: Pedagogy', in C. Carson and P. Kirwan (eds), *Shakespeare and the Digital World: Redefining Scholarship and Practice*, 58–62, Cambridge: Cambridge University Press.
Landsberg, A. (2018), 'Post-Postracial America: On Westworld and the Smithsonian National Museum of African American History and Culture', *Cultural Politics* 14, no. 2: 198–215.
Little, A. (2016), 'Re-Historicizing Race, White Melancholia, and the Shakespearean Property', *Shakespeare Quarterly* 67, no. 1: 84–103.
Lumsden, K. and E. Harmer, eds (2019), *Online Othering: Exploring Digital Violence and Discrimination on the Web*, Cham, Switzerland: Palgrave Macmillan.
Morris, S. M. and J. Stommel (2017), 'Open Education as Resistance: MOOCs and Critical Digital Pedagogy', in E. Losh (ed.), *MOOCs and Their Afterlives: Experiments and Access in Higher Education*, 177–97, Chicago: University of Chicago Press.
Morrison, T. (2014), 'A Humanist View', speech, Portland State University, 30 May 1975, https://soundcloud.com/portland-state-library/portland-state-black-studies-1. Talk transcription: https://www.mackenzian.com/wp-content/uploads/2014/07/Transcript_PortlandState_TMorrison.pdf.
O'Halloran, K. (2014), 'Corpus-Assisted Literary Evaluation', in D. L. Hoover, J. Culpeper and K. O'Halloran (eds), *Digital Literary Studies: Corpus Approaches to Poetry, Prose, and Drama*, 120–45, New York: Routledge.

Shakespeare, W. (2009), *Titus Andronicus*, in *The Complete Works of Shakespeare 6th edition*, D. Bevington, ed., 966–1004, New York: Pearson.
Stoever, J. (2016), *The Sonic Color Line: Race and the Cultural Politics of Listening*, New York: New York University Press.
Thompson, A. (2011), *Passing Strange: Shakespeare, Race and Contemporary America*, Oxford: Oxford University Press.
Thompson, A. (2016), 'Shakespeare and Race', in *Illuminating Shakespeare*, Oxford: Oxford University Press, https://www.youtube.com/watch?v=NsUoW9eNTAw.
Voyant, https://voyant-tools.org/docs/#!/guide/about.

5

Diversifying Shakespeare

Intersections of Technology and Identity

Meg Lota Brown and Kyle DiRoberto

Overview

As faculty teaching in a US state bordering Mexico, we have recently begun framing our Shakespeare courses with the concept of 'mestizaje', the pluralist identity that resists binary thinking in Gloria Anzaldúa's *Borderlands/La Frontera*. Students in our classes applied this concept to two Shakespeare plays that were chosen because of their compelling resonance for contemporary communities in Arizona: *Titus Andronicus* and *The Merchant of Venice*. Given our proximity to the Mexican border and our state's restrictive laws regarding race, ethnicity and sexual orientation, we explored Shakespeare's work within the context of our students' own demographic and cultural diversity.[1] *Titus Andronicus* prompted analyses of race, law, gender and other important topics that confront the members of our regional – and global – communities. Similarly resonant in *The Merchant of Venice* was the problematic construction of minority identity within a larger dominant culture. Examining the (im)possibility of assimilation, the construction of stereotypes and the criminalization of difference, the play enabled critical discussion about inequality and oppression that is particularly relevant to communities in Arizona.

Technology was a primary medium in and through which students investigated representations of identity in both Shakespeare's plays and modern communities. In our lower-division course, 'Diversifying Shakespeare: Engaging Beyond Boundaries', students designed digital teaching projects that incorporated a wide range of technological tools.[2] First, they explored the research function of digital tools in literary analysis. While developing open-source teaching modules, they discovered the capacity of technology to simulate Anzaldúa's principles of inclusion and critical thinking by drawing learners into interactive engagement with multiple perspectives. Technology specialists at the University of Arizona library introduced students to a wide range of digital resources from which they could choose tools to incorporate into their capstone group projects on identity construction in Shakespeare's plays.[3] Students were vigilant about not allowing the 'wow factor' of technology to obscure critical analysis. They wanted to highlight the capacity of technology to make information accessible, focusing on how best to switch the interpretive dynamic from a white male-dominated production of knowledge – whether in the field of literary studies or engineering – to a more inclusive model.[4] In reflective journals, students stressed the importance of the participatory capacity of digital tools. They observed that the collaborative and interactive potential of technology allowed for polyphonic and multimodal exploration. While the digital resources themselves were simply tools, the groups' deployment of them led to the investigation, enactment and promotion of diverse approaches to Shakespeare's plays.

During technological 'jam sessions', students experimented with software applications and web-based platforms as well as hardware and 3-D printing. Short tech assignments guided their discovery of each tool's capacity (see Applications section below). With the virtual reality system HTC Vive, students 'tried on' different identities. For example, one game allowed a player to jump into different bodies and experience different perspectives, as well as interact with other characters and with objects in the game's virtual world. Players could see in a mirror whom they became when they inhabited new bodies. By synching the player's mouth with that of the animated character, the game suggested interesting possibilities for students who were considering adaptations and performance. Gamers' words echoed in the virtual world, and portions of this experience could be filmed, saved, edited and played back. In weekly assessments, course evaluations and class discussion, students noted that the VR simulations deepened not only their understanding of why and how identities are constructed but also their awareness of the power structures and cultural values that define groups and individuals.

In the following pages, we explore a few applications that the students found to be particularly suited to their inquiry into mestizaje and Shakespeare. One application that all of the groups chose to incorporate into their teaching projects was TouchCast, an interactive, video-based presentation tool. Students enjoyed its complex capacity for layering media, its green screen applications and its interactive properties referred to as vApps.[5] Fully interactive video applications, vApps can be integrated into a presentation to encourage viewers' responses. Students found the participatory capacity of the application especially engaging, and they discovered that in TouchCast they could both investigate the value of diverse approaches to Shakespeare and enact the polyvocal nature of that investigation.

Description

The multifaceted capacity of TouchCast allows users to integrate images, sound files, maps and videos. Collaborative groups in the class created presentations that embedded a variety of digital tools in the interactive application. One presentation, entitled 'Representation, Borders, and Violence in Shakespeare', included green screen, videos, social media links, pdf files, maps, images and the language visualization tool Voyant (described in more detail below; see also Chapter 4). The presenters drew on Anzaldúa's theory of the third space and 'la conciencia de la Mestiza' to interrogate social divisions and the constructedness of identity; they then traced these concepts in Shakespeare's work. Using the green screen, students projected themselves onto the border between Arizona and Mexico. They simulated a news cast that compared social divisions in *The Merchant of Venice* with partisan politics in America, focusing particularly on some conservatives' opposition to immigration as well as support for further militarizing the border. Recognizing in our own culture the 'otherizing' violence that informs early modern anti-Semitism and gender oppression, the students performed literary analysis as an educational mode of social activism.

Students preferred TouchCast to similar applications, such as ThingLink and Padlet, because of its greater capacity for active learning. For example, in 'Representation, Borders, and Violence in Shakespeare', viewers can engage with a variety of materials while the student presenters shrink to one side of the screen, still present but not dominant. Touching the screen (in the mobile version) or clicking (in the desktop version) allows users to scroll through *Borderlands/La Frontera*, read scholarship about Anzaldúa, engage with others about her work through the social media reading-group application Goodreads and watch a short film posted on YouTube. The latter is inspired by Anzaldúa's work and includes people discussing their experiences in various kinds of borderlands. In the course of the presentation, then, users enter a multifaceted virtual learning community. A curated sequence of tools helps with navigation. After the presentation ends, presenters can continue to interact with viewers by way of social media links embedded in TouchCast.

Along with TouchCast, nearly every group of students chose to incorporate Voyant into their final teaching project. With this open-source, browser-based, language visualization application, they generated scatterplots, collocated graphs and produced cirrus word clouds in order to analyse the language of corpora and the linguistic construction of identity. They were excited about Voyant's ability to formulate the first steps of interpretation by reading 'at a glance'. Moreover, the application manifests linguistic evidence in a modality that is accessible for learners who might, for example, have language barriers. It was one of the most popular tools in the course, perhaps because its primary focus on linguistic analysis resonated with Shakespeare's and Anzaldúa's shared emphasis on language as a critical arena for examining social violence. One project highlighted the capacity of Voyant to make visible the anti-Semitic construction of identity in language: students created word clouds that represented the most prevalent descriptions of Shylock in *The Merchant of Venice*. 'Devil', 'flesh' and 'Jew' dominate the cirrus visualization, highlighting the Christians' conjunction of the Semitic and the carnal, and making manifest 'at a glance' the demonizing of Shylock (see Figure 5.1).

Students also embraced geographical visualization. Groups imported into their TouchCast modules geographical mapping tools, such as ArcGIS StoryMaps, in order to examine stage representations of Shylock across centuries and continents. They mapped performances of *The Merchant of Venice* from the earliest recorded interpretations to the most recent film adaptation set in America. The maps make visible the persistent history of flattening Shylock's character, of performing him as an anti-Semitic stereotype despite Shakespeare's exposing of stereotypes as problematic and violent. Connecting characterizations of Shylock to the cultural moments in which his role was performed, they supported their analysis with pop-up images, videos and graphs. Like the dramatic device of a play within a play, they expanded the viewers' understanding by creating presentations within a presentation. For example, during one TouchCast teaching module, a vApp of interactive pushpins pops up on the geographical map of performance locations. Presenters invite viewers to touch or click on the pin that signifies

FIGURE 5.1 *Screenshot of TouchCast presentation.*

Charles Macklin's eighteenth-century performance of Shylock. When the pushpin is activated, the teachers shrink to the side and the screen fills with an account of Macklin's influential rendition of a darkly villainous Jew.

Pins on the map of America bring the viewer centuries forward. Presenters examine twenty-first-century productions that expose the Christian Venetians in the play as hypocritical and vicious. One of the pins points to Edward Hall's 2009 production. Set in an all-male prison in Brooklyn, the film emphasizes entrapment and futility in a socio-economic system that organizes people into predatory tribes. Students compare this culture to the brutal mercantilism of *The Merchant of Venice*. The ArcGIS StoryMap and interactive vApps, embedded in the overarching narrative on TouchCast, draw students into the exploratory process of learning as they click on videos, pdfs, newspaper articles, theatre reviews and grotesque images of Shylock with a prosthetic snout and demonic features.

Similarly arresting was the presentation 'Andronichess', which explored the socio-political world of *Titus Andronicus* by adapting the play to a chess game. The students' examination of social violence in Roman politics – and by thinly veiled extension, the politics of early modern England – included close attention to similar forms of violence in their own culture. The game was filmed with commentary and fully interactive vApps that pop up from time to time, inviting the participation of the audience. Students used a 3-D printer to fabricate chess pieces that represented the exclusion of Aaron. His and his son's avatars were the only black pieces on a board of white (Roman) and brown (Goth) figurines. While the other markers were conventional chess shapes, Aaron's was fashioned as a bottle, which the students explained signified both poison and medicine. The artefact suggested not only the deadly and restorative alternatives of the pharmakon but also the multivalent function of diversity in the play. For example, the group noted that one way to read Aaron is as the cause of turmoil, a poison of radical difference; another view is that he is more akin to a scapegoat, a catalyst who forces his audience to recognize their own violence. As the chess game plays out on film, the voiceover 'sportscaster' considers whether the scapegoat might cause the cyclically violent society of difference to collapse and then to regenerate an alternative dynamic. Aaron's child, represented as a wounded bird because of the crippling exclusion that he faces, evokes the potentiality of a future that will be determined by our own ethical choices. Highlighting the resonance of *Titus Andronicus* in their own culture, the group added an Instagram vApp with hashtags to 'Black Lives Matter' and other contemporary discussions of racially motivated violence.

Student learning

Student assessments of the course, both in their final reflections on the process of digital collaboration and in their anonymous course evaluations, were uniformly positive. They remarked on discovering the potential of technology to manifest social inequities.[6] The opportunity to explore multiple modes of inquiry and to communicate in varied formats augmented their understanding and created new avenues for engaging with a wide range of interlocutors. In addition, students reflected that bridging the digital and print, the academic and the popular, the canonical and the marginalized, performance and close reading made them more aware of the critical processes that lead to solving problems or creating new knowledge.

When enlisting digital tools to experiment with different identity formations – whether casting a white female as Aaron in a VR game or printing a 3-D chess piece that signifies social status – students were struck by how these experiences alerted them to the power of unexamined assumptions about identity. As a business major in the class observed, Portia's courtroom question – 'Which is the merchant here? And which the Jew?' (4.1.176) – strikingly calls attention to the fact that identity is socially conferred rather than essential. Recognizing cultural constructions of difference and power, she noted, enriches our understanding of early modern literature, but it is also urgently necessary in order to navigate our current moment.

In a capstone collaboration, each group in the class showcased their work in a state-wide conference that we organized on digital pedagogy. We invited undergraduates and faculty from all three state universities and every community college in Arizona to include digital pedagogy in their curricula and to participate in the conference. One of our objectives was to bring together learning communities in higher education that intersect too rarely. We hoped to strengthen institutional synergies and foster creative collaborations among a diverse population of students. Participants marshalled a variety of instructional modalities, pedagogical methodologies, cultural and theoretical perspectives, digital technologies and disciplines. The process enriched the immersive classroom engagement of our state-wide community of practitioners and undergraduates. In anonymous class evaluations, students repeatedly pointed to two aspects of their learning experience that were most successful. One was the course format of deploying digital tools in collaborative discovery. The other was interacting with other undergraduates and faculty from diverse institutions throughout the state. Both experiences, they observed, fostered a strong sense of their place in an intellectual community.

Application

What follows are several assignments that introduce students to three of the digital tools featured in this chapter: TouchCast, StoryMaps and Voyant. Also provided below are links to a sample student project and to the conference programme; course resources; and our syllabus (minus the boilerplate language about accessibility, grading policy, academic integrity, absence policy, etc.).

Building an interactive TouchCast presentation

This assignment teaches students how to create an interactive presentation with multimedia digital tools using TouchCast. A professional-grade editing application, TouchCast allows for the incorporation of interactive vApps, which connect the viewer to maps, polls, social media and more in the midst of a presentation. Students will need access to a green screen, an iPad (with the TouchCast Studio application installed) and a tripod. Recording, editing and creating special effects are all done in the app; for presentations of up to one hour, the application is free.

Preparing for your TouchCast recording

1 **Create an overview of your group presentation by identifying what you want your audience's key takeaways to be.** Suggestion: ask yourself what experiences, textual evidence, data, etc. would be most effective and memorable for conveying your findings. You might create an outline or preliminary sketch of what you want your presentation to look like. For this, you could use a storyboard format to map your actions, script your dialog in the teleprompter, sketch your graphics and special effects and add your interactions. [7]

2 **Make a list of the digital tools, websites and other resources that might best facilitate your discussions of diversity.** Suggestion: watch examples of TouchCast on your iPad and interact with the pop-ups, so you get a sense of what your audience will experience. Think about what combination of digital tools will best reach your audience and why. TouchCast's vApp library is an open-source platform, and you can customize or modify the tools as needed. Discuss these options with your group. For short presentations (10–15 minutes), select no more than three or four vApps, so as not to overwhelm your audience. Prepare in advance the data, images and graphics for each application that you will import into your presentation. On the following page, tutorials guide you through the steps for using two vApps: Storymaps and Voyant.

Creating and editing your TouchCast recording

1 **How to record your video in TouchCast:** start by setting up your recording space. Once your green screen is in place, make sure you have good lighting. Natural lighting is ideal, but artificial lighting will work fine. Put your iPad on its tripod and open the TouchCast Studio app. Select 'start from scratch'. Tap 'new project', name it and start recording the video. After recording, make sure to save clips. You can edit them in the app as well.

2. **How to Add vApps**: Once you have recorded your presentation, you can go back into the application and open your project by double clicking on the image of the recording and selecting play. It is here that you can add vApps, sounds, whiteboards and other features. You just have to select your video on the small panel at the bottom of the frame. It will light up green, and the '+vApp' option will become white, signifying that it is active. Click the 'add vApp' prompt. Once you have imported your vApps, you can edit them, deciding when they appear and their duration. You can also add titles and other special effects. Once you have all that configured, in the 'edit vApp' space (which you can leave and come back to as often as you need) you record your final version with the vApps appearing in the size, place and duration you have determined. Congratulations, your presentation is done!

Suggested vApps

1. **StoryMaps** This tutorial focuses on adding Storymaps to TouchCast. Building a map with a narrative can be an excellent tool for exploring everything from Shakespeare and colonial imperialism to cultural exchange. Whether you use StoryMaps to represent Shakespeare's global reach or to explore adaptations and performances on stages across the world, maps can inspire your audience to start thinking about the plays in terms of transhistorical and international perspectives.

    a. Navigate to ArcGIS Storymaps on the internet, sign up and build your map.

    b. Once you build your map, return to the TouchCast application and access your recording by choosing 'my project' at the right top of the app. Tap the recording to which you want to add the vApp, and in the pop-up, click on the arrow. Select the image of the recording near the bottom of the screen. It will be outlined in green when selected. 'Add vApp' will appear. Select it.

    c. You will see a selection of vApp icons. Choose the 'website' vApp. In the upper left of the dialogue box, there is an option to search Google. Search it for StoryMaps. It will take you to the site where you sign in, choose your map and select the green 'use' in the upper right-hand corner. You can now edit.

    d. Don't forget to rerecord the clip after arranging your vApps. There is a small red and white 'record' button near the bottom of the screen for that purpose. If you forget and exit, the vApps will not appear in your presentation. They are still there, but they won't appear until you have recorded with them in place.

2. **Voyant** This corpus analysis tool generates word clouds as well as other visual representations of word frequency and colocation. In so doing, it provides data that can aid in discussing the nuances in linguistic constructions of identity. To use Voyant,
    a. Navigate to the Voyant website and type, copy or paste a text or an URL, or upload an optimized pdf into the 'add text' box.
    b. Once your corpus is uploaded, a variety of visualizations, called 'skins', are automatically generated. 'Stop words', such as 'the' and 'from', are pre-emptively suppressed. This option can be modified to produce more targeted representations of texts. To do this, hover over the second visualization, called 'reader', and click on 'edit list', which will allow you to add to the list of suppressed words. Experiment with excluding and then including the names of characters in an uploaded script; discuss the results of those changes. You can add this vApp into TouchCast following the same steps that you followed for StoryMaps above.

SAMPLE FINAL PROJECT

https://v2.touchcast.com/testua/representation_borders_and_violence_in_shakespeare

Conference program

https://tinyurl.com/rybqw5g

Digital resources

Examples of student digital humanities projects

- Exploring the Influence of the Museum of Modern Art, http://www.moma.org/collection.com/.
- Origins of the NY Philharmonic, https://nyphil.org/about-us/history/archives-collections.
- NY Tenements: How Images Enact Change, https://www.tenement.org/blog/whose-project/.
- Introducing American Fashion: Examining the Development and Commodification of Style in America, https://fashionhistory.fitnyc.edu.

Examples of Shakespeare-related digital humanities projects

- Map of Early Modern London, http://mapoflondon.uvic.ca/.

- Network visualization: mapping Shakespeare's tragedies (using Gephi), http://www.martingrandjean.ch/network-visualization-shakespeare/.
- To See or Not to See: An Interactive Tool for the Visualization and Analysis of Shakespeare Plays, http://www.thomaswilhelm.eu/shakespeare/output/hamlet.html.

Examples of Voyant projects
- <u>Lincoln Logarithms: Finding Meaning in Sermons</u>, http://disc.library.emory.edu/ lincoln/voyant/.
- A Republic of Emails: What are the contents, https://www.maxkemman.nl/2016/11/a-republic-of-emails-what-are-the-contents/.

General digital humanities tools
- <u>Hypothesis (web annotation)</u>, https://web.hypothes.is/.
- <u>Timeline JS</u>, https://timeline.knightlab.com/.

Examples of digital mapping projects
- The Emotions of London, https://litlab.stanford.edu/LiteraryLab Pamphlet13.pdf.
- Exploring the literary map: an analytical review of online, http://onlinelibrary.wiley.com/doi/10.1111/gec3.12303/full.

Digital mapping tools
- Story Maps, https://storymaps.arcgis.com/en/.
- StoryMap JS, https://storymap.knightlab.com/.

Virtual reality guide
- <u>Overviews, tutorials and links tps://docs.google.com/document</u>, https://tinyurl.com/v923smn.

Syllabus

Diversifying Shakespeare: engaging beyond boundaries

Dr David Sterling Brown	ENGL-310
Dr Meg Lota Brown	Studies in Genres
Dr Kyle DiRoberto	Tu/Th 3:30-4:45
(Contact information and office hours in D2L)	Room: ILC, 137

Students in this tech-focused course will read Shakespeare's *Titus Andronicus* and *The Merchant of Venice* in terms of the theories and concepts articulated in W. E. B. Du Bois's *The Souls of Black Folk* and Gloria Anzaldúa's *Borderlands/La Frontera*. Students will earn 100 per cent Engagement credit while developing critical skills that will enable them to manage effectively the challenges of diversity and identity beyond the classroom. In a semester-length project, students will collaborate with one another to develop digital teaching tools and then present their work at a state-wide conference; the three instructors' NEH-funded grant includes the opportunity for students to contribute their projects to the Folger Shakespeare Library's online suite of shared teaching tools and digital assignments. In addition to the semester-long project, students will produce weekly written reflections. Assessment of the reflections will be based on how students 1) communicate their understanding of diversity and identity through textual interpretations and personal experiences; and 2) translate their understanding into digital teaching tools.

Required texts

W. E. B. Du Bois	*The Souls of Black Folk*
William Shakespeare	*Titus Andronicus*
	The Merchant of Venice
Gloria Anzaldúa	*Borderlands/La Frontera*

Course schedule

Thursday, Jan. 12: Syllabus Review and In-class Small Group Mixers: Frederick Douglass' 'The Color Line'.

Tuesday, Jan. 17: Du Bois, *The Souls of Black Folk* (Forethought and Chapters 1–4).

Thursday, Jan. 19: Du Bois, *The Souls of Black Folk* (Chapters 6, 9 and 11); *Titus Andronicus* Act 1); Journal assignment is due by 3:30 today; Quiz.

Tuesday, Jan. 24: Du Bois, *The Souls of Black Folk* (Chapters 13–14 and Afterthought); *Merchant of Venice* Act 3, Scene 1; Quiz.

Thursday, Jan. 26: Gloria Anzaldúa, *Borderlands/La Frontera*; Quiz.

Tuesday. Jan. 31: Technology Tool Time; Peer review #1 is due by 3:30 today; Tech assignment in class.

Thursday, Feb. 2: Technology Tool Time; Journal assignment is due by 3:30; Tech assignment in class.

Tuesday, Feb. 7: Technology Jam Session.

Thursday, Feb. 9: Technology Jam Session and Presentations; Peer review #2 is due by 3:30; Tech assignment in class.

Tuesday, Feb. 14: *Titus Andronicus*, Acts 1–5; Quiz.
Thursday, Feb. 16: *Titus Andronicus*; Journal assignment is due by 3:30; Quiz.
Tuesday, Feb. 21: *Titus Andronicus*.
Thursday, Feb. 23: *Titus Andronicus*; Peer review #3 is due by 3:30.
Tuesday, Feb. 28: Technology Tool Time; Tech assignment in class.
Thursday, March 2: Technology Jam Session; Journal assignment is due by 3:30.
Tuesday, March 7: Technology Jam Session and Presentations; Tech assignment in class.
Thursday, March 9: *The Merchant of Venice*, Acts 1–5; Peer review #4 is due by 3:30; Quiz.
March 11–19: SPRING BREAK
Tuesday, March 21: *The Merchant of Venice*; Quiz.
Thursday, March 23: *The Merchant of Venice*; Journal assignment is due by 3:30.
Tuesday, March 28: *The Merchant of Venice*.
Thursday, March 30: Textual Intersections; Peer review #5 is due by 3:30.
Tuesday, April 4: Textual Intersections.
Thursday, April 6: Digital Tool Development: Shakespeare, Identity and Diversity; Journal assignment is due by 3:30.
Tuesday, April 11: Digital Tool Development: Shakespeare, Identity and Diversity.
Thursday, April 13: Digital Tool Development: Shakespeare, Identity and Diversity; Peer review #6 is due by 3:30.
Tuesday, April 18: Digital Tool Development: Shakespeare, Identity and Diversity.
Thursday, April 20: Digital Tool Development: Shakespeare, Identity and Diversity; Journal assignment is due by 3:30.
Saturday, April 22: Engagement in the State-wide Conference.
Tuesday, April 25: No Class (comp time for Saturday conference).
Thursday, April 27: Reflection and Synthesis: student presentations. Journal Assignment is due by 3:30.
Tuesday, May 2: Reflection and Synthesis: student presentations. Journal Assignment is due by 3:30.

* * *

Components of final course grade

Participation	10%
2 Five-Minute Tech Presentations (both by week 8)	5%

5 Tech Assignments (all 5 tech assignments by week 8)	10%
7 Quizzes (5 quizzes by week 8)	15%
Engagement in the State-wide Conference	15%
6 Journal Entries and 6 Peer Reviews (review of diction, voice, subordination, organization, sentence structure, clarity and punctuation)	35%
Final presentation	10%

Engaged learning course

This is an 'Engaged Learning Course', in which you will participate in significant experiential learning and reflection designed to prepare you to apply skills and knowledge to the types of problems you may encounter beyond the classroom. If you earn a grade of C or better, you will earn the notation 'Engaged Learning Experience Completed' on your UA transcripts. The completion of this course will also appear on your Student Engagement Record in UAccess.

This course has been designated with the following **Engaged Learning attributes:**

ØEngagement Activity: **Discovery** – Students involved in independent or collaborative inquiry that contributes to a wider sense of understanding, the development of solutions to challenging problems or the creation of new knowledge.

ØEngagement Competency: **Diversity** – Students develop explicit understandings of the sociocultural, linguistic, economic and political experiences of diverse groups representing varying identities and societies, both their own and others, and apply those understandings in work related to a wide range of communities. Diversity and Identity as a Competency is based on developing an appreciation for differences and a sense of an inclusive community.

Course assessment and expected learning outcomes

Critical thinking
- Exercise synthetic, analytic and/or computational reasoning as needed to solve problems.
- Raise salient questions about the evidence, inferences and conclusions of inquiries, including one's own inquiries.
- Infer and assess the ambiguities, assumptions, values and purposes at issue in inquiries, including one's own work.

Effective communication
- Interpret and clearly present information in varied formats, including digital technology, oral presentations and multimedia projects.
- Compose correct and clear written material in multiple formats such as research logs, researched reports, exam answers and reflective essays.
- Improve written and visual documents in response to feedback.

Understanding and valuing differences
- Assess how different modes of inquiry and expression are appropriate in varied cultural and disciplinary contexts.
- Examine how differences in cultural and individual viewpoints expand our understanding of human experience.

In accordance with the UA Tier II Humanities Learning Outcomes and Objectives, the course will enable students to develop the following skills and competencies:

- Identify and analyse the impact of cultural and historical factors on the creation and reception of artistic and literary works.
- Relate arguments and ideas from literature and historical documents to the circumstances under which they were written; read primary documents and be able to place them in their historical context; identify disparate ideas from the evidence of these documents.
- Describe how the development of philosophical and religious thought has influenced human civilization.
- Use appropriate vocabulary for written and oral descriptions and analyses of literary works.

In addition, students will:

- Collaborate with a diverse and interdisciplinary group of educators and peers.
- Identify current challenges regarding human identity – locally and beyond Arizona's borders.
- Distinguish different literary genres and construct textual interpretations.
- Create digital teaching tools that explicitly translate experiences of diverse groups.
- Survey user experiences with digital teaching tools.

Notes

1. For example, in 2010, the Arizona State Legislature passed what was at the time the strictest and most comprehensive anti-immigration bill in the nation, S.B. 1070. In the same year, the Governor and the State Legislature approved a law that targeted ethnic studies in public schools. Mexican-American Studies, in particular, was held to be seditious and un-American. The curriculum, comprised primarily of courses in history, literature and art, was proven to have significantly reduced the drop-out rate of minority high school students, improved their test scores and increased their rate of college attendance. But the Tucson Unified School District was forced to ban the program or lose 10 per cent of its state funding. In 2017, a US District Court ruled that the ban was not motivated by 'legitimate pedagogical concerns' but 'by a desire to advance a political agenda by capitalizing on race-based fears' (Gonzáles v. Douglas 269 F. Supp. 3d 948). Nevertheless, the original programme was never reinstated.
2. Our collaboration included David Sterling Brown, who has contributed to this volume the preceding chapter on a course that he developed separately.
3. The technological expertise and teaching effectiveness of the UA librarians were invaluable. Special thanks to Niamh Wallace, Anthony Sanchez and Jennifer Nichols.
4. The class was comprised of a variety of majors, including business management, English, information science, education, journalism and computer science.
5. TouchCast is designed for the iPad. We allotted funds from one of two grants to buy iPads for our students and then donated the hardware to our university library's makerspace so that the equipment is now free for any student to use. Special thanks are due to the National Endowment for the Humanities, the Folger Shakespeare Library and the University of Arizona's Office of Student Engagement for their support of our project.
6. Student comments were not limited to considerations of technology. They also reported that the focus of literary studies on the nuances of language improved their writing, honed their critical thinking and enabled them to recognize more fully the benefits and challenges of diversity.
7. https://commons.wikimedia.org/wiki/File:Storyboard_Template.jpg.

References

Anzaldúa, G. (1987), *Borderlands/La Frontera: The New Mestiza*. San Francisco: Aunt Lute Books.
Gonzáles v. Douglas 269 F. Supp. 3d 948, 2015.
Shakespeare, W. (2005), *Titus Andronicus*, Folger edition, Barbara Mowat and Paul Werstine, eds, New York: Simon and Schuster.
Shakespeare, W. (2009), *The Merchant of Venice*, Folger edition, Barbara Mowat and Paul Werstine, eds, New York: Simon and Schuster.

6

The British Black and Asian Shakespeare Performance Database

Reclaiming Theatre History

Jami Rogers

Overview

The British Black and Asian Shakespeare Performance Database (BBASPD) is an open access, digital humanities project developed for the AHRC-funded Multicultural Shakespeare project at the University of Warwick.[1] It documents the contributions of practitioners of African-Caribbean, south Asian and east Asian heritage from 1930 to, as of this writing, 2021.[2] The database's pedagogical resources include the biographical information of relevant practitioners; a catalogue of over 1,300 productions (at the time of submission) in which relevant practitioners have been involved; tools that monitor casting practices and persistent inequality in British classical theatre, for example the timeline and the roles counter; select oral histories embedded on the people pages; and excerpts from reviews of many productions listed in the database. These can form the basis for a number of exercises through which the material can be explored, expanding students' understanding both of received ideas about plays and characters as well as the practices that have served to exclude actors of colour and, by extension, women.

As well as entries detailing the work of individual performers of colour, the database also displays information in such a way as to illustrate the historical arc of inclusion in British Shakespeare. For example, each of

Shakespeare's plays has its own page, accessible via the 'plays' tab on the database's main page. The 'plays' section first shows the four categories of Comedy, History, Tragedy and Adaptation and these bars expand to display the individual works, which will allow the user to click on an image in order to be taken to information related to *The Tempest*, *Othello* or *Henry V*, for example. Every play webpage lists productions in which there has been minority ethnic participation since 1930, in chronological order. What is also displayed is what the Multicultural Shakespeare project's team informally has called a 'roles counter', a visualization of each part and the number of times African-Caribbean, south Asian or east Asian performers have played those roles since 1930. Listed in descending order, this feature shows immediately the casting bias towards parts such as Caliban and Ariel in *The Tempest*, Hippolyta in *A Midsummer Night's Dream* or the witches in *Macbeth*. The feature also shows that comparatively very few of these performers have appeared in the history plays at all. The database is thus also an important tool in documenting the glass ceiling that persists for performers of colour in Britain, well into the twenty-first century.

The main remit of the database from the start was to highlight the wealth of talent in the United Kingdom from communities that have been frequently marginalized and their history in the country poorly documented. It was designed as a celebration of their work that was more geared towards fleshing out the historical record rather than with any pedagogical use in mind. This chapter will primarily highlight key features of the British Black and Asian Shakespeare Performance Database in terms of research and creation. It will also illustrate how this historical resource can enhance and expand the teaching of Shakespeare, which will also help to decentre whiteness as the theatrical norm.

Description

The construction of the database occurred on two parallel tracks: research and technical development. The bulk of the research for the database occurred in theatre archives around the United Kingdom, including the Victoria and Albert Museum's Theatre and Performance archive, the Royal Shakespeare Company archive and the Shakespeare Institute Library's (SIL) programme collection in Stratford-upon-Avon. The Multicultural Shakespeare project also had a generous research budget, which meant it was feasible to visit the archives of the country's major regional theatres, including Manchester's Royal Exchange Theatre, the Crucible Theatre in Sheffield, the Octagon Theatre in Bolton, the Birmingham Rep and the Bristol Old Vic.

As the research for the British Black and Asian Shakespeare Performance Database progressed, the theatre programme evolved as the definitive source of information. The reasoning for this decision is relatively straightforward, because programmes contain full cast lists (including minor characters and supernumeraries) which most reviews and other online sources do not. Using the theatre programme as the definitive source in choosing who belongs in a database specifically devoted to practitioners from African-Caribbean, south Asian and east Asian heritage is not without its pitfalls, however. In order to ensure the accuracy of the information in the database, other methods to confirm practitioners' heritage were also employed. This included seeking confirmation from secondary sources such as the Spotlight pages[3] for individual actors, the actors' agents' websites and biographical information from media reports and/or the Internet Movie Database. As the entertainment industry – and the wider culture – views even mixed-race people as belonging to minority groups (e.g., categorizing Barack Obama as the first African American President, although his mother was white), it was also decided to enter practitioners of mixed heritage in the database.

While this research was under way, the physical database also began to take shape. With the Multicultural Shakespeare project set to be completed in 2015 (as it officially was), a sustainable platform was needed to ensure that the British Black and Asian Shakespeare Performance Database would be available long after that end date. Given the need for sustainability, along with the range of data the team was looking to amass and the decision that the database should have an easily accessible public interface, Drupal was chosen as its infrastructure. Since the database would be housed on the University of Warwick's domain name, Drupal was also chosen because it was a platform the university's IT department was willing and able to support on a long-term basis, crucial after the formal end of the Multicultural Shakespeare project.

The development of the database was greatly enhanced by regular communication between the technical and research personnel. While originally envisioned as a database that concentrated on performers, as my research progressed it became clear that people of colour had also made contributions in roles such as assistant director, designer, movement director, composer and fight director. Thus, Steve Ranford, who oversaw technical development, added these categories to the database.

Crucial to the database's pedagogical usefulness would be effective design, both of the visual representations of the data and of the ways in which its components are compartmentalized. The Multicultural Shakespeare project was fortunate enough to have the resources that allowed us to hire an external designer, Pat Lockley, who had far more experience working with Drupal than anyone else involved. In another instance of research and technical team collaboration, Tony Howard, Susan Brock, Steve Ranford and I all met with Lockley in a free-ranging session that essentially provided him with a 'wish list' of what we would like the database to 'do' – or, perhaps more accurately, to display. In a nutshell, what you see when you type in the database's URL is the result of this brainstorming session and Lockley's expertise. The areas that are clearly displayed are the key data categories, visible through the tabs at the top: people, productions, companies and roles (or parts).

The features designed by Lockley enable the user to see two key pieces of data in visual terms. First, the 'roles' tab shows a timeline that counts the number of parts cast using a performer of colour in any given year since 1930 using a series of bars that denote each year. This helps to visualize the gradual increase in integration of Shakespeare in Britain. A second feature that was built into the pages for each Shakespeare play (accessible via the 'plays' tab) is the previously mentioned 'roles counter', a visualization of each part and the number of times African-Caribbean, south Asian or east Asian performers have played those parts since 1930. This feature shows immediately that there is a bias (as noted above) towards parts such as Caliban and Ariel, Hippolyta and the witches – that is, 'exoticized' roles. In collaboration with the team and outside technical expertise, the British Black and Asian Performance Database became a resource that not only showed the history of integrated casting in Britain, but one that also unearthed the levels of discrimination that persist in Britain against classical performers of colour.

The British Black and Asian Shakespeare Performance Database was officially launched in January 2016 at the Tricycle Theatre – now the Kiln Theatre – in Kilburn, north London. The design elements that were incorporated to show the levels of discrimination for performers of colour in British classical theatre were those that had the most immediate impact for the wider public, gaining national and international press coverage. The critic Lyn Gardner wrote a column for the *Guardian* titled 'Colour-blind casting: how far have we really come?' that laid out some of the key research findings from the database, including that only seven performers of colour had played Hamlet by the end of 2015 in the more than eighty years since 1930.[4] The *Independent* also ran a feature about the database, highlighting the finding that the glass ceiling persists, with performers of colour cast more often as servants such as Ariel and Caliban rather than leading roles like Prospero, even decades after they entered the mainstream workforce in Britain. *The Stage* also ran a front-page article and a follow-up reaction piece that foregrounded the inequalities that persist within classical theatre for actors of colour, speaking to Noma Dumezweni, Paterson Joseph, Cynthia Erivo and Kobna Holdbrook-Smith. The impact of the database in the wider context also highlights the many ways in which student learning can be enhanced by its use in the classroom.

Student learning

One of the database's potential impacts on student learning is as a way to decentre whiteness as the default for theatre history. Out of seventy-four contributors to the six-volume *Players of Shakespeare* series, Adrian Lester and Ben Kingsley are the only performers of colour writing about their experiences of playing Shakespeare's characters. While *Players of Shakespeare* has ceased publication, newer volumes follow a similar format. Julian Curry has published two similar volumes under the umbrella title *Shakespeare on Stage*, which include only two actors of colour – Adrian Lester and Chiwetel Ejiofor – out of twenty-five performers in total. These editorial decisions contribute to the diminishment and even erasure of Black and Asian performers from the historical record and maintain the status quo fiction that Shakespearean performers are white. The British Black and Asian Shakespeare Performance Database has embedded within it multiple narratives that can be used as pedagogical tools that serve as an antidote to a mainstream theatre history that focuses almost exclusively on white performers; these narratives include the importance of regional theatre to the growth of integrated casting, the performance history of *Othello* juxtaposed with that of other major tragedies, and interviews which provide an oral history of integrated casting.

The British Black and Asian Shakespeare Performance Database also paints a more nuanced picture of inclusion, as it shows that regional theatres were far ahead of the Royal Shakespeare Company, the National Theatre and – as of its 1997 opening – the 'rebuilt' Shakespeare's Globe. For example, while the RSC gets credit for its 1986 casting of Hugh Quarshie as Banquo in Adrian Noble's production of *Macbeth*, David Thacker's version at the Young Vic preceded it by two years and was far more adventurous. At a time when African-Caribbeans appearing as Othello was still rare, Thacker cast seven African-Caribbeans in his 1984 *Macbeth* as the thanes who opposed Macbeth, including an African-Caribbean Malcolm (Brian Bovell) who becomes King at the end of the play.

The casting of *Othello*'s tragic hero is another of the multiple narratives that can be observed in the British Black and Asian Performance Database. The first entry within this resource is African American Paul Robeson's performance as Othello at London's Savoy Theatre in 1930. While in Britain it is now expected that Othello will be played by an African-Caribbean, the database clearly shows the exclusion of performers of colour from the part until the 1980s. After Robeson's 1930 appearance, only five African-Caribbeans and one south Asian played the title role in the play for the next fifty years. After 1980 regional and London fringe theatres were once again at the forefront of inclusion, with the Northcott Theatre, Exeter, London's Young Vic and the Lyric Hammersmith theatres as well as theatres in Chester, Colchester, Edinburgh, Bristol and Lancaster among those that cast an African-Caribbean as Othello before the RSC (1990), the National Theatre (1997) and Shakespeare's Globe (2007) did. The huge inequalities at the top of the classical canon are also visible, as the database shows especially clearly through its 'roles counter' feature. The disparity can be illustrated through the number of performers of colour who have played the title roles in major tragedies, with Othello far outpacing the others as of this writing: Othello (ninety-three), Romeo (twenty-five), Macbeth (thirteen), Hamlet (eight), King Lear (seven) and Antony (four).

Along with the production data, the British Black and Asian Shakespeare Performance Database also houses selected interviews with some of the major British classical actors of colour and other key individuals who helped shape its historical narratives, carried out by members of the project. This includes Adrian Lester discussing his portrayals of Rosalind and Hamlet; Paterson Joseph on his early work with Cheek By Jowl and the RSC as well as his playing Brutus in the 2012 African-set *Julius Caesar*; Lucian Msamati on his performance as Iago opposite Hugh Quarshie in the RSC's 2015 production of *Othello*; the white director David Thacker recalling his casting of Rudolph Walker, only the fourth Black man to have played Othello in the capital since 1833, at the Young Vic in 1984 (see exercises below); and white director Bill Alexander talking about his work with the Birmingham Rep in the 1990s, including his 1994 *Tempest*, the pedagogical application of which can also be seen below.

Given its origins and my circumstances as research lead, the history to date of the British Black and Asian Shakespeare Performance Database is primarily the creation of an archive with potentiality for student learning, rather than a project or tool primarily conceived with the classroom in mind. But precisely as such, it may suggest ways Shakespeare pedagogy could now 'repurpose' a wide array of archives and other digital materials originally designed for research, deploying their content to make visible to student learners new narratives in what often seems an 'old' field. In this way, as well as in documenting persistent racial inequities in theatrical performance, the database is poised to play its own important role in reforming Shakespeare's history, revealing how digital archives can assist in urgently needed social change – on stage, in research . . . and in the classroom.

Application

In order to illustrate the ways in which the database can help to decolonize the curriculum, I lay out below a series of provocations that can serve as a springboard for wider conversations in the classroom. These may also suggest models for other instructors to create comparable activities using other plays in the database, as best fit their syllabi and curricular requirements.

Exercise 1: casting stereotypes

Jonathan Miller's 1970 production of *The Tempest* remains important because of its introduction into mainstream theatre of a postcolonial reading of the play. Miller's concept was influenced by the French anthropologist Octave Mannoni's *Prospero and Caliban: The Psychology of Colonialism*, which explored a thesis about 'the effect of the paternal white imperial conqueror on an indigenous native population' (Miller 1986: 159). Moreover, this production was staged within months of the end of the Biafran separatist war, with its horrific costs in lives and the fate of the postcolonial nation. In retrospect, Miller's production is problematic, particularly through its co-option of Nigerian cultural conflict as shorthand that mirrored contemporary Britain's attitude to its former colonies. In Miller's *Tempest*, Ariel was representative of the civil servant class (an Ibo) while Caliban was viewed as more primitive (an Hausa), both stereotypes of subservience.

In order to fulfil his vision, Miller cast two Black men, Norman Beaton and Rudolph Walker, as Ariel and Caliban. This was the first time either part had been played by a person of colour in Britain. It is important to balance Miller's use of stereotypes with the overall conditions of the time for actors of colour aspiring to classical theatre, who were almost completely excluded from Shakespearean production. Norman Beaton in 1979 described this state as a 'closed shop' for Black actors and Rudolph Walker recalls 'what I faced as a young actor in this country is that Shakespeare – and especially the leading role in Shakespeare – wasn't meant for us, as Black actors' (interview with author). Miller's production was a breakthrough for Walker and Beaton and those that came after them, even as it also relied on tribal stereotypes. It should also be remembered that Ariel and Caliban remain the two parts in which Black and Asian performers are most frequently cast in *The Tempest* well into the twenty-first century. The breakthrough has become the stereotype.

Questions for students' discussion about The Tempest

- Explore other productions of *The Tempest* in the database. How many have used a Black or Asian actor to portray Ariel and Caliban?
- Ariel and Caliban function in Miller's production as Prospero's servants. How many other servant roles are also more often cast using an ethnic minority performer? [There are several roles that conform to this expectation, including Lucius in *Julius Caesar*, Margaret in *Much Ado About Nothing*, Speed and Lucetta in *Two Gentlemen of Verona*, Maria in *Twelfth Night*.]
- Contrast the casting of Miller's *Tempest* with that of Glen Walford's 1984 Liverpool Everyman and Bill Alexander's 1994 productions. What does having a Black central family (Prospero, Miranda, Antonio) with a white Caliban do to the dynamics of the play? Who is uncomfortable with a Black man playing a leading role? How many times has a Black or Asian person played Prospero versus the number of times performers of colour have played Caliban and/or Ariel?

- Are these patterns still operative in the twenty-first century? Explore Dominic Dromgoole's 2016 production at Shakespeare's Globe in terms of integrated casting. Is his casting more open than Jonathan Miller's in terms of the roles available to actors of colour? What message was sent by costuming an actor of African-Caribbean heritage as Caliban in animal fur while the rest of the cast is wearing Elizabethan clothes?
- Jonathan Miller's production was staged in the aftermath of the Nigerian Civil (or Biafran) War, an event that had gained worldwide attention. As a former British colony, there was particular interest in the war in the British press. The intersection of theatre, contemporary events and postcolonial Britain could provide the basis for a research project for more advanced students.
- Jonathan Miller also revived his production of *The Tempest* in 1988, with Rudolph Walker again reprising Caliban. How had the production changed? How had it remained similar to the original 1970 production?

Exercise 2: *Othello* and the tragedies – performance history

Between 1833 – when African-American Ira Aldridge played Othello at the Covent Garden Theatre – and 1980, only three Black men had played Othello in London, two African Americans and one Trinidadian-born British subject: Aldridge himself, Paul Robeson in 1930 at the Savoy Theatre and Errol John at the Old Vic in 1963. The lack of entries for *Othello* in the British Black and Asian Shakespeare Performance Database before the early 1980s is indicative of what Norman Beaton phrased as a 'closed shop' for actors of colour in British classical theatre. Beaton wrote this description in an op-ed piece in the *Guardian* in 1979 after it had been revealed that the African American actor James Earl Jones had been cast to play Shakespeare's Moor for the BBC Television Shakespeare series. As I have noted elsewhere, the BBC claimed that there were no Black British actors capable of playing the role, to which the actors' union, British Actors' Equity Association, strenuously objected (Rogers 2017: 111; the white actor Anthony Hopkins would eventually be cast as Othello). While the database shows that there were few actors of colour who had been given the opportunity to participate in professional Shakespeare productions, it was blatantly false to say that there were no actors capable of playing Othello – several already had.

The database shows a major shift in the production history of *Othello*, which begins in the early 1980s; furthermore, it contains an invaluable resource for contextual purposes in the form of an audio recording. In an interview with the director David Thacker, he recounts in detail his casting of Rudolph Walker as Othello for the Young Vic in 1984. This is an historically important moment because Walker was then only the fourth Black actor to have played the part in a major theatre in London since Ira Aldridge. Thacker also relates the resistance he encountered at the Royal Shakespeare Company five years later when he was trying to cast Walker as Gower in the 1989 production of *Pericles* in Stratford. With this resource, students can be introduced to the difficulties that actors of colour have had when attempting to achieve parity with their white counterparts.

Othello's performance history can also be used as a springboard to widen an examination of what roles actors of colour are allowed to play. While Othello has become almost exclusively a role for Black men, what are the other major roles that African-Caribbean, south Asian and east Asian actors are allowed to play regularly? There are ninety-six productions of *Othello* in the British Black and Asian Shakespeare Performance Database at the time of writing and Othello has been played ninety-three times by a performer of colour. By contrast, the other tragedies tell a story of exclusion: the database shows that out of the sixty-seven productions of *Hamlet* currently included in the database in which African-Caribbean or Asian practitioners participated, only eight performers of colour have played Hamlet across seven productions. This fact poses questions about what other roles, apart from Othello, ethnic minority actors have access to; it ties in with the layers of stereotyping that go into the casting process, which mean that very few actors who are not white have been included for consideration to play the major roles in the Shakespearean canon. How does the strength of the stereotypes translate onto the Shakespearean stage, if not through Hamlet? Why is there more representation in the comedies than the histories and tragedies? Why are actors of colour still playing Othello more often than they play Hamlet or Henry V? Why do African-Caribbean men play characters known primarily as aggressive or violent, such as Tybalt or Demetrius? There are a multitude of questions that the British Black and Asian Shakespeare Performance Database can help students begin to unpack, providing material for further research, writing and textual analysis.

Questions for students' discussion about Othello

- Using the reviews of numerous productions of *Othello* in the database, trace the shift in attitudes about Black actors' performance of Shakespeare through the decades. Analyse the data and think about how racism may be encoded and how that relates to questions such as 'Who owns Shakespeare?' and 'Who is allowed access to Shakespeare?'
- Why were reviewers repeatedly using the phrase 'genuinely black Othello' about entries in the database? What stereotypes are

associated with 'genuinely black rage', which was how one reviewer described elements of Rudolph Walker's performance in 1984?
- Use elements of David Thacker's interview to discuss the question of received ideas about what 'Shakespeare' is, particularly his recollections about casting Rudolph Walker in 1984 and the fact that British society in the 1980s was resistant to the idea that a Black man with a West Indian accent could play Shakespeare. What does this say about the questions 'Who is allowed access to Shakespeare?' and 'Who owns Shakespeare?'
- Use Adrian Lester's discussion of playing Othello to investigate some of the issues that occur when playing the part, particularly those to do with stereotypes. (Two resources complement each other here – the interviews Lester did with Tony Howard and Ayanna Thompson, the former housed on the database and the latter in *Shakespeare Survey* 70 (Lester 2017).)
- Lucian Msamati's audio interview with myself in the British Black and Asian Shakespeare Performance Database can be used to provoke further questions about race and identity through his discussion of playing a Black Iago opposite Hugh Quarshie at the RSC in 2015.

* * *

With thanks to Tony Howard, Steve Ranford and Susan Brock for filling in the informational gaps about the genesis of the British Black and Asian Shakespeare Performance Database when it was in its gestational period.

Notes

1 The Arts and Humanities Research Council is one of Britain's main research funding bodies.
2 The terminology in this chapter is that employed in Britain in terms of race and ethnicity. South Asian here refers broadly to the Indian subcontinent, and east Asian primarily encompasses (but is not limited to) people of Chinese, Japanese, Korean, Indonesian, Filipino heritage.
3 Spotlight is the UK's primary casting tool, which was once published in book form but now is a premium online service where professional actors list their acting experience, skills, age and what is euphemistically known as 'characteristics', under which umbrella ethnicity is placed.
4 Eight performers of colour had played Hamlet by the end of 2016, including Paapa Essiedu and Raphael Sowole for the RSC and Black Theatre Live, respectively. Cush Jumbo was set to become the ninth performer of colour to play Hamlet in 2020 at the Young Vic, which was postponed due to the coronavirus pandemic. With Greg Hersov's production rescheduled for

25 September–13 November 2021, she should have achieved that milestone by the time this volume goes to print. For context, in the four years between 2015 and 2018 alone, there were at least thirteen professional productions of *Hamlet* with white actors playing the lead in Britain, including Maxine Peake, Benedict Cumberbatch, Andrew Scott and Michelle Terry.

References

Beaton, N. (1979), 'A taste of nothing much', *The Guardian*, 9 February, 13–14.
The British Black and Asian Shakespeare Performance Database, Jami Rogers (ed.), University of Warwick/Arts & Humanities Research Council, https://bbashakespeare.warwick.ac.uk.
Gallagher, P. (2016), 'Shakespearean black and ethnic minority actors "still only getting minor roles"', *The Independent*, 16 January, https://www.independent.co.uk/news/uk/home-news/shakespearean-black-and-ethnic-minority-actors-still-only-getting-minor-roles-a6816941.html.
Gardner, L. (2016), 'Colour-blind casting: how far have we really come?', *The Guardian*, 13 January, https://www.theguardian.com/stage/theatreblog/2016/jan/13/colour-blind-casting.
Gould, M. (2013), *The Biafran War: The Struggle for Modern Nigeria*, London and New York: I.B. Tauris.
Hutchison, D. (2016), 'Shakespeare database reveals "massive failure" in minority casting', *The Stage*, 8 January.
Hutchison, D. (2016), 'Casting snub for black actors in Shakespeare: theatre stars react', *The Stage*, 14 January.
Lester, A. (2017), 'In Dialogue with Ayanna Thompson', *Shakespeare Survey* 70: 10–18, Cambridge: Cambridge University.
Miller, J. (1986), *Subsequent Performances*, London and Boston: Faber and Faber.
Olusoga, D. (2016), *Black and British: A Forgotten History*, London: Macmillan.
Rogers, J. (2013), 'The Shakespearean Glass Ceiling: the State of Colorblind Casting in Contemporary British Theatre', *Shakespeare Bulletin* 31, no. 3: 110–21.
Rogers, J. (2017), 'David Thacker and Bill Alexander: Mainstream directors and the development of multicultural Shakespeare', in Delia Jarrett-Macauley (ed.), *Shakespeare, Race and Performance: The Diverse Bard*, 110–21, London: Routledge.
Rogers, J. (forthcoming), *British Black and Asian Shakespeareans: Integrating Shakespeare, 1966–2018*, London: Arden Shakespeare.
Schwarz, W. (1969), 'Biafra's bitter tale: Next week Parliament will debate the Nigerian War', *The Guardian*, 6 December.

# 7

Reading Interculturality in Class

Contextualizing Global Shakespeares in and through A|S|I|A

Eleine Ng-Gagneux

Overview

Digital performance archives have facilitated the accessibility and study of Global Shakespeares worldwide. They are useful resources when teaching intercultural and cross-cultural Shakespeare productions in classrooms, which are often distant from the physical locales and contexts where these local performances were originally staged. For many students, watching Shakespeare productions through scholarly performance archives, video-sharing websites (e.g., YouTube) or online streaming services (e.g., the Globe Player) forms their first encounter with Global Shakespeares. For some, viewing Shakespeare through digitized video-players actually marks their first experience as an audience of any Shakespeare performance. The means by which we understand (global) Shakespeare productions are increasingly being mediated, and it has become equally important to address these alternative spectatorial frameworks as the production and reception of Shakespeare continue to shift with technology.

A major challenge in teaching Asian Shakespeare performances to students unfamiliar with Asian theatre is the tendency to perceive *Shakespeare*, rather than local performance practices, as the centrical force that engenders the adaptive paradigms of these productions and their global digital flow (see O'Neill 2018: 129). The lack of contextual information and (translated) data on diverse performance strategies hinders students from fully considering the cultural exchanges and conditions that determine and shape such adaptations. Furthermore, the unavailability of translated scripts means students are unable to analyse how these productions culturally and creatively engage with the Shakespearean text in a comprehensive way. Thus, the reading of these productions can often perpetuate exoticized notions of traditional Asian art forms or fail to account for the ways in which Shakespeare's canonical status is challenged by contemporary interpretations of his work.

Digital Shakespeare projects can, at times, affirm the problematic acceptance of Shakespeare's cultural authority and supposed universality (Estill 2019: 2). However, multilingual and collaborative digital archives like the Asian Shakespeare Intercultural Archive (A|S|I|A: http://a-s-i-a-web.org) are productive in-class resources that shift this Shakespeare-centrism.[1] These digitized mediums reframe Shakespeare's global presence as an effect of an evolving paradigm of cultural interchange and prompt students to (re) contextualize his cultural prominence. In this chapter, I look at how A|S|I|A can be adopted as a pedagogic tool to study the different types of (inter/cross-)cultural exchanges involved in Asian Shakespeare performances. When used to teach Global Shakespeares, A|S|I|A also helps to interculturalize learning environments, which can be overly determined by monolingual and monocultural ways of thinking. I discuss how a learner's understanding of Global Shakespeares is impacted by the interactive components in A|S|I|A, and explore in which ways these features encourage student-users to recognize the plurality of intercultural Shakespeare production and the implications of their own cultural and spectatorial positions on the study of such performances.

A|S|I|A includes sixty-two full-length recordings of Shakespeare productions from East and Southeast Asia. This online database also archives publicity materials such as production programmes and photographs, and holds performance data and original performance scripts, which are mainly translated into English, Mandarin, Japanese and Korean. As a collaborative digital project, A|S|I|A relies on a team of scholars, practitioners, translators, students and technical experts from various scholarly fields and countries (e.g., China, Japan, South Korea, Singapore and the United Kingdom). The team's focus on creating a multilingual digital environment and performance data collaboratively offers users different entry points into the study of intercultural Shakespeare performances, which cultivates comparative research across contexts and languages.

The interculturality of A|S|I|A is informed by a collective process of data creation, and is virtually manifested in the digital platform's readability and the interactivity of its worldwide users. In addition to its multilingual and extra-performance components, this searchable database includes interactive tools like a personal My Toolbox function where members are able to bookmark and retrieve clips of specific performance segments. A|S|I|A's Forum (a message and discussion board) enables users to share and exchange information and ideas as well as generate new occasions for collaboration by way of a virtual research community. In the classroom, these interactive functions not only support student-users to be 'information producers rather than just information consumers' (Casey 2019: 14) but also establish a virtual space that could lead to real-world collaborations. Here, the digital archive is no longer just a 'dissemination platform' but an online meeting place that fosters cross-cultural communication (Carson and Kirwan 2014: 247). Being able to discuss productions with other international users allows students to encounter the complex dynamics of intercultural exchange first-hand, and more crucially, invites them to be part of the dialogue that surrounds Global Shakespeares.

A|S|I|A has maintained a significant focus on providing its users with detailed performance data and full script translations in the website's featured Asian languages.[2] The translation of these different types of data and the function to navigate between the various language interfaces in this parallel language website foreground both the cultural specificity of the archived productions and the cultural subjectivity of its online audience. These diverse positionalities are further emphasized through the archive's video interface. The video-streaming interface, which was conceived by Yong Li Lan and Alvin Lim, provides users with the option to read and switch between any one of the translated scripts while watching the video-recordings. As Yong posits, 'a viewer in any language is aware of watching the video in the co-presence of a watching experience in (at least) three other languages, virtually and perhaps actually at the same time' (2017), which heightens one's cognizance of the multiple spectatorial perspectives a single production can generate. While one experiences watching a live theatrical event and an online video recording quite differently, this virtual engagement with Shakespeare initiates alternative modes of watching, replaying and (re)interpretation.

The Notepad that appears alongside the video-player screen affords users and editors of A|S|I|A the ability to leave either private notes or comments that can be made public there, each of which are time-stamped and appear when the video-recording reaches an annotated moment. Included in the Notepad is a group notes function (i.e., 'Group Code'), which can be used to facilitate virtual and live group discussions. These commentaries serve two important purposes: first, the notes left by editors provide users with additional information that is not in the script or performance data (e.g., details on specific musical instruments); second, the presence of remarks and questions by other users on the Notepad panel as one watches forms a visual trace of alternative spectatorship and underscores the multiplicity of an intercultural watching experience. This feature is helpful when teaching students to recognize their own positionality and the context of their watching environment.

The archive is intercultural in its content, design and archiving methods, and as Lim suggests, 'provides a way to think of interculturality in a digital way' (2018: 209). The diverse interactive features built into A|S|I|A further extend its interculturality by forming new Shakespearean nexuses that are based on the local and the global and, when used in classroom settings, ask student-users to participate in these discursive networks. Online archives like A|S|I|A do not merely store memories of the original event but continue to create new engagements with Shakespeare through intercultural modes of enquiry that are made possible by digitization.

Description

The collaborative framework of A|S|I|A is premised on cultural and analytical plurality, and its performance data evinces this intercultural practice of archival research. Editors with extensive knowledge in one or more theatre culture(s) create this data, which allows specialized knowledge to be sharable and searchable by diverse users from different linguistic, cultural and scholarly communities. Each data-map is usually produced in the same language as the studied performance and simultaneously in English by at least two editors before it is translated into the other languages of the website. Although the accessibility to Global Shakespeares has increased, there still seems an authorial stronghold of specialized opinion emerging from critics from distinct national, cultural and intellectual territories, which contradictorily limits intercultural Shakespeare scholarship to an area studies paradigm (see Prescott 2013). The extensive collaboration between the editors and editor-translators when developing data, however, reflects a research methodology that actively resists unilateral perspectives and ideological binaries.

Performance data protocols provide teachers and students with a formalized discursive vocabulary to use in examining modes of adaptation, performance strategies and the contextual dimensions of a production. Metadata in A|S|I|A is divided into four main categories: Art/Forms (i.e., the language, performance forms and staging strategies used in each production); Production (i.e., data regarding the creation and staging of the featured performance); Points of Reference (i.e., contextual information that a production refers to, in terms of the Shakespearean play and its new staging environment); and Reception (i.e., responses to the live performance event). The structural organization of these categories highlights different ways a production can be read and understood, and comprises 'the field of discussion surrounding each performance'.[3]

Most of the primary information in the Reference and Art/Forms categories have secondary data that are detailed as 'Distinctive usage of' data. This information individualizes specific staging strategies that inform the entire performance, and foregrounds the diverse nature of Shakespeare production in Asia. For example, to illustrate to my students how multilingualism references idiosyncratic cultural and performative signs within different dramatic and extra-dramatic contexts, I examine the use of language in two productions by Singaporean directors Mohammed Najib Soiman and Ong Keng Sen. The use of multiple Asian languages, namely English, Bahasa Melayu, Mandarin and Cantonese, in Soiman's *Ma' Ma Yong: About Nothing Much To Do* (an adaptation of Shakespeare's *Much Ado About Nothing*) is linked expressly to Singapore's multicultural and multilingual society (A|S|I|A). The same use of various Asian languages like Thai, Japanese and Mandarin in Ong's *Lear*, however, while also associated with a particular cultural frame of reference, is representative of the distinctive Asian traditional performance forms adopted in the production, such as *noh* and *jingju* (Beijing Opera). This use of multilingualism in Ong's *Lear* referenced the production's larger multicultural framework, rather than alluding to a specific local geography or epoch. The different significations of performing multilingualism in these two productions demonstrate how comparative study simultaneously emphasizes the intersections and divergences between discrete Asian Shakespeares, reminding us that the 'global narratives' which gloss Shakespeare's circulation 'need to be reconfigured as [a] series of linked and contextualised local ones' (Dawson 2002: 188). This differentiation between similar staging strategies is important when studying intercultural Shakespeares, as such performance models, which can be easily subsumed under a broad and oversimplified 'Global Shakespeare' approach, can now be studied as particularized engagements with a Shakespeare that is made global through heterogeneous localized processes.

Encouraging comparative research through the searchability of digital databases enables students to identify nuanced differences in the use of performance styles and strategies within specific cultural and theatrical contexts. A quick search of the keywords 'Korean folk culture' in A|S|I|A will list a number of Korean productions as search results. This data, 'Korean folk culture', is recorded in the broader Reference category as a 'non-Shakespeare' cultural reference entry in both the National Changgeuk Company of Korea's (NCCK) *Romeo and Juliet* and Yohangza Theatre Company's *A Midsummer Night's Dream* data-maps. The distinctive usage of this particular Reference data, however, is markedly unalike, as the two productions are aimed at different performative outcomes and work within different semiotic systems. In NCCK's *Romeo and Juliet*, traditional Korean folk culture is represented through the use of 'festive entertainment', like *talchum* (mask dance) and *kkokdu noleum* (puppetry). In Yohangza's *Dream*, reference to folk culture is translated through *shinmyoung puri* (a release of high spirits), which is manifested in the 'aesthetic principle in the [production's] dances and music' and can be experienced by both the performer and the audience. Though both productions evoke Korean folk culture to create distinct imaginative worlds onstage, the former performance presents this contextual reference to

Korean culture as art form, whereas in Yohangza's *Dream*, an aspect of indigenous folk culture is expressed as a shared communal spirit, evoked through the creation of and participation in the theatrical event. Databases and their extensive collections urge student-users to notice the performative variance of Asian Shakespeare production that occurs within and beyond a single theatre culture. This awareness of the intracultural dimensions of intercultural theatre also helps limit generalized and essentialized views that tend to persist within Global Shakespeare discourse.[4]

The methods by which we discuss and record intercultural Shakespeare performances online shape new research perspectives in this scholarly field. A well-designed database, as Stephen Ramsay posits, 'contains not static information, but an entire set of ontological relations capable of generating statements about a domain' (Ramsay 1995: 195). Hence, how datasets are organized, data-maps are presented and data is retrieved fosters patterns of connections and seeing. Through repeated searches of the A|S|I|A database, student-users can learn to refine their keyword queries and, in doing so, gain interpretative insight into what constitutes the complex web of Global Shakespeare production.

In order to improve the searchable capacity of A|S|I|A's expanding database, the team revised the archive's existing data structure and entries during the 'Mapping Asian Shakespeares: Asian Intercultural Digital Archives Metadata Workshop' (2015).[5] As a single term can denote diverse meanings in different (theatre) cultures, the team also re-evaluated how searchable keywords were reflected in the archival database. The example below of a 'Single/Plural performance form' data entry from Yohangza's *Dream* illustrates how the revised data structure now permits more details to be included:

Original data entry
Single/Plural performance form → Multiple forms → Distinctive feature: Korean traditional dance → Distinctive usage of: –

Revised data entry
Single/Plural performance form → Multiple forms → **Performance type**: Classical → **Performance form**: Korean traditional dance → Distinctive usage of: Loo's fan dance, which presents his sadness after being rejected by Beok in Scene 5

The reconceptualization of new sub-fields (i.e., 'performance type' and 'performance form') aims to facilitate greater data granularity and allow a framework for comparison to emerge. Although 'performance form' entries record practices specific to distinct theatre cultures, the broader 'performance type' sub-field enables a larger group of data to be catalogued together.

The standardization of categorized keywords recorded in the database's sub-fields (e.g., 'performance type', 'stage design', etc.) and the reorganization of its data structure allowed a pie chart feature to be developed. While the details listed in the data-maps help student-users to better understand the diverse contexts that inform specific creative productions, the pie charts of the Art/Forms categories present the comparative intersections between the performances in the database via visual representation (Figure 7.1). The pie charts enable students to locate patterns of adaptation strategies shared among these archived Shakespeare productions. This simple form of data visualization displays how the vast amount of information in A|S|I|A is connected. More materially, it makes visible to student-users the branches of local knowledge and artistic practices that configure Shakespeare as a site for interculturality.

A user can access different pie charts either by clicking on the 'Single/Plural Performance Forms' or 'Language of Performance' link, or choosing from a dropdown menu of 'Distinctive Staging Strategy' properties (e.g., costume design, stage design), which are found at the top of the pie-chart display page. Navigating the website through the pie charts motivates student-users to formulate their own research pathways, which are determined by individual discursive topics and their own research interests. For example, a student who was curious about the usage of coloured costumes in Yohangza's *Dream* wanted to explore how this production's costume data entry, which falls under the 'symbolic colour' sub-category, related to other production data entries that were similarly classified. Clicking on the 'colour' slice segment of the main costume design pie chart showed the student that the 'colour' category in the database was divided

FIGURE 7.1 *Screenshot of pie-chart display page. Courtesy of the Asian Shakespeare Intercultural Archive.*

into three sub-categorical types: 'symbolic colour', 'colour coded' and 'single colour'. While the student first perused the various data entries listed on the 'colour' pie-chart display page exclusive to the 'symbolic colour' sub-category, the observation that coloured costumes functioned as a prominent performance strategy in many of the productions in A|S|I|A prompted her to expand her research to include the analysis of data recorded under the 'colour coded' and 'single colour' sub-categories. By offering users multiple points of entry to examine the performative dimensions of Asian Shakespeares, the pie charts also encourage a mode of research that works to decentralize Shakespeare as the sole catalyst for intercultural exchange (and international circulation): users can construct diverse trajectories of research that need not start and end with Shakespeare.

Student learning

I taught Intercultural Shakespeare as part of a larger first-year theatre history and performance module in the United Kingdom.[6] For many of my students, learning about a range of intercultural theory and performance practices was challenging. These concepts existed outside their horizons of knowledge and required them to contextualize different performative frameworks and become conscious of their own spectatorial positions. Citing data from the 'Shakespeare' sub-field of the Reference category was especially effective when concretizing the aesthetic, cultural and linguistic interactions that transfigure a Shakespearean play into an intercultural performance.

The data in this sub-field organizes a production's adaptation of a Shakespearean play into three broad categories: plot, character and text. The taxonomy of a performance's correlation to these dramatic elements is further classified into three branches, which delineate the varying degrees of closeness an adaptation has to Shakespeare's play(s): first degree, over 80 per cent (translation); second degree, 20–80 per cent (adaptation); and third degree, under 20 per cent (allusion). The first-degree classification is generally applied when an adaptation largely remains faithful to the Shakespearean play, while the third-degree classification designates a production that substantially reconfigures the original play's linguistic and dramatic context. The percentage range allotted to the second-degree classification is intentionally kept expansive as it allows for a broader scope of adaptive approaches to be accounted for in this bracket. This medial classification is used to denote a production that reimagines Shakespeare's play through alternative language(s) and theatre culture(s) without either source materials being erased or completely dominating the adaptation process. Together with this codification, the 'Distinctive usage of' data elaborates on the exact ways in which a performance reworks and treats the Shakespearean plot, character and text.

The information in the 'Shakespeare' sub-field categories systematizes the aesthetic and cultural intersections between a Shakespearean play and its new interpretation. Take, for instance, the data for NCCK's *Romeo and Juliet*. The plot category for this production was given a first-degree classification, as the performance's plot followed the Shakespearean play very closely, with the Capulet and Montague feud being recontextualized through the regional conflicts between two Korean provinces (A|S|I|A). The production was assigned a second-degree classification in its character category as it retained the main Shakespearean characters, and some minor characters (Capulet and Lady Capulet, Montague and Lady Montague, Paris, the Apothecary and Friar John, who was reimagined as a female shaman). The third-degree classification was assigned to the production's text category. The production was based on an original script, by Park Sung-Whan, which modernized the Shakespearean language to contemporary Korean vernacular and transposed 'Shakespeare's text into Pansori [a storytelling-singing art form] verse and local contexts'. Since this production adapted *Romeo and Juliet* mainly through *Changgeuk* (Korean opera), Park's script consisted of verse, prose and lyrics, spoken and sung, which drastically transformed the Shakespearean text.

While showing performance clips in class provided extensive examples of the ways in which Shakespeare could be rewritten, a majority of my students found it difficult to expound on the links between a performance's adaptive framework and the more abstract models of intercultural exchange reviewed in class (e.g., Patrice Pavis's hourglass, Rustom Bharucha's pendulum and Jacqueline Lo and Helen Gilbert's intercultural models). The Reference data in the 'Shakespeare' sub-field, however, became a productive rubric in scaffolding my students' understanding of the relationship between Shakespeare and the theatre cultures that reinterpret him and how to theorize such intercultural engagements.

When asked which of the three theoretical frameworks of theatrical interculturalism studied in the module best expressed the cultural exchange exemplified by Yohangza's *Dream*, many students used the second-degree classification of its plot, character and text categories to support their choice of Bharucha's pendulum model (see Figure 7.2). Bharucha's model sees interculturalism evoking 'a back-and-forth movement, suggesting the swing of a pendulum' and entails, in ideal cases, an evenly balanced process of cultural exchange (1993: 241). My students considered second-degree classifications across the three dramatic properties in this production's 'Shakespeare' sub-field data as being indicative of the 'two-way street' adaptation paradigm suggested by Bharucha's pendulum imagery (1993: 2). To some, this correlation between Shakespeare's play and Yohangza's *Dream* corresponded directly with the pendular flow of cultural interchange Bharucha's proposes, which describes 'a mutual reciprocity of needs' shared between a source and target culture (1993: 2). This information helped my students evaluate how Shakespeare's original was still recognizable in the

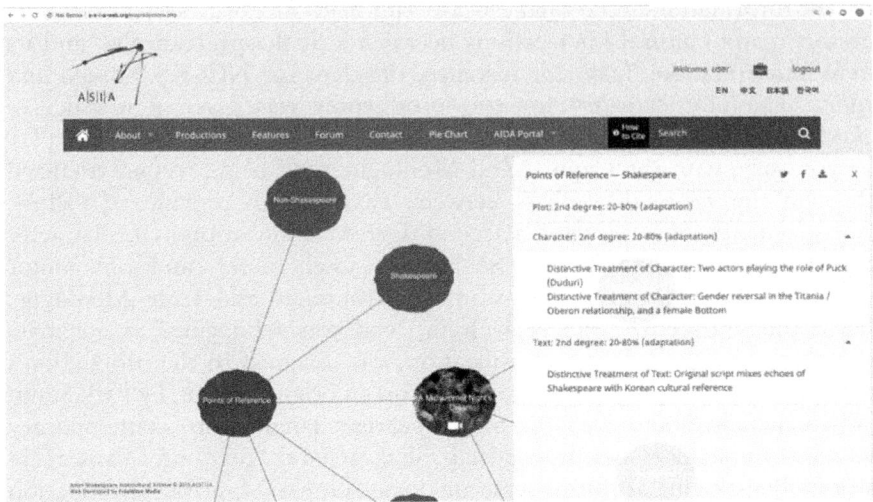

FIGURE 7.2 *Screenshot of the Points of Reference data display and 'Shakespeare' sub-field of the Yohangza Theatre Company's* A Midsummer Night's Dream *data-map. Courtesy of the Asian Shakespeare Intercultural Archive.*

new performance script and how the different performance styles and new Korean cultural references added an alternative reading of the Shakespearean play. To put it simply, students were able to observe in this adaptation that Shakespeare simultaneously remained and was made anew.

Although this assessment of Bharucha's theory only touches the surface of his concept of theatrical interculturalism, it became a basis for my students to engage with the more complex ideological principles we studied.[10] The classification scheme was an accessible means for students to learn and compare different modes of adaptation in intercultural Shakespeare production. It charted the 'intellectual terrain covered in the area being classified' (Sperberg-McQueen 2004: 162) and illustrated the underpinning values assigned to discrete adaptive strategies.

In addition, for their final written assessment, many students who chose to write a short intercultural adaptation of a scene from *A Midsummer Night's Dream* used this taxonomic model to clarify their artistic conception in the commentaries that accompanied their script submissions. This rubric not only provided students with a discursive framework to explore larger theoretical ideas covered in class, but also allowed them to form their own perspectives on intercultural Shakespeare (re)production and become self-reflective about their creative decisions. Furthermore, the assessment underscored the value of creating activities that combine knowledge acquired through digital pedagogy with more formal written work. Such multimodal exercises prompt students to learn through diversified ways of knowing and doing in order to apply their 'theoretical understanding *in practice*' (Beetham and Sharpe 2007: 3). As surveyed from a sample of written commentaries, the classification scheme offered students a user-friendly way to read interculturality and bridged the gap between theory and practice. The concepts of knowledge which are embodied in the interface design and data structure of A|S|I|A demonstrate how digital resources don't just support teaching but can become key tools that encourage independent knowledge creation and shape new opportunities of learning.

Application

Lesson topic	Evaluating intercultural practice and theory
Level	Second-year undergraduate students (Theatre Studies)
Class type	Seminar (120 minutes) *based on a class of twenty students*
Learning outcomes	**Students will be able to:** ➢ Apply A|S|I|A's classification scheme ('Shakespeare' sub-field data) to their understanding of theatrical interculturalism. ➢ Analyse the key characteristics of intercultural Shakespeare adaptation. ➢ Assess critical intercultural theatre approaches and theories.
Materials	• William Shakespeare's *A Midsummer Night's Dream* • Asian Shakespeare Intercultural Archive (http://a-s-i-a-web.org) • Richard Schechner's 'Global and Intercultural Performances' in *Performance Studies: An Introduction*
Prior knowledge	**Students have been introduced to:** • Patrice Pavis's hourglass model, Rustom Bharucha's pendulum model and Jacqueline Lo and Helen Gilbert's intercultural model. • A|S|I|A's performance data-maps and classification scheme. • Yohangza Theatre Company's *Dream* performance (video-recording on A|S|I|A).
Learning environment	• Students to be in groups of five • Computer access • Projection and screen

Duration	Lesson development	Assessment	Resource
20 mins	**Trigger activity** • Teacher to review different theatrical models of cultural exchange. • Students to peruse the Yohangza's *Dream* data-map. • Class discussion: ➢ Identify the ways in which Shakespeare's play is reinterpreted through Korean theatrical and cultural contexts. ➢ Explore why this performance can be considered an intercultural Shakespeare adaptation.	Students should: • Elaborate how 'Shakespeare' sub-field classification scheme relates to intercultural theatre theories and practice studied in the module.	A|S|I|A data-map: → Art/Forms category → Reference category
35 mins	**Main activity** Groups will: • Conceptualize and present an intercultural adaptation of a scene in Shakespeare's *Dream*. • Explain how they would adapt the Shakespearean plot, character and text. Prompts (for groups) • Students to share their cultural and linguistic backgrounds with their groups. • Consider how they would approach the following: ◦ Monolingual or multilingual performance language(s) ◦ Single or plural performance form(s) and/or style(s) ◦ Setting, costume and stage design, music, etc. • Decide which type of intercultural exchange they want to model their adaptation after. • Use pie charts for examples of different staging strategies that shape intercultural Shakespeare adaptation.	• Demonstrate how their adaptations reflect an intercultural approach. • Relate their creative choices to the different theatrical models of cultural exchange studied.	→ Reference category → Pie charts

Duration	Lesson development	Assessment	Resource
45 mins	10 mins group presentations including time for Q&A	• Reflect on and explicate their creative concepts of intercultural practice. • Give peer feedback and raise questions about the rationales behind another group's concept.	
10 mins	**Wrap-up (teacher-led)** 1. Compare and contrast the different adaptive approaches adopted by the various student-groups. 2. Relate their creative concepts to larger theoretical discussions about intercultural Shakespeare explored previously. 3. Highlight the complexities of defining intercultural Shakespeare.		
10 mins	Briefing of follow-up lesson (**optional**) In their existing groups, students are to: • Examine the staging strategies and 'Shakespeare' sub-field classifications of another *Dream* performance in A|S|I|A. • Compare and contrast this performance with Yohangza's *Dream* (groups should focus on the same scene chosen for their main activity). • Use the Notepad group notes function to annotate the same scene of both performances. This full list of notes can be downloaded and studied in the following seminar. • Discuss the responses to the scenes, paying close attention to how their own positionalities impact their reading of these performances.		→ Notepad function (see 'Features' page on A|S|I|A for information on how to create a 'Group Code')

Notes

1 A\|S\|I\|A is part of three research projects supported by the Singapore Ministry of Education (Relocating Intercultural Theatre, MOE2008-T2-1-110; Digital Archiving and Intercultural Performance, MOE2013-T2-1-011; and Digital Performance Scholarship, MOE2018-T2-2-092).
2 See 'About' page in A\|S\|I\|A.
3 See 'Database' page in A\|S\|I\|A.

4 Rustom Bharucha's understanding of 'intracultural' illustrates the interactions between cultures within national borders rather than encounters outside national contexts, and suggests that the identification of a nation as being intrinsically monocultural is problematic (2000: 9).

5 The Asian Intercultural Digital Archives is a group of digital archives of East and Southeast Asian performance materials based at the National University of Singapore (NUS): A|S|I|A, the Contemporary Wayang Archive (CWA; http://cwa-web.org/), led by Miguel Escobar Varela, and the Theatre Makers Asia archive (TMA; http://tma-web.org/), led by Alvin Lim. This workshop was held at NUS and attended by Yong Li Lan, Hwang Ha Young, Alvin Lim, Takiguchi Ken, Lee Chee Keng, Suematsu Michiko, Choi Boram, Shreyosi Mukherjee, Miguel Escobar Varela and Jiang Liheng (FreeWave Media).

6 The term 'Module' is used to describe a course of study in universities in the United Kingdom and corresponds with the term 'Course' used in the United States.

References

Asian Shakespeare Intercultural Archive (2015), *Asian Shakespeare Intercultural Archive*, 3rd edn, http://a-s-i-a-web.org.

Beetham, H. and R. Sharpe (2007), 'An introduction to rethinking pedagogy for a digital age', in Helen Beetham and Rhona Sharpe (eds), *Rethinking Pedagogy in the Digital Age: Designing and Delivering E-Learning*, 1–10, London and New York: Routledge.

Bharucha, R. (2000), *The Politics of Cultural Practice: Thinking through Theatre in an Age of Globalization*, Hanover, NH: Wesleyan University.

Bharucha, R. (2003), *Theatre and the World: Performance and the Politics of Culture*, London: Routledge.

Carson, C. and P. Kirwan (2014), 'Conclusion: Digital Dreaming', in C. Carson and P. Kirwan (eds), *Shakespeare and the Digital World*, 238–57, Cambridge: Cambridge University Press.

Casey, J. (2019), 'Digital Shakespeare is Neither Good Nor Bad But Teaching Makes it So', *Humanities* 8: 1–19.

Dawson, A. B. (2002), 'International Shakespeare', in S. Wells and S. Stanton (eds), *The Cambridge Companion to Shakespeare on Stage*, 174–93, Cambridge: Cambridge University Press.

Desmet, C. (2017), 'The Art of Curation: Searching for Global Shakespeares in the Digital Archives', *Borrowers and Lenders* 11, no. 1: 1–11.

Estill, L. (2019), 'Digital Humanities' Shakespeare Problem', *Humanities* 8: 1–16.

Lim, A. E. H. (2018), 'Digital Environments for Intercultural Content: A Case Study on the Asian Shakespeare Intercultural Archive', in Sarah Whatley, Rosamaria K. Cisneros and Amalia Sabiescu (eds), *Digital Echoes: Spaces for Intangible and Performance-based Cultural Heritage*, 191–211, n.p.p.: Palgrave Macmillan.

Lo, J. and H. Gilbert (2002), 'Towards a Topography of Cross-cultural Theatre Praxis', *Drama Review* 46, no. 3: 31–53.

Mohammed, N. S. (2008), *Ma' Ma Yong – About Nothing Much to Do*, in *Asian Shakespeare Intercultural Archive*, http://a-s-i-a-web.org.
O'Neill, S. (2018), 'Shakespeare's Digital Flow: Humans, Technologies and the Possibilities of Intercultural Exchange', *Shakespeare Studies* 46: 120–33.
Ong, K. S. (1997), *Lear: An Intercultural Theater Collaboration of Six Asian Countries*, in *Asian Shakespeare Intercultural Archive*, http://a-s-i-a-web.org.
Park, S.-W. (2009), *Romeo and Juliet*, in *Asian Shakespeare Intercultural Archive*, http://a-s-i-a-web.org.
Pavis, P. (1992), *Theatre at the Crossroads of Culture*, London: Routledge.
Prescott, P. (2013), *Reviewing Shakespeare: Journalism and Performance from the Eighteenth Century to the Present*, Cambridge: Cambridge University Press.
Ramsay, S. (2004), 'Databases', in S. Schreibman, R. Siemens and J. Unsworth (eds), *A Companion to Digital Humanities*, 177–97, Oxford: Blackwell.
Sperberg-McQueen, C. M. (2004), 'Classifications and its Structures', in S. Schreibman, R. Siemens and J. Unsworth (eds), *A Companion to Digital Humanities*, 161–76, Oxford: Blackwell.
Yang, J. U. (2012), *A Midsummer Night's Dream*, in *Asian Shakespeare Intercultural Archive*, http://a-s-i-a-web.org.
Yong, L. L. (2017), 'Translating Performance: the Asian Shakespeare Intercultural Archive', in J. C. Bulman (ed.), *The Oxford Handbook of Shakespeare and Performance*, 619–40, Oxford: Oxford University Press.

PART THREE

Teaching with Traditional and Modern Archives

8

Shakespeare at Basecamp

Kristen Poole, with Jake Cohen

Overview

My favourite pedagogical digital tool is the online project management platform Basecamp. Widely used in the corporate world, Basecamp has become an industry standard partly because of its simplicity: the visual presentation of the platform makes it easy to use, and it clearly displays everyone's activity on a project. For teachers, the intuitive nature of the site and the ease of tracking participation make it an ideal classroom tool. While the newer Basecamp 3 has more bells and whistles, I find the simpler Basecamp 2 more suitable for my pedagogical needs. Importantly, Basecamp is free for educators and students.[1]

Through the years I have used several course management platforms – Blackboard, Sakai and Canvas, the current platform at my university. I have also used a rival Basecamp product, Asana, as part of a project development team. This experience with other platforms has helped me appreciate the particular merits of Basecamp, which I first encountered while doing volunteer work. Basecamp's robust discussion threads – on which it is simple to embed images, music and film clips – make it ideal for teaching textual and film analysis. The Basecamp 2 app enables students to communicate and keep up with collaborative projects through their phones, sometimes productively blurring the lines between work and play. This 'fun factor', which systems like Canvas lack, allows Basecamp to foster social and intellectual community.

In what follows, I describe Basecamp 2 and how I have used it to teach Shakespeare in very different contexts, ranging from an advanced undergraduate seminar on the Henriad and archival research to a first-year writing seminar on *Hamlet*. I also discuss a course on political rhetoric and *Julius Caesar* that was suddenly moved entirely online during the pandemic of 2020. For this last course, one of the participating students, Jake Cohen, writes from the student's perspective.

Description

A Basecamp 2 site has three key features: discussion threads, to which can be uploaded documents; an area for posting documents; and 'text docs' which resemble yellow legal pads or shared pads of virtual 'paper' upon which everyone can write. There are additional features, like a calendar and to-do lists which can help in coordinating projects. One interesting feature of this platform, and part of what makes it feel so intuitive, is that in various ways the site mimics the functionality of paper. In addition to the simulated yellow legal pads, clicking one on the available conversation threads takes the user to what looks like another piece of paper with all of the available threads. These conversation threads clearly separate out exchanges on a particular topic. My students say that they find this overview of threads preferable to fishing through modules in Canvas.

I find a number of Basecamp 2 features valuable for teaching. First, everyone on a Basecamp site can initiate discussion threads; it is an egalitarian rather than authoritarian (top-down) platform. This means the reins can be handed to the students for various activities. It allows them ownership of class experiences: for collaborative projects, the students can determine how they go about accomplishing a task. They can also initiate threads in which they post pictures of their pets or put together a pandemic playlist, blurring the lines of academic work and social media; while such threads might seem trivial, they encourage friendship and draw students to voluntarily check in on Basecamp regularly. For courses that are entirely online, Basecamp allows for the easy subdivision of a group: a class of thirty can be broken into three groups of ten, for instance, or a twenty-two-person composition class can be divided into four groups of five to six students. These smaller class sizes allow students to really get to know each other and to feel mutually accountable and supportive. When complemented by frequent Zoom meetings, the small subgroups can allow me to get to know my students even better than in a traditional classroom.

A feature of particular interest for the pedagogy of writing is the visibility of all documents posted on the site. On other teaching platforms I have used, uploaded assignments are only accessible by the teacher, which perpetuates the idea that student writing is largely a private discursive form targeted at an audience of one. By contrast, the open sharing of assignments on Basecamp teaches by modelling, helps college students segue into public professional writing and encourages students to produce their best work.

Another advantage of Basecamp is simply its novelty, at least at my institution. As I write this during a period of widespread online teaching, I have been hearing from my students that there is something of a Scylla and Charybdis to online platforms: on the one side, there is platform overload, with students being bombarded by new platforms they have to figure out; on the other side, there is platform monotony – my students have complained of Canvas fatigue, in which all of their courses look and feel the same. (One of my students described her Canvas-dominated online education as 'feed the beast', continuously throwing assignments into the ever-gaping Canvas maw.) While I can understand the institutional need for a centralized institutional platform, sometimes variety is the spice of life, and the ease and availability of Basecamp makes it easy to throw in the mix.

There are also pragmatic reasons I appreciate the platform. As mentioned, it is simple to establish new 'projects', as a Basecamp site is known, and to switch between them (I put each in a different tab; see Figure 8.1).

By contrast, my university Canvas account allows only one site per class. I also appreciate that Basecamp will display a detailed activity log for each student, including the full text of all their posts, which makes assessment of online participation much easier. In courses where I have relied on Basecamp, platform activity usually accounts for 30 per cent of the student's course grade. Basecamp threads are incredibly easy to archive; each site maintains open and archived threads, which can be reopened at any time. It is simple

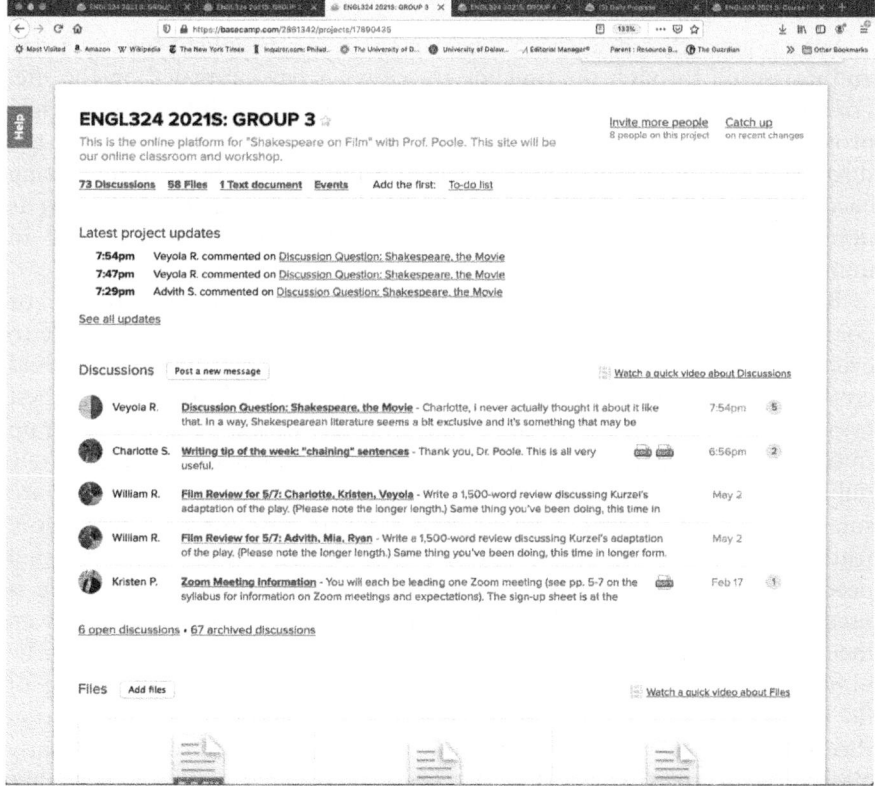

FIGURE 8.1 *Screenshot of Basecamp site, showing discussion threads; University of Delaware, 5 May 2021.*

to copy threads across multiple sites: I can show one group an exemplary thread from a previous semester to model expectations, and I copy threads I might reuse in future courses onto a separate, private course prep site. Another pragmatic concern is student buy-in: for students at my university, many of whom pursue 'vocational' degrees as opposed to the liberal arts (degrees like mechanical engineering, criminal justice, nutrition science, etc.), the real-world project management aspect of Basecamp can be appealing. They understand that they are learning the hard and soft skills of professional project management – working together as a team, developing their professional online voice and persona, managing deadlines, practising leadership and so on. The content of the course might be Shakespeare's history plays, but many are interested in the experience of project management, and this investment in 'real world' applicability paradoxically makes them more engaged in analysing sixteenth-century texts.

Finally, because everything can be contained on the site, Basecamp greatly reduces the need to communicate via email; individual posts can be tagged so that they are also sent to students' emails, but I use that feature sparingly. A 'progress' tab at the top of the site provides a running timeline of all activity (see Figure 8.2).

For students, this means that they can check in a couple of times per day and just scroll through the timeline to see what has happened on the site. For me, the progress tab makes it easy to monitor all activity across multiple projects, which all stream into the one timeline. I check the 'progress' tab throughout the day, popping in with a contribution to a discussion, offering encouragement, sharing a picture of my pets, or prodding and reminding as needed. I have established a 'Bat-signal' thread for questions that need an immediate response, so that I can easily see them in the timeline.

Basecamp may not, of course, be appropriate for all course formats or goals. As stated earlier, Basecamp makes all uploaded documents visible to everyone on the site; while this has great pedagogical advantages, it could create sensory overload for larger courses. I have found that it works best for small seminars (up to fifteen), although I have used it successfully for up to twenty-two students in a writing seminar; again, when teaching entirely online during the pandemic, I had great success dividing larger sections into smaller groups. I have not had much luck using Basecamp as an 'add on' feature of a course; from my experimenting thus far, it seems like Basecamp needs to be all or nothing – it works as the central course platform that is used continuously both inside and outside of the classroom, but not as an incidental side bar to the course, since not enough students will use it. The nimble movement of Basecamp threads, with the continuous posting of documents, comes at the cost of ongoing site curation, as conversation threads need to be regularly archived and documents need to be frequently cleared out so that the site does not become cluttered and unmanageable. This curation is easy to do (click on 'archive' next to a thread or 'delete' next to a document), but one needs to spend time maintaining a neat, functional

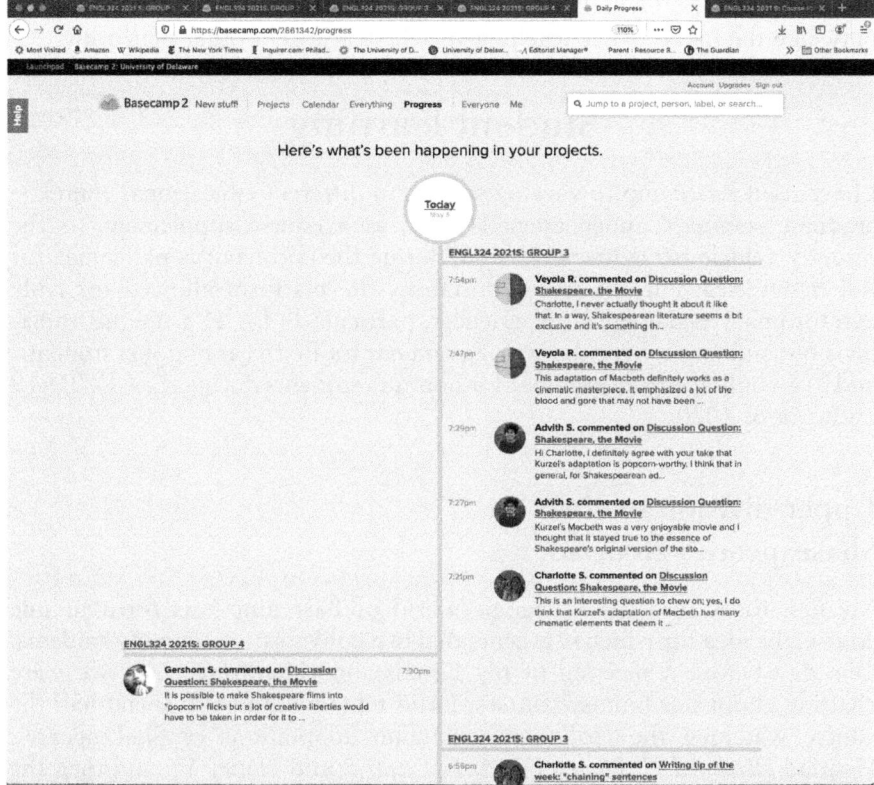

FIGURE 8.2 *Screenshot of Basecamp progress view; University of Delaware, 5 May 2021.*

site. And since the platform revolves around continuous dialogue, the instructor also needs to budget time for reading and responding to the various threads (although Basecamp assignments can substitute for traditional assignments necessitating time-intensive assessment). Following all of the posts on multiple active Basecamp sites can feel a bit like flying down the freeway, and I can't always keep up with the speed of the discussion or fully participate – but the flow of posts also means that the students are actively conversing with each other. The platform does not have some of the pedagogical conveniences of course management platforms like Canvas: it cannot gather together assignment submissions in a quick and easy way; it does not allow for in-site peer editing; it does not automatically coordinate with my university Zoom account; and there is no online grade book, among other Canvas tools. I have come up with alternatives for some of these features; for instance, I just share the URL for my Zoom mini-lectures and I post a template of my Excel grade sheet so students can track and calculate their own grades. Overall, the benefits of having engaged, active students outweigh the loss of some teaching-specific features of other platforms.

Student learning

I have used Basecamp to varying success in different educational contexts: graduate seminars, independent studies, as a course supplement, as the primary vehicle for coursework and, during the coronavirus pandemic, for full remote learning. In several instances the platform allowed for truly extraordinary pedagogical experiences, particularly for 1) a unique upper-division seminar; 2) a regular writing seminar for first-year honours students; and 3) an online writing seminar for honours students during the COVID-19 outbreak of 2020.

Upper-division seminar on Shakespeare's Henriad

My first foray into the pedagogic world of Basecamp was for a unique course, the idea for which was generated in a conversation with my students. One day before a meeting of my Renaissance Literature class, we were chatting about our fantasy courses; I said mine would be to spend half the course watching the *Hollow Crown* film adaptations of Shakespeare's Henriad (*Richard II*, *Henry IV, Parts 1 and 2* and *Henry V*), and then the other half working with original sixteenth-century archival materials in my university's Special Collections library. And we would eat doughnuts. The idea was pretty much a joke, but the students were extremely enthusiastic about the prospect and the next term the course came into being.

What followed was perhaps the most rewarding pedagogical experience of my career. For the first half of the course, we met in the theatre-like media viewing room of the university library and used virtually all of the class time to watch the *Hollow Crown* films (which were not otherwise readily available to the students). With class time used for screenings, the play-reading and discussions moved online to Basecamp. Each week I subdivided the group into working teams of four students (with the membership of the teams changing every week), set up a discussion thread and assigned them the task of generating exam questions on the playtexts and the film adaptations. The act of putting together an exam became its own mode of discussion, as students needed to think through essential knowledge about the plays, how to read them, how to ask questions about them. They had to think creatively about exam formats. Every week each group had to post a document on Basecamp that listed possible exam questions, the rationale for choosing those particular questions, and what they considered to be the larger concerns raised by the play, using textual evidence. I wasn't sure what to expect, but the Basecamp threads quickly came alive with serious, thoughtful intellectual work that naturally integrated textual close readings and students' knowledge from other contexts. While I had been hesitant about using all of the class time to watch movies, the intense Basecamp conversations would have filled each period several times over. The students began watching the films with an eye towards sharing their observations with their peers online, and it was clear that they were reading the plays in an active way, pulling out relevant lines and words as they shaped their questions. The success of this particular assignment was due to the fact that the students were highly motivated learners, but also that they were given a real and genuinely collaborative task: the exam consisted of a selection of their questions, and thus preparing these questions became its own mode of studying for the exam. Since the class met in a darkened theatre and on Basecamp, I established 'Doughnut Hour', an optional (but always well-attended) weekly in-person gathering to eat doughnuts and just have conversations. These periodic gatherings were crucial to fostering the online community.

The second half of the course was held in the university's Special Collections, where students learned to handle and read sixteenth-century archival materials. With the help of the librarian (Alex Johnston), the group worked with Holinshed's *Chronicles*, Edward Hall's *The Union of the Two Noble and Illustre Families of Lancastre and Yorke* and sundry other texts (recipe books, medical texts, bestiaries, alchemical treatises, sermons, etc.) that provided a sense of the plays' cultural context. The ultimate course goal was to share the students' close readings and historical and archival research on a public website. Research projects and writing styles were adapted for a web-based platform and a reading public, and the students coordinated the project using Basecamp. Based on the students' skills, interests and talents as manifest in Basecamp participation, class discussion, and, yes, Doughnut Hour, I appointed them to the roles of project manager, general editor, copy-editor and web development team. They took over the project, divided the labour, established deadlines, cheered each other on, covered for each other during illnesses and generally rose to the challenge. The experience of the first half of the semester in developing exam questions had made them comfortable with collaborative work and they were adept Basecamp users. The result was a website that is chock-full of high-quality researched content.[2] Several of the students included the website and their Basecamp experience on their resumés and cover letters when they were seeking jobs.

First-year composition course on *Hamlet*

Given the clear success of using Basecamp for a specialized upper-division course, I decided to try the platform in a completely different context: a twenty-two-person Honours section of Critical Reading and Writing, a mandatory university requirement for first-year students. Whereas the course on Shakespeare's Henriad had been comprised of advanced undergraduates, most of whom were specializing in the humanities and all of whom had elected to take a challenging course, the *Hamlet* group were first-term students, most of whom were in STEM fields such as chemical engineering and most of whom (it was later revealed) had not selected the seminar as one of their top choices. Very few of the students were enthusiastic about taking a composition course and most of them (again, it was later revealed) dreaded having to spend an entire term studying *Hamlet*. Many of the students were not comfortable writing or analysing language. If the Henriad course was populated by upper-level, motivated students who enjoyed writing in its many forms, this course consisted of largely unmotivated students who were there by compulsion and who took more delight in numbers than in words.

Not surprisingly, then, their initial engagement with Basecamp discussion threads was minimal and lacklustre. The students dutifully performed their assigned task but were not genuinely conversing with each other. Through a process of trial and error, I discovered that they responded well to film clips, which are very easy to embed in a Basecamp thread. While they were finding *Hamlet* tough reading, they were comfortable viewing and commenting on short clips of film productions (imported from YouTube). As before, I put them in smaller groups on a discussion thread, which allowed for more interaction. These early conversations loosened things up for more involved textual work later. I have found that the more fun and humour are integrated into Basecamp – the more it mimics some of the community-building functions of social media – the more students use it productively for coursework. Also, when students begin to feel comfortable taking the initiative to start their own conversation threads, they are more active on the platform.

I used Basecamp in a variety of ways. Students discussed the assigned textbook readings in three- or four-person threads; these seemed to ensure that students actually read and absorbed the material. (In pre-Basecamp courses, I had assessed reading with tests and quizzes, which always felt inadequate and punitive.) Students also workshopped paragraphs and thesis statements over Basecamp. In the classroom, group work could be done using the text doc feature; with the site projected, everyone could see the progress of the different groups, which spurred them to be more productive. To ensure that these classroom exercises weren't just work for work's sake, I integrated the in-class Basecamp work with their outside assignments. For instance, as preparatory work for their individual essays, during class the students could analyse a particular passage by identifying different verbal patterns. This use of Basecamp both in and outside of the classroom allowed for a sense of course continuity and a balance of crowd-sourcing and independent thinking. By the end of the term, the students had become a tight-knit group, their writing skills were vastly improved and there seemed to be near-universal appreciation of their deep knowledge of *Hamlet*.

Teaching with Basecamp in the COVID pandemic of 2020

In the spring of 2020 I had begun teaching another Honours composition course, this one focused on political rhetoric (covering Cicero, Shakespeare's *Julius Caesar* and modern American political speeches). I had integrated Basecamp into the original course syllabus, using much of what I had learned in the *Hamlet* seminar. Only four weeks into the term, we were hit by the coronavirus pandemic and all university courses were suddenly moved entirely online. In my case that meant my courses were moved entirely onto Basecamp, supplemented with periodic teleconference (Zoom) meetings. Here, one of the students, Jake Cohen, gives an account of his learning experience with Basecamp.

* * *

Even before the COVID-19 pandemic forced our class to go exclusively online, I knew that Basecamp would be a unique educational resource. In all of the English courses I had taken before, I found that the nature of writing was very impersonal: I would write something for an assignment, revise it on my own, submit it in-person or via Canvas and then get a grade for it, with the occasional comment or two from my teacher. I never liked this format of writing. Instead of writing to express my own analytical interpretations of a literary work, I wrote to satisfy the requirements of a standardized rubric that was used to grade my essay – a method that, in my opinion, completely devalued my authorial voice and defined my work solely by my instructor's response to it.

When I walked into this course, however, the dynamic changed – primarily due to Basecamp. Most of our initial assignments were through Basecamp, where Dr Poole would assign us a reading from our texts (Cicero's *The Art of Argument* and Rosenwasser and Stephen's *Writing Analytically*), pose a few questions prompting a deeper understanding of the reading and have us respond to the questions in Basecamp threads of roughly three to four students. For a multitude of reasons, these Basecamp threads were very beneficial to me and drastically different from assignments I had in previous English courses. First, these group threads minimized the pressure I felt before to write for a grade, allowing me instead to respond freely to the prompts on my own accord. The open-ended questions became enjoyable for me to answer because I knew I could analyse from the heart and not from a restrictive set of instructions. Secondly, the collaborative nature of these Basecamp threads required a different type of writing. Because we were writing to and with one another, these Basecamp assignments steered us away from the infamous 'five-paragraph essay' form and pulled us toward discussion-oriented writing – writing that values each contributor's voice equally in the group's joint purpose to find deeper meaning in the reading. In these ways, the Basecamp assignments during the period when our class met in-person (pre-COVID-19) were still intellectually challenging, yet so 'egalitarian' (to quote Dr Poole's earlier description) in their nature that I was for once able to reflect analytically without worrying about my instructor's final judgement.

When the class shifted online because of COVID-19, we not only used Basecamp significantly more but also used it significantly differently than before, as the class was split into four separate working groups, each with their own Basecamp site and collaborative projects, all overseen by Dr Poole and supplemented with weekly Zoom video meetings. We entered an unprecedented form of learning through Basecamp.

The first week of online instruction was very much a trial run. Dr Poole had assigned us to our separate projects and appointed a weekly group leader, whose responsibilities included translating that week's goals and tasks from the syllabus into Basecamp action (such as determining what discussion threads were needed). My group (consisting of five students) nominated me to be team leader for this first, transitional week in our new course format. I realized quickly that the tasks before me were analogous to what Dr Poole had been managing for so long in her other projects, including the first month of our course. It was a major learning curve for me to look at what our group needed to do over the course of the week and figure out how to assign the tasks in the most fair and effective way possible. However, the most stressful part was being a team leader when half of my group clearly was not as active as they should have been on our Basecamp project, with one student largely absent. Dr Poole recognized his inactivity and soon removed him from the project; our productivity improved dramatically and I felt that my efforts as team leader were finally being reciprocated. It was at this point that I learned perhaps the most important lesson about Basecamp: because it is a digital tool inherently based on group collaboration, Basecamp works effectively if (and only if) everybody on a project is active.

Our collaboration improved over the following weeks and we used Basecamp for a major course project: writing a collaborative essay analysing one of Mark Antony's speeches in Shakespeare's *Julius Caesar*. This type of group work was completely foreign to me and the other group members, as most of us had had small collaborative writing assignments in the past but nothing to this extent. Aware of our inexperience, Dr Poole broke up this project into smaller assignments. First, we each wrote a paragraph analysing a different aspect of Mark Antony's speech, then established a thesis for our work and finally wove our paragraphs together with an introduction and conclusion to produce a co-authored essay. From the start to the end of this essay, we used Basecamp in countless ways: we delegated tasks, peer-reviewed, set mini-deadlines, scheduled Zoom meetings and communicated when we each planned on submitting our work. We also learned that Basecamp works extremely well with Microsoft Word. In order to conduct peer reviews, we used Word to suggest edits and comment on one another's paragraphs, then uploaded these so our entire group could discuss revisions.

While I would not say that my group did this seamlessly (it was our first major project in such an unprecedented time), we definitely learned so much from working collaboratively. Our course was originally not supposed to be this collaboration-intensive, but I think this outcome was for the better. Although the circumstances for the move to complete online coursework were unfortunate, Basecamp exposed me to a new way of learning and a new style of writing that prepared me for the professional world. I noticed that my writing became more intentional; I now pay attention to how my writing serves the larger purpose of the group, no longer hyper-focused on meeting the requirements of my instructor. In addition to this sense of group responsibility, Basecamp forced me to take a more active role in my class. There was not a sense of anonymity as there was for in-person classes, because all of our voices were crucial for the advancement of the course. That said, while I missed interacting with the eighteen other students in my class, I truly valued how Basecamp made me perceive my class in a more intimate setting. I enjoyed getting to know the members of my group through their writing, and I have found it very powerful that we made all of our authorial voices blend into one for our group essay. At its core, Basecamp promotes the true purpose of writing to engage with others. My class's shift to Basecamp may have been a response to the COVID-19 crisis, but I hope that it eventually becomes a new normal for instructors worldwide to adopt as a viable alternative to in-class instruction.

* * *

Jake's account of his learning experience on Basecamp reinforces many of my own observations of how the students benefitted from the format and also reveals student concerns I had not fully processed. This was the first time that I had students write a major essay collaboratively, and the results were stellar. My original intent was merely to keep them engaged with the course and give them a continued sense of community in the new online format, but I discovered how quickly they became sensitive to often abstract ideas like authorial voice as they blended their constituent parts of the work together. But I had not fully recognized the stress experienced by student group leaders because of inactive peers. In the subsequent semester I instituted some safeguards that ensured a higher likelihood of successful groups: I assigned the groups (as opposed to letting students choose, which had led to strong students clumping together); I made more frequent Basecamp performance assessments, including one at the end of the second week; I established a protocol for removing inactive students from a group after two warnings, placing them on their own Basecamp site where they would take the course as an independent study, but with a hefty penalty to their Basecamp grade; and early in the semester I held Zoom tutorials on how to use the platform. This early intervention and facilitation of group dynamics has led to more uniformly high-performing groups.

Application

A key component of my project-management approach is letting students figure out how to accomplish a set of goals. Rather than setting specific deadlines, the syllabus lists what needs to be done, and the week's leader needs to think about how to break up tasks, how to pace the week and how to set up Basecamp discussion threads to manage the workflow. Below, for instance, is a sample week for the co-authored essay on Mark Antony's speech that Jake discussed.

WEEK 7: POLISHING YOUR PAPER

Here are the week's goals:

1) To refine your essay's thesis, introduction and conclusion as you polish the whole; 2) To ensure that your essay holds together and is coherent, especially in transition sentences that link one paragraph to the next; 3) To work on making the prose of your essay more concise.

Here are your tasks:

- Read Joseph Williams' *Style*, chapter 7 on 'Motivation'. On a Basecamp thread, discuss how you might want to revise your introduction and conclusion in light of this chapter.
- Read *Style*, chapter 8 on 'Global Coherence'. On a Basecamp thread, discuss the biggest takeaways from this chapter.
- Revise your essay in light of these two chapters, using Word mark-up. How you do this is up to your group. You might want to have one team work on the intro, one on the conclusion and one on the coherence. (Separately rewritten intros and conclusions could be pasted into a final document, if it is tricky to sequence the passing around of the document.)
- In your revision, you might need to revise the content of some of the paragraphs if there are redundancies or sharp breaks in tone.
- By the end of the week, post your final, polished essay on Basecamp. This is worth 10 per cent of your course grade.

Notes

1 See https://basecamp.com/discounts.
2 See https://shakespeareshenriad.weebly.com/. Unfortunately, perhaps due to a change in Weebly's policy or pricing, the beautiful photos of the archival

materials that originally illustrated the site have been removed. This illustrates the pitfalls of digital decay and perhaps of relying on commercial products. Biographies of the students who created the site are available at https://shakespeareshenriad.weebly.com/biographies.html.

References

Cicero, M. T. ([early 50s BCE] 2016), *How to Win an Argument: An Ancient Guide to the Art of Persuasion*, ed. and trans. J. M. May, Princeton, NJ: Princeton University Press.

Rosenwasser, D. and J. Stephen (2019), *Writing Analytically*, 8th edn, Boston: Cengage.

The Hollow Crown (film) (2012), dir. Rupert Goold, Richard Eyre and Thea Sharrock, United Kingdom: Neal Street Productions and NBC Universal for BBC.

9

The Victorian Illustrated Shakespeare Archive

Art to Enchant

Michael John Goodman

Overview

Digital resources present us with an opportunity to reimagine teaching and scholarship anew and to do things differently. However, if we are not going to, as the philosopher of computing Jaron Lanier dramatically suggests we might, become a 'numb mob' (2010: xiii), we must work with digital technology in the classroom in a way that meaningfully engages our students' intellectual curiosity and not just use technology for technology's sake. By approaching the digital in this way, we do not become passive observers of the most significant cultural change since the Industrial Revolution or get swept along a digital river whose current is increasingly becoming more rapid (and monetized: 'Big Tech' is encroaching on our classrooms very quickly) – but, instead, we actively help to shape what the digital is, what it does and what it means. The affordances of the digital allow us not just to critique cultural works but also to create those cultural works themselves for the benefit of all, especially those involved in education.

In a 2011 profile in the *New Yorker* magazine, published soon after his *You Are Not A Gadget*, Lanier revealed his way of thinking about technology and the consequences of what might arise from it: 'I've always felt that the human-centered approach to computer science leads to more interesting, more exotic, more wild, and more heroic adventures than the machine-supremacy approach, where information is the highest goal' (Kahn). It is an approach that I have aspired to with the creation of my own digital resource, the *Victorian Illustrated Shakespeare Archive* (*VISA*).[1] My own interpretation of what Lanier means by the 'human-centered' approach (2011) is that at all times the digital designer should foreground the end-user in the decisions that they make, even if that comes at the expense of being able to achieve more complicated computational functionality. The end-users I ultimately had in mind were both students and educators, who in my experience rarely have the time or the inclination to learn the ins and outs of (often) very complex digital resources.

The archive was created for two main reasons: first, to introduce and make accessible to educators and students over 3,000 illustrations taken from the four most significant illustrated editions of Shakespeare's Complete Works in the Victorian period; and second, to challenge the assumption that something that has been digitized and is available online is an achievement in and of itself. Over the years, as an undergraduate student and then as a postgraduate researcher, I have become increasingly frustrated with digital resources that are poorly designed, ill thought-out and challenging to use. In short, they make learning and research difficult. With *VISA* I wanted to demonstrate that by focusing on human-centred design, and with some imagination, it is possible to create digital resources that are user-friendly, accessible for a variety of needs and enjoyable to use with no restrictions. Good digital design, I contend, facilitates good digital pedagogy.

VISA, then, makes available online over 3,000 wood-engraved Shakespeare illustrations and allows students, researchers and members of the public to explore an innovative image archive and ask new questions about this material: for example, how did the Victorians depict certain characters and plays pictorially? How does this portrayal differ across the Victorian era? Are particular characters or plays illustrated more than others? Does this signify the popularity of these characters or plays? Are there pertinent gender, identity or colonial implications in these representations?

But there is one more important question that needs to be answered: why these illustrations? For Stuart Sillars, 'Victorian Shakespeare, with its complexes of authenticity, actuality and identity, is an intensely visual construction' (2012: 1). He observes how technology enabled Shakespearean images to be produced and disseminated around the world:

> [T]he most recent technology made such images instantly transmissible. The steam press, wood-pulp paper, wood engraving, the stereo plate and, in the later years, steel engraving and chromo-lithography, facilitated the production of images in vast numbers; railways transported them throughout the kingdom, steamships took them across the Atlantic. The past, once Imaged, became available to all through the temporal ordering of the present.
>
> 2012: 18

Shakespeare in Victorian visual culture, then, was entwined with new technologies. Not only was the availability of pictorial Shakespearean material accessible to more and more people through new means of transportation such as the railway, but also the very mode of representation (wood-engraved illustrations, for example) allowed for such material to be produced in high quantity and became affordable to a large section of the Victorian public.

Victorian Shakespeare illustration is particularly significant because the illustrated editions of the Complete Works would have been the first encounter with Shakespeare that many readers had. As Sillars also observes, 'the illustrated edition was the broadest channel by which the reading public gained an acquaintance, whatever its nature or intensity, with the plays of Shakespeare' (2008: 28–9). They were sold relatively cheaply and were affordable to members of the working classes, a group of people that may not have been able to experience Shakespeare in the London theatre. Consequently, their experience of Shakespeare was often based on these illustrated pages rather than the stage. As such, these editions played an important part in how the Victorian population thought about and constructed Shakespeare. Indeed, from 1840 to 1870 the illustrated edition becomes a theatre of the book where words and images combine in complex interaction, just as they do on the stage.

Finally, what is the significance of the illustrations being wood-engraved? Like the web today, wood-engraving touched upon all aspects of society and allowed for knowledge to be disseminated in new ways and across all social classes. Because the wood used to engrave the images was usually boxwood, it was very durable and the wood blocks could be set alongside type in the printing press, allowing for word and image to be combined on a single page (Wakeman 1973: 20). As Brian Maidment notes, 'Wood engraving vastly extended the possibility of integrating text and image into the same printed page using cheap and technically simple methods' (2001: 15). Wood-engraving, combined with more efficient printing techniques, meant that the publishing business was transformed into a mass-produced commercial industry and, for the first time, illustrated books became affordable to working- and middle-class families.

Before the development of wood-engraving and the printing technology that allowed for the mass circulation of illustrated texts, Shakespeare's Works often contained just a single frontispiece or a few illustrations per play printed on different pages than the text. In the Victorian period, however, we witness not only more integration between word and image (as seen in many of the illustrations in *VISA* by Kenny Meadows), but also a vast increase in the sheer quantity of illustrations in these editions.

The four Victorian editions that make up the *Victorian Illustrated Shakespeare Archive* are what Stuart Sillars calls the 'major editions' (2008: 253). These editions stand out because no other editions from the period illustrate the plays so extensively and as visually coherently as these works, with each containing at least 800 illustrations. Additionally, they represent an important intersection between Victorian book technology and history, readership, the visual arts and Shakespeare. The first of these editions was by Charles Knight, called *The Pictorial Edition*, originally published in fifty-six parts between 1838 and 1843, and eventually collected in eight volumes.[2] The second edition, by Barry Cornwall with illustrations by Kenny Meadows, was originally published in 1843. This was followed by the Howard Staunton edition with illustrations by John Gilbert, originally issued in parts between 1856 and 1860 and published in three volumes between 1858 and 1860. Finally, there is the edition by Charles and Mary Cowden Clarke with illustrations by Henry Courtney Selous. This final edition was originally published in parts and volumes between 1864 and 1868. All four editions are visually quite distinct and interpret the plays in different ways.

Charles Knight's edition, for example, takes the approach of treating the plays as if they had an actual historical reality. That is to say, Knight is far less concerned with interpreting characters or scenes from the plays than in depicting the landscapes as well as the costumes and the objects the characters would have worn and used had they been real-life people living in the times the plays were set. The first illustration in *Julius Caesar*, for example, does not depict any of the characters from the play, but instead shows two generic 'Roman Standard Bearers', while the rest of the illustrations from the play are mostly landscapes of ancient Rome. In this way, Knight's *Julius Caesar* is characteristic of his editorial approach to all the other plays in this edition. Furthermore, when taken as part of a larger body of material that includes the three other Shakespeare editions, Knight's *Pictorial Edition* begins to take on a fascinating new dimension, as these illustrations became involved in a dialogue with the other editions. So a search in the archive for *Julius Caesar*, for example, will bring up all the illustrations in the archive that have been keyworded as 'Julius Caesar', and a user can then appreciate the illustrations of Knight's edition in a much broader and far more compelling context, allowing them to track how they may have influenced later illustrators' interpretations and to experience them as part of the rich matrix that was Victorian visual culture.

Description

The digital archive allows images that have been separated by both time and space – either by being on different pages of the same edition, or by being created by a different illustrator in a different edition – to be brought together to generate new meanings and offer potentially new insights. By incorporating the wondrously weird and surreal illustrations of Kenny Meadows, the more novelistic interpretations of John Gilbert and the more dramatic interpretations of the plays by H. C. Selous alongside those of Knight's edition, *VISA* presents students and educators with a treasure trove of visual Shakespearean material that invites students to find their own ways into the plays that echo the responses of readers and students centuries ago, immersed as they were in a world of visual Shakespeare.

Every illustration in the archive has been described and keyworded using extensive bibliographical and iconographical metadata and keywords. The bibliographical data provides users with the name of the illustrator (where available), the name of the engraver (where available), the size of the illustration in millimetres and inches, the title of the edition from which the illustration is taken and the publisher and place of publication of that text. Iconographical keywords allow students to search the archive intuitively for the material they seek. A search for *Julius Caesar*, as described above, will bring up all the illustrations in the archive that have been tagged as that play, in a user-friendly and effective way that hitherto would have involved a trip to a special research library and much time and effort spent searching for all the images. Additionally, students can also search for those more general aspects of the illustrations that are not directly associated with Shakespeare's plays that, nevertheless, might be important for telling us something about them or Victorian illustration and culture, such as 'Chairs', 'Reading and Writing' or 'Books'.

An additional element of humanity baked into the design is its interpretability. When *VISA* has been demonstrated at conferences, I have often been asked why I have not tagged the illustrations thematically to include such attributes as 'love', 'revenge' and 'politics'. I avoided this approach in order to keep the keywords as objective as possible rather than imposing my own subjective interpretation on the illustrations. As one consequence, students have to decide the thematic content of the illustrations themselves, encouraging them to think deeply and critically about the images without any editorial guidance from myself. What we decide to leave out of our pedagogical resources is just as important as what we put in.

All the illustrations in the archive have been digitized, by hand, to a resolution of 300 dpi (dots per inch), which is an industry standard for image publication. As a result, students can print out the illustrations and include them as part of their course work or other projects and the illustrations will retain their quality. In the archive itself, students can also view the images at full size and zoom in on them. This magnification of the illustrations and the clarity that results enables students and other users to engage with details of the engraving that would be difficult to appreciate in the printed book. All this information enables students to investigate and analyse Victorian Shakespeare illustration in a way that is unprecedented.

VISA was designed to be as accessible as possible and to allow students to find these historical illustrations with as few mouse clicks as necessary. Additionally, the archive contains transparent metadata which showcases to students the archival creation process, offering them a chance to understand how digital archives such as this are created. The multiple entry points into the archive, while focused on Victorian Shakespeare editions, can be applied to any other corpus of material, and I hope the following description inspires educators, or other curious readers, to develop their own archives in their own work and pedagogical practice.

There are several ways students can navigate *VISA* depending on their requirements: either through the 'Start Looking' drop-down menu, word clouds or through the illustrator links at the top of the homepage. Rolling the mouse over the name Kenny Meadows, for example, will bring up a menu consisting of 'Comedies', 'Histories' and 'Tragedies', which in turn offers a pop-up menu of the plays that have been categorized under those terms. Clicking on 'A Midsummer Night's Dream' in the Comedies menu will bring up a new page displaying all the illustrations of the play from that edition in thumbnail form and in the order that they appear in the text. A student can then decide whether they want to explore the set of illustrations from the beginning (in order) by clicking on the first illustration that appears in this thumbnail gallery, or, alternatively, choose any other illustration in the gallery that they want to investigate further. This pathway through the archive is the most efficient way for students wishing to explore a single play from a single edition.

By clicking on one of these thumbnail illustrations, the archive will then display this set of illustrations in a carousel view that enlarges the images and allows users to cycle through them conveniently and effectively. Beneath each illustration in the carousel view is the metadata for that particular image, allowing students to easily identify the archive's information about it, meaning that students can clearly learn how the archive is structured and organized.

Each illustration is also numbered out of the total number of images that make up that play, providing students with important information so that they can easily ascertain exactly where an image appears in its broader pictorial context. For example, the illustration by John Gilbert, 'Bottom as an Ass', is catalogued as number 12/19. It is the twelfth illustration in a series that contains nineteen, so a student can surmise at a glance where this image appears in relation to the other illustrations from that play.

The 'Start Looking' menu allows students to search directly for certain characters, plays, illustrators or genres (and a few more attributes). As opposed to the way of searching, described above, where a user clicks on the play by the illustrator, the 'Start Looking' menu allows for a much more advanced and nuanced way of searching for specific qualities associated with Shakespeare's plays. This way of searching draws from *all* the illustrations in the archive, which are then presented to the user in a useful grid format. If, for example, a student wanted to investigate the different ways the Victorian illustrators interpreted the character of Miranda from *The Tempest*, they would click on the 'Start Looking' menu and scroll down until they came to the section called 'Characters' and would click on

'Miranda'. The archive would then retrieve every illustration of Miranda contained within it, allowing them to compare and contrast the different illustrations of that character.

In addition, next to the name 'Miranda' in the 'Start Looking' menu is a number in parentheses, revealing how many illustrations of Miranda are in the archive (in this case eighteen). This information allows students to see which characters or plays were the most frequently illustrated in these editions, helping them to determine which character to write about in an essay, for example. It also encourages them to investigate the broader Victorian context in which these plays were embedded and to ask questions such as: are there large numerical discrepancies between genders? What play has the most illustrations? What play has the least? What does this tell us about Shakespeare in the Victorian period?

The final way of navigating the archive is through word clouds, which visually indicate the frequency with which a keyword is used within the archive by its size. Rolling the mouse over a word displays the exact number of illustrations that have been tagged under that keyword. 'History', unsurprisingly, is quite large, with 943 illustrations keyworded under that term, whilst 'Birds' is much smaller with only sixty-eight illustrations.

In an interview I gave for the online arts magazine *Hyperallergic*, Carey Dunne (2016) wrote about the archive:

> The beauty is not just in the illustrations themselves, but in the way the archive is organized: A word cloud lets you search the illustrations by motif, from the magical (witches, fairies, ghosts) to the grim (death, daggers, beheadings). It reveals how, despite all the intricacy of his works, Shakespeare built all of his plays from a limited set of basic elements. With categories like Clowns, Castles, Horses, Kings, Moons, Musicians, Ships, and Swords, the word cloud reads like a list of Jungian archetypes.

Dunne has identified here one of the effects of the human-centred design approach I took in constructing the archive. By making visible in a word cloud – a feature students are very familiar and comfortable with – how *VISA* is organized, it allows them to feel unafraid about using it.

Student learning

In the past eighteen months I have been using *VISA* to engage students visually with Shakespeare's plays. By moving away from the 'sanctity' of Shakespeare's text (from the page to the screen, from the text to the visual), in a similar way to how film and performance studies instructors have achieved, my students' exploration of the plays has become far more sophisticated, imaginative and thoughtful than had previously been the case, and has helped them to understand and appreciate that Shakespeare's plays generate meaning in different time periods in distinctive ways that are unique to that particular era. What follows are two case studies where the archive has been used in creative ways in class and the learning outcomes that have been accomplished.

Word and image

Learning outcome: Analyse the differences between Shakespeare's words and Victorian Shakespeare illustrations

A very simple classroom activity that is effective in developing student's critical analysis skills both of the play text and the illustrations is to select a passage from the play the students are studying and invite them to compare that passage to the illustrations of that scene. This activity works well when students are divided up into groups, given different scenes or characters to analyse, and present their discoveries to the rest of the class at the end of the seminar. This scaffolding encourages students to learn that Shakespeare's plays are not monolithic and can be interpreted and presented in many different ways. In practice, this has resulted in some astute observations: one student observed that in Kenny Meadow's illustrations for *The Taming of the Shrew*, Petruchio and Katharina are often depicted as being a cat and a dog, which allows the illustrator to 'get away' with depicting scenes that they would not have been able to otherwise, such as the final scene where the cat and dog are shown cuddled up under a table, with the clothes the characters have been wearing throughout on top of the table. The comedic implication is that they have gone to bed. Another student has noted the problematic portrayal of Caliban throughout all the illustrations, while another once commented that some of the frontispieces acted as 'spoilers', revealing far too much about key moments from the plays, and 'Shakespeare would not like that.' All these examples, obviously, then act as prompts for further discussion of Victorian culture and the period's values and ideologies, and also our own assumptions and biases. One of the most rewarding moments for me as an educator was when a student told me that this exercise helped her to visualize the play she had been studying (*Measure for Measure*) in a way that she had been unable to before, and as a result felt far more comfortable with Shakespeare's language. The visual had provided her with a way into the text and empowered her to engage with Shakespeare. Finally, a student once commented in a presentation that by being able to see a visual representation of Sycorax, it had enhanced that character's status in the play for him and made him reassess her significance to *The Tempest*, where she is only mentioned and never seen.

Word cloud

Learning outcome: Development of original research

A quick and rewarding in-class exercise is to ask the students to click on a random word or term in the word cloud to see if we can make any interesting connections with the illustrations in the archive. By clicking on the tag 'Walking Sticks', for example, we can see that certain pictorial themes begin to emerge: the characters who feature the most often with walking sticks are, on the whole, overweight men from the genre of Comedy, such as Dogberry from *Much Ado About Nothing*, Sir Toby from *Twelfth Night* and Falstaff from *The Merry Wives of Windsor* and *Henry IV*. We can then use this discovery to ask further questions and broaden the scope of our research. For example, were walking sticks used on the Victorian stage for particular comedic purposes? Did Victorian actors and performers use walking sticks as a comedic trope to elicit laughter from the audience? Did the Victorian illustrators of Shakespeare's plays (because they were part of that culture and familiar with the stage use of this prop) include them in their images as it was the 'obvious' thing to do? Moreover, was there a particular Victorian actor associated with the roles of Dogberry, Sir Toby and Falstaff? This example demonstrates just how useful the word cloud can be. By exploring certain visual motifs – those motifs that we could very easily overlook – we have broadened our field of study to potentially encompass Victorian stage and performance history so that we might be able better to understand contemporary Victorian stage practice. Students have found this activity useful because it enacts in a visual and easily understood way how research ideas can arise and develop. Indeed, by thinking of items in this manner, it allows us to then think about our own contemporary period, and ask what item of clothing we might be taking for granted in a similar fashion to walking sticks on the stage. Baseball caps perhaps?

Application

The following teaching plan for a two-hour seminar brings together everything this chapter has discussed and can be adapted or changed depending on the desires of the educator and the students' needs and abilities.

TEACHING PLAN

Title: Introduction to *Victorian Illustrated Shakespeare*
Time: two-hour seminar

Objective: to introduce postgraduate students to illustrated Victorian representations of Shakespeare's plays by using *VISA* and to demonstrate how these illustrations can be used in their own essays, projects and research.

Students will:

- Become familiar with *VISA*.
- Gain an understanding of the importance of Shakespeare in Victorian visual culture.
- Be able to place these illustrations in a broader Victorian cultural and historical context.
- Compare and contrast illustrations by focusing on a single play and a single character.
- Identify potential areas of interest for their own research.

Directions

−30 mins   Demonstrate to the class *VISA*. Ask a student what their favourite play is and use that as the focal point to explain how to navigate the archive. Be sure to show to the students how the images can be magnified.

30–50 mins   Explain how these illustrations are part of a wider Victorian obsession with images and Shakespeare. Give an explanation of what wood-engraving is and how important the technology was in allowing illustrated editions to be purchased cheaply by all classes of society and how, for the first time, it offered many people a chance to engage visually with Shakespeare's plays in a meaningful way in their home.

50–60 mins   Break

60–90 mins   Ask the students to get into groups of three or four. In their groups have them choose a character and look at the various illustrations of them in the archive. Prompt the students to think about the different styles of illustration, the way the characters are presented and what the implications are of this presentation. Ask the students to think about how they could write an essay on this topic.

> 90–120 mins Each group presents their findings to the rest of the class. After each presentation, have a brief question and answer session led by the students. Guide the students into thinking about how these representations reflect or contribute to Victorian culture.
>
> *For next week:*
> Ask the students to read Barbara Hodgdon's article 'Photography, Theater, Mnemonics; or Thirteen Ways of Looking at a Still' and choose two twentieth-century photographs of famous Shakespeare actors in a role and compare it to images of the same character in *VISA*. How do these representations differ? What can we learn about the media and time that produced them? In class we will use Hodgdon's article as a way to discuss the problems inherent in analysing Shakespearean images, how useful the article might be when applied to Shakespeare illustrations, and the historical claims we can make about them.

Notes

This chapter includes several sentences drawn from my previously published comments at 'Shakespeare, Wood Engraving and New Media, Part I' and 'Part II', Cardiff Book History, https://cardiffbookhistory.wordpress.com

1 The *Victorian Illustrated Shakespeare Archive* is available at www.shakespeareillustration.org.
2 The edition that I have used in the archive is undated, and I therefore use dates provided by the British Library for the first edition. Full citations for Knight and the volumes that follow in the text are available in the References.

References

Cornwall, B., ed. (1846), *The Works of Shakespeare revised from the best authorities with a memoir, and essay on his genius, by Barry Cornwall: and, annotations and introductory remarks on the plays, by distinguished writers: illustrated with engravings on wood, from designs by Kenny Meadows*, London: William S. Orr and Co.

Cowden Clarke, C. and M. Cowden Clarke, eds (1864–8?), *Cassell's Illustrated Shakespeare, The Plays of Shakespeare, Edited and Annotated by Charles and Mary Cowden Clarke*, 35 Parts, London, Paris and Melbourne: Cassell & Company Limited.

Dunne, C. (2016), 'To Browse or Not to Browse? 3,000 Victorian Illustrations of Shakespeare Published Online', *Hyperallergic*, https://hyperallergic.com/326101/

to-browse-or-not-to-browse-3000-victorian-illustrations-of-shakespeare-published-online/.

Hodgdon, B. (2003), 'Photography, Theater, Mnemonics; or, Thirteen Ways of Looking at a Still', in W. B. Worthen and P. Holland (eds), *Theorizing Practise: Redefining Theatre History*, London: Palgrave Macmillan, 88–119.

Kahn, J. (2011), 'The Visionary', *New Yorker*, http://www.newyorker.com/magazine/2011/07/11/the-visionary.

Knight, C. (1839–42?), *The Pictorial Edition of the Works of Shakspere. Edited by Charles Knight*, 8 vols. London: Charles Knight and Co.

Lanier, J. (2010), *You Are Not A Gadget: A Manifesto*, London: Allen Lane.

Maidment, B. (2001), *Reading Popular Prints 1790–1870*, Manchester: Manchester University Press.

Sillars, S. (2008), *The Illustrated Shakespeare, 1709–1875*, Cambridge: Cambridge University Press.

Sillars, S. (2012), *Shakespeare, Time and the Victorians*, Cambridge: Cambridge University Press.

Staunton, H., ed. (1865–7), *The Works of Shakespeare. Edited by Howard Staunton; The Illustrations by John Gilbert; Engraved by the Dalziel Brothers*, 3 vols, London: George Routledge and Sons.

Wakeman, G. (1973), *Victorian Book Illustration: The Technical Revolution*, Newton Abbot: David and Charles.

10

Student-Curated Archives and the Digital Design of Shakespeare in Performance

Marcia McDonald, Joel Overall and Jayme M. Yeo

Overview

Many Shakespeare classes offer students the opportunity to attend a local live production. Particularly for students in regional and rural contexts, these productions may be the only experience of live Shakespeare – and sometimes of live theatre generally – that they have. Yet despite the breadth of scholarship on performance pedagogy in the Shakespeare classroom, as Jessica Winston has recently pointed out there is a relative scarcity of work on the pedagogy of the local live performance (2019: 290–1, 322, n. 3). In our own iteration of this classroom activity, we wanted students to accomplish two primary learning objectives: to develop critical tools for exploring the multimodality of Shakespeare in performance, and to identify how a specific theatrical interpretation of a play contributes in a small way to an evolving global understanding of Shakespeare's work. These goals were both inspired by the productions of our regional Shakespeare company, the Nashville Shakespeare Festival, which tends to stage shows featuring artistic choices deeply rooted in Southern culture and in Nashville's vibrant music scene.

We wanted to explore with our students how these productions, with their original music written by local singer-songwriters, might be in conversation with Shakespeare productions around the world, available through what Alexa Alice Joubin calls 'Global Shakespeare 2.0'. As Joubin notes, this wave of global Shakespeare blurs 'the boundary between traditional notions of live and virtual performances' (2011: 40) through video simulcasting and archiving. Over the past decade, with the rise of social media Shakespeare, YouTube Shakespeare and, in the wake of the coronavirus pandemic, Zoom Shakespeare, these technologies are increasingly connecting audiences with new interpretations of Shakespeare's work. We wanted to approach local live performance through a lens that would help students understand the role this digital environment has played in shaping Shakespearean interpretations worldwide while simultaneously encouraging sophisticated multimodal textual analysis. We found the perfect solution for these desires in the form of an online archive, created by our students, that enables them to curate, annotate and compare the production elements of their local live performances with Shakespeare plays staged worldwide. This chapter describes how we conceptualized, implemented and developed learning outcomes for the *Nashville Shakespeare Performance Archive (NSPA)* project, a student-curated online archive of Shakespeare productions staged in Nashville, Tennessee.[1]

We initially designed our project in an application for an NEH-funded mini-grant through the Folger Shakespeare Library. From the outset, we conceived of a multi-year archive with new productions added each year; the project has now been running since 2016–17, with occasional shifts to the timeline or assignments. To build the archive, our course 'Shakespeare: Representative Plays' partnered with another English class, 'Digital Literacies', which also engages students in multimodal close reading and provides the technical skills of website design and creation. Digital Literacies was developed in part to offer humanities-based professionalization to our majors and introduce students to HTML coding, audio/visual design and multimodal rhetoric. The two courses are usually offered consecutively to span a single academic year, although we have more recently offered both classes concurrently.

Each course sets out a sequence of assignments and collaborative projects that build toward the final archive. The Shakespeare class typically collects digital artefacts from the production in the first weeks of the term, including conducting interviews and obtaining performance footage, photos and other data. They then give this material to the Digital Literacies class, which uses the data to create and edit videos and build a website for the archive in the second half of term. While both classes are offered within the major, they are also available for general education credit and tend to attract different student populations, with the Shakespeare class drawing education or theatre majors and Digital Literacies attracting students from media studies or marketing. To support this diversity, each class is taught separately. While each maintains its own specific learning outcomes, we facilitate communication and (when possible) meetings between the two classes, and together we strive to give students the experience of constructing and contributing their knowledge to the global dialogue about Shakespeare performance through digital humanities. We hope that this collaboration awakens students – majors and non-majors alike – to the breadth of disciplinary possibility within the field of English studies. While this collaboration has been key for accomplishing the project at our institution, the archive can also be scaled down for a stand-alone Shakespeare class using website creation and hosting services such as WordPress.

Over the years, our project has involved multiple institutional and community stakeholders. Our most important partner for the project is the Nashville Shakespeare Festival (NSF), which produces two shows each year: a free summer show in the park and a ticketed winter show housed at Belmont University's Trout Theater. We work with NSF prior to the start of the term to review the logistics of documenting the production and the intellectual property protocols involved in creating the archive. We also work closely each year with our university library's instructional technology staff as we build the website; the archive itself is housed within the Belmont library's digital collections.

In our classes, we explore the scholarly stakes of the project with our students by contextualizing our archive alongside other digital performance archives of Shakespeare, from internationally-focused archives such as MIT's Global Shakespeares or the Asian Shakespeare Intercultural Archive (A|S|I|A – discussed in Ng-Gagneux's chapter) to more localized archives such as the Cleveland Press Shakespeare Photographs: 1870–1982 or Shakespeare and the Players. These technologies preserve and expand access to local productions around the world, giving students and scholars the ability to assess a play's cultural engagements long after the production has closed. We discuss with our students how our access to these plays reshapes normative performance options as new productions and technologies open avenues for meaning in Shakespeare's plays. We explore how such Shakespeare archives preserve the theatrical interpretations of smaller and/or non-professional productions similar to those staged in Nashville, creating an informal network of multilocal performances that multiply the cultural and interpretive engagements of the work of Shakespeare around the world. Discussing this creative and scholarly investment with our students helps them understand their own work as contributing in a small but meaningful way to a global conversation about Shakespearean interpretation.

While this context gives critical meaning to the work of our students, the primary investment of this project is to help students identify, analyse and in a limited sense reproduce the interpretive multimodality of performance. Through identification, classification and curation of the visual, aural and verbal elements of the production, our students become more attuned to the interpretive nature of theatrical performance, in part as they come to think of the archive as itself a kind of interpretation. As rhetorician K. J. Rawson reminds us, 'there are both policies and politics involved in archival selection' (2018: 332). Rawson examines the importance of understanding the organizing principle of 'archival description' as a means of 'telling a story about records' (2018: 328). As students become aware of their role as 'translators' of a production, they begin to appreciate and articulate the interpretability – the adaptability – of Shakespeare's work. They are, in other words, connected to a reinvigorated 'liveness' of performance that emerges in the interplay of traditional and new media as they catalogue and curate a theatrical performance for an online platform.

While we direct our pedagogical intentions toward student understanding of theatrical interpretation, we also preserve some 'messiness' in allowing students to conceptualize the content for each new production archived. We believe that by keeping the content and the digitalization in students' hands, we put them in the nexus of multiple interpretive crossings: stage play and play text; live production and digital archive; literary theory and digital humanities; fluid performance and stable archive; theatre stage and computer screen; local production and global access. It is in this nexus, this carnival space, that students can explore, experiment and construct a repository of Shakespeare in performance which affirms that, as one student noted, 'after all this time, people are still playing with Shakespeare in a way that makes this work *new*'.

Description

The overview of the class assignments and structure below is divided between the 'Shakespeare' class and the 'Digital Literacies' class for clarity.

Shakespeare

The upper-level Shakespeare course, required for English majors but open to all majors, has as its catalogue course description, 'Traces the development of Shakespeare's career through the study of representative tragedies, histories, comedies, and romances'. While this generic description allows for the reading of six to ten plays and varied pedagogies over a fourteen-week semester, it does not prepare students for a project on the scale of the *NSPA*. To meet the challenge of integrating this project into a Shakespeare survey, the class read eight plays (one to two fewer than normal). A second challenge requires placing this project first in the semester to coincide with NSF's August and January production schedule. Thus, students 'warm up' to reading Shakespeare by first engaging with images from productions as they explore a range of archives. One additional initial step is informing students of their rights and options concerning the use of materials they author in the archive and for our use in research on the project. Each student signs (or declines to sign) a permissions form; students who prefer not to sign are offered the option of alternative assignments that are not used for the website or in publications about the project.

The Shakespeare course uses a five-step sequence of assignments:

1. Attend the play and write a performance review.
2. In groups of four to five, review an assigned Shakespeare performance archive and propose categories of content for *NSPA* (i.e., 'costumes', 'venue', 'music').
3. Plan for and collect materials, interviews, visual and audio recordings.
4. Present content and, as a class, propose content priorities for the Digital Literacies class.
5. Reflect on the project in a paper (see 'Reflective Essay' below).

This logical sequence belies the messiness of the project: interviews may fall through, equipment fails to record, no one's schedule coordinates well, rain cancels a performance. These stumbling blocks, inherent in group projects, give students valuable experience in improvising and revising plans. Also, the experience often produces something of value – an interview with an actor because a show is rained out, or a new idea triggered by observing set design.

For the first assignment, reviewing the NSF production, students have an open-ended prompt: 'comment on anything that is significant to you about how the performance interprets the play and how the context of Shakespeare in the park influences your reaction to the performance'. Rather than setting out a template, this prompt asks students to make a first act of interpretation by simply noticing what creates meaning for them, trusting the production to convey a coherent meaning for a text they likely have only a limited understanding of at this point. Once they articulate how the production enabled them to understand the play, they have entered into the dynamic of production as interpretation – and of engaging Shakespeare as a 'live' text.

The second assignment requires students to critique archives ranging from MIT's *Global Shakespeares* to the *Globe to Globe Hamlet* and *Shakespeare on the Road* (see 'Shakespeare: archive as genre' below). Groups post responses on a discussion board, thus generating topics for in-class discussion. Students then use their insights to consider what information might be important for the *NSPA*, for instance, interviews with actors; photographs of sets, props and costumes; musical scores and songs. As a result of this assignment, students see their 'local' festival in light of the range of productions made available by archives and appreciate its artistry. All of a sudden, 'New York Shakespeare' and 'London Shakespeare' are not always already superior – just different. Also, by framing the critical exploration of existing performance archives as a means of teaching how to 'read' productions, the archive project accelerates students' engagement with live theatre.

The messiness of discussion board posts, class discussion, reading and viewing the play ultimately yields to consensus on proposed categories for the digital archive (i.e. 'costume', 'venue', 'music'). Students create groups to collect data and we use equipment we purchased with the Folger grant funds to conduct professional interviews and provide a stipend to the NSF for coordinating actors' time and granting us access to other materials (in recent years, actors and staff have also donated their time to the project). We also give students brief instructions on how to frame videos and capture audio effectively. This material, along with the proposals for the priorities of the archive, is ultimately transferred to the Digital Literacies class. For this project's first iteration, the Folger grant also funded the assistance of a graduate student working on Shakespeare and social media: Alyssa Wynans. Because she was deeply versed in both the language of Shakespeare and the digital environment, she helped the students bridge the 'boundaries between the knowledge or discourse communities they already belong to [social media] and the knowledge or discourse communities they aspire to join [Shakespeare]' (Bruffee 1993: 85) – and she formed the same bridge for an instructor who knows Shakespeare but was less confident in digital literacy.

Digital Literacies

Drawing on the work of students in the Shakespeare class, students in the Digital Literacies course incorporate the images, video clips, interviews and other written elements into the final website. Digital Literacies is a relatively new course for Belmont's English major and follows the lead of other US universities in examining how disciplines in the humanities can use digital tools to expand knowledge beyond the written word. Specifically, using key terms from the subfield of Multimodal Rhetoric, the course emphasizes how visual, aural, spatial and gestural modalities convey meaning as a complement, an enhancement or even in contrast to the linguistic mode (Ball, Sheppard and Arola 2018: 34). For instance, a student might craft an archive's logo, conveying one meaning in writing while colour, arrangement and size add other layers of meaning. As such, coursework in Digital Literacies highlights how layers of image, sound and organization convey meanings alongside or in addition to linguistic symbols – the perfect pairing for a digital project on Shakespeare in performance. Student contributions to the *NSPA* occur through four stages:

1 Draft a logo and website design as a part of an individual blog assignment.
2 Create student groups based on potential menu items for the archive, such as 'sound design' or 'cast'. Each group gives a three- to five-minute pitch presentation that makes the case for their contribution, with storyboard and site mock-up visual aids.
3 Write a final draft of the HTML/CSS web page(s) and video with a website launch presentation.

4 Complete an individual portfolio that includes a critical introduction and weblinks to the individual work each student creates for the project.

The first half of the course involves assignments and in-class activities that help students learn basic technical skills in image creation, web design and video production. Each of these opening assignments provide novices with an opportunity to experiment with new technology such as Photoshop, HTML/CSS code and video editing tools. These early exercises, which often include group work, help students develop collaborative and substantive skills necessary for the later creation of an original contribution to the *NSPA*.

The second half of the course challenges students in Digital Literacies to use their newfound technical skills to create original content for the *NSPA* by creating a new section in the archive with a new set of webpages for the assigned play. While the learning outcomes of this particular course require students to use industry-standard software such as HTML/CSS code and Adobe Creative Cloud programmes, the following activities could easily be accomplished through user-friendly web design and video production tools. As the first activity for creating an original contribution to the *NSPA*, each student conceptualizes a logo and site mock-up, crafted through Adobe Photoshop, for the class to entertain as a possible design schema for the archive. This activity compels students to learn more about the play, more fully understand the local and global *NSPA* audiences and draw upon rhetorical and design terms to explain their visual concept. As part of the logo design assignment, each student also writes a design justification (see 'Digital Literacies: *Shakespeare Performance Archive* logo and site layout' below) that makes the argument for why their design is the preferred version for the audience and situation of the *NSPA*. Once all students have read each other's submissions, they vote on one version or a combination of versions for the upcoming pitch proposals.

After the design of the new play section in the archive has been set, students examine the materials collected by the Shakespeare course and arrange the content as they see fit into five to six different categories, assigned to groups of three to four students. These categories often, but do not always, replicate the categories created by the Shakespeare class. In the past, categories have included 'director', 'costume', 'actors', 'script adaptation' and 'songwriting', and students have incorporated a number of elements (images, videos, script comparisons, acting profiles, etc.) to effectively archive the play based on the audience and purpose. Although students in Digital Literacies attempt to preserve the original intent of the groups from the Shakespeare class, they have creative license to craft the project as they see fit so long as they justify why in their pitch proposals and later in the critical introductions of their individual portfolios. In recent iterations of this project, when we have been able to teach both courses concurrently in the same academic term, students in both classes negotiate the archive categories together.

Student learning

Student learning in Shakespeare

Because the archive changes the content of the Shakespeare survey, it necessarily augments the content-focused learning outcomes generally associated with traditional survey classes. The most significant added learning outcome is understanding the digital archives of Shakespeare's plays as a curated body of knowledge, indeed as a genre. A second outcome is an ability to articulate a complex understanding of theatrical production as interpretation.

We candidly admit that, especially for the first iteration of this collaboration, 'confusion' may have been a prominent learning outcome. Shakespeare students in the autumn of 2016 expressed difficulty understanding the assignment at the beginning; however, with the unveiling of the archive in spring 2017 at a mini-conference that included presentations from students in both classes, all students could see the product of the long arc of their work: a 'live' digital archive. At that point, 'confusion' turned into a sense of accomplishment. With the archive in place, students in the next Shakespeare survey–Digital Literacies sequence in 2018–19, which archived *Hamlet*, were able to begin with a concept of the project.

Each Shakespeare class requires a short essay, informed by course readings on archives, identifying what the student learned through participating in the project (see 'Shakespeare: project reflection essay' below). The essay responses confirm the students' understanding of the 'generic' qualities of an archive, and some students grasped how archive construction resembles theatrical interpretation. Much like a director, they made distinct decisions about what was important to highlight about the performance:

> It wasn't just the production itself that redefined my understanding of an interpretive act, as the gathering of resources and the eventual construction of an archive also helped with redefining my understanding. [. . .] By participating in the construction of a digital archive, we make decisions on what to include, feature and focus on, which is all an act of interpretation. Thus, in a sense, our digital archive will be an interpretive act of an interpretive act.

Another student queried:

> Do we choose to focus on *Hamlet* as political thriller because of our own turbulent political atmosphere? Do we focus instead on the gender politics literally at play because of the ways gender is still a topic of debate today? [. . .] In this sense, by archiving this production of *Hamlet* we create a time capsule of our thoughts and selves as they relate to *Hamlet* in the early months of 2018.

These excerpts show that the students recognize themselves in the conversation about Shakespeare and theatrical interpretation, because the digital archive makes visible their choices in the historical moment of both production and archive and, potentially, subjects their archival choices to interpretive critique.

In understanding the production as interpretation, students also discern the cultural connections of the particular production. The NSF's Nashville setting for the 2016 *The Comedy of Errors* prompted one student to note the 'sweet tribute' that the staging offered the iconic Nashville honky-tonk Tootsie's Orchid Lounge: 'Tootsie's became the Porpentine, a local haunt in the world of the play. Bonnie Keen, who played [. . .] the proprietress [. . .] said that she took inspiration for her role from the real-life owner of Tootsie's [. . .] Because it had a natural counterpart in the text, the choice to include a Tootsie's-esque setting avoided feeling clumsy or forced'.[2] For another student, the archive linked Nashville to a global culture and to a 'presentist' experience of Shakespeare:

> Shakespeare becomes even more accessible when it is put into mediums that we use every day, like the internet [. . .] I really do believe that finding the right avenue for Shakespeare, whether that be online, in the theatre or in print, makes a huge difference in how people receive him as a writer – this is why this archive is so important.

Student learning in Digital Literacies

Digital Literacies outcomes addressed by the project include demonstrating proficiency in digital production tools and developing sophisticated rhetorical skills. But the learning outcome that most overlaps with the Shakespeare class is obtaining a deeper understanding of the interpretive power of selection, organization and labelling in the archive using multiple modes of meaning: linguistic, visual, aural, spatial and gestural.

Like their counterparts, students in Digital Literacies quickly recognize the generic and interpretive elements of building an archive. Through writing descriptions and keywords, and through organizing content, students come to understand their work as creative and generative rather than merely descriptive. Part of this realization happens through close interaction with the librarian in charge of Belmont University's digital repository. An in-class presentation from the librarian brings students behind the scenes of library metadata creation, where they gain vital technical and analytical knowledge regarding the creation of metadata and search engine optimization (SEO). This knowledge in turn provides them with a deeper understanding of the epistemological role that selection, organization and labelling play within the larger scheme of content management.

Furthermore, the class's focus on design and technology transforms students into multimodal authors who interpret the play and organize the archive for various stakeholders such as students in the Shakespeare class, casual fans of the Nashville Shakespeare Festival and even those involved in the play's production. From image manipulation in Adobe Photoshop to video editing skills in Adobe Premiere Pro, students can confidently list proficiency in a number of these Creative Cloud applications as well as HTML/CSS code. More importantly, students gain valuable experience using multiple modes of meaning for a variety of audiences, which is a foundational goal of the course. For instance, students archiving *Hamlet* thought it vital to convey the dark mood and family turmoil of the play through the modes of sound and image in the opening frames of each video of this archive iteration. To do so, a few students edited together a ten-second introductory clip with ominous music and an animated *Hamlet* logo that slides apart in the middle. The layered meanings in this example were both interpretative and dynamic. In their capstone assignment for the course (see 'Digital Literacies: individual portfolio and critical introduction assignment' below), students justify these interpretive choices by explaining how they used various modes of meaning to convey themes of the play, translating Shakespeare for those who will access the archive.

Application

The *Nashville Shakespeare Performance Archive* – https://shakespeare.belmont.edu – contains the digital archives of four productions by the Nashville Shakespeare Festival: *The Comedy of Errors* (summer 2016), *Antony and Cleopatra* (summer 2017), *Hamlet* (winter 2018) and *The Tempest* (summer 2019). We also provide four assignments, two from the Shakespeare and the Digital Literacies courses, respectively.

Shakespeare: archive as genre

Each of the project groups will be assigned a digital Shakespeare performance archive to review. On our class 'Learning Management Software', in the space designated for your archive, post your critical appraisal of the archive, using criteria developed in our class discussion and readings on the function of archives and concepts of local and global Shakespeare. You should also use your own experience working with websites; what meets your expectations and is truly informative? What distracts or enhances the website's functionality? In what ways does the specifically 'digital' archive structure a user's access to a performance? How did this archive teach you about Shakespearean performance?

Shakespeare: project reflection essay

In this paper, you will describe your part of the archive project and discuss how your contribution helps create an interpretation of *The Comedy of Errors*. This paper should include whatever you 'produce' for this project (i.e., questions for interviews, rationales for still photographs, audio and videos to include, draft content language for the archive), your description of the group process and timetable involved and your analysis of how your contribution is an interpretive act. This essay should cite the article by Alexa Alice Joubin or another article on digital Shakespeare to help you theorize or analyse your contribution. Conclude by providing an analysis of or reflection on the project as a whole.

Digital Literacies: *Shakespeare Performance Archive* logo and site layout

For your second blog post, you will individually envision and create a logo and site layout for the *Nashville Shakespeare Performance Archive*. Your final proposed site mock-up should include one sample web page with your logo and should be posted on your blog site as a jpg file. In addition to the site mock-up, you should include a 300+ word blog entry that explains your logo and site layout within the context of the Nashville, Shakespeare, Belmont and global audiences that will likely access the site. Remember, a design justification is more than an analysis; it is a chance to argue to your classmates, the Shakespeare class and *NSPA* stakeholders why your site design is the preferred version. Be sure to explicitly use the design terms (contrast, repetition, alignment and proximity) to justify every element of the site. Logos and site design will be evaluated based on specificity and visual appeal.

Digital Literacies: individual portfolio and critical introduction assignment

This individual component of the project is your chance to make a compelling argument for your participation in the *NSPA* project. First, you should design a basic HTML page that showcases your work in the project. By linking to or including images of your work for this project, you are detailing your strong participation in its creation.

In addition, your HTML page should include a 1,000+ word critical introduction explaining your work on the project. In particular, this introduction should explain how you were influenced by other Shakespeare archives, videos or websites. Also, your introduction should trace your creative process of developing, revising and finalizing your contribution to the archive. Finally, using specific examples from your own work, explain how you paid attention to the design principles we've been discussing all year.

Notes

1 The *NSPA* can be accessed at https://shakespeare.belmont.edu/. Another essay exploring the development of this archive appears in Yeo (2021).
2 For more on the local nature of this production, see Yeo (2017).

References

Ball, C., J. Sheppard and K. Arola (2018), *Writer/Designer*, 2nd edn, New York: Bedford St. Martin's.

Bruffee, K. (1993), *Collaborative Learning: Higher Education, Interdependence, and the Authority of Knowledge*, Baltimore, MD: Johns Hopkins University Press.

Cleveland Press Shakespeare Photographs: 1870–1982, Michael Schwartz Library, Cleveland State University, https://engagedscholarship.csuohio.edu/shakespeare/.

Donaldson, P. and A. Huang Joubin (n.d.), *Global Shakespeares: Video and Performance Archive*, MIT Global Shakespeares Project, Massachusetts Institute of Technology, https://globalshakespeares.mit.edu/.

Huang Joubin, A. (2011), 'Global Shakespeare 2.0', in P. Holland (ed.), *Shakespeare Survey 64: Shakespeare as Cultural Catalyst*, 38–51, Cambridge: Cambridge University Press.

Rawson, K. J. (2018), 'The Rhetorical Power of Archival Description: Classifying Images of Gender Transgression', *Rhetoric Society Quarterly* 48, no. 4: 327–51.

Shakespeare and the Players, Center for Digital Scholarship, Emory University, https://shakespeare.emory.edu/.

Winston, J. (2019), 'Situated Interpretation: Teaching Shakespeare with Live Performance', *CEA Forum* 48, no. 1 (Winter/Spring): 290–333.

Yeo, J. (2017), 'The Comedy of Errors' (review), *Shakespeare Bulletin* 35, no. 2 (Summer): 350–5.

Yeo, J. (2021), '"Shakespeare is for Everyone": Teaching Regional Productions through the Digital Performance Archive', roundtable, *CEA Forum* 49, no. 2 (Summer/Fall).

Yong, L. Lan, A. Eng Hui Lim, K. Takiguchi, Y. Hwang Ha, L. Chee Keng, M. Suematsu, K. Kobayashi and H. Lee (2016), *Asian Shakespeare Intercultural Archive* (A|S|I|A), 2nd edn, http://a-s-i-a-web.org/en/home.php.

PART FOUR

Teaching in Hybrid and Online Learning Environments

11

Performance and Pedagogy

The Global Shakespeares Online *Merchant of Venice* Course

Sarah Connell

Overview

In the summer of 2016 *The Merchant of Venice* was performed in the Venetian Ghetto for the first time, commemorating both the 500 years since the Ghetto's foundation and the 400th anniversary of Shakespeare's death. A team from the Massachusetts Institute of Technology travelled to Venice to film this site-specific piece of theatre, recording not only rehearsals and performances but also interviews with the cast and crew. The footage from Venice is now a key component in an online course that was released to an initial group of collaborators in the autumn of 2016 on MITx, MIT's domain within the edX Massive Open Online Course (MOOC) platform. 'Global Shakespeares: Re-Creating the Merchant of Venice' was designed to test out the possibilities of teaching Shakespeare and dramatic performance in an online environment, foregrounding a multiplicity of perspectives while making use of the MITx platform's distinctive pedagogical capacities.

The Venice footage offers a solid foundation for the course's emphasis on performance, with an array of exemplars and perspectives from theatrical professionals. The production also provides a distinctive model of theatrical polyvocality, with five actors playing Shylock and many different languages interspersed with Shakespeare's text.[1] The course's final assignment, in which students stage and film a scene from *Merchant*, is key to its pedagogical goals of helping students to construct their own authority in working with Shakespeare, while thoughtfully analysing the many decisions at stake in theatrical productions and carefully considering their own choices as actors and directors. This chapter discusses how the *Merchant* course was designed around three core foci – polyvocality, performance and prototyping digital pedagogies for the humanities – sharing materials and strategies that can be adapted for online Shakespeare teaching in many contexts.

The course follows a five-part structure, organized as follows: Reading Drama and Poetry; Close Reading and *The Merchant of Venice*; Production Choices and *The Merchant of Venice*; Designing Your Own Productions; and Preparing for Live Performance. Early in the design process, the initial development team – Professor Diana Henderson, Sarah Connell and Cathleen Nalezyty – determined that the course should support both independent scholars and students in classes that integrate portions of the course's content. To address these different learning environments, we included core foundational materials in the course, providing learners who may have little previous experience of Shakespeare with a solid introduction to scansion and reading verse, the historical and literary contexts of Shakespeare's works, and other key topics.

Within its five-part structure, the course is divided into thematic units; for example, the first part includes a section on recent debates about staging *Merchant*, an introduction to Shakespeare and his language and a guide to reading Shakespeare and early modern drama. These units themselves contain the individual components of the course, many of which are performance videos, such as footage from the Venice production, videos from MIT's *Global Shakespeares Video & Performance Archive* and other digital collections, and example student projects. Other videos include interviews, conversations, instructor presentations on some key topics, and 'professor's cut' segments with voiceover commentary by MIT faculty accompanying scenes from stage and film productions of *Merchant*. The course also includes textual introductions to core concepts, topics for analysis and some of the debates surrounding *Merchant*. Students contribute their own content to the course by writing posts for discussion fora, with open responses as well as guided activities. In each part, there are several sets of questions designed to help learners think about Shakespeare in new ways as well as opportunities for students to annotate the play. Finally, the course team developed several digital tools for experimenting with Shakespeare's language, including one for scansion and another for listening to and identifying sounds.

Because it is so central to the course, some background on the Venetian production of *The Merchant of Venice* will be helpful here. The play was directed by Karin Coonrod and was a production of the Compagnia de' Colombari international collective of performing artists. A key aspect of this production was the performance space: it was staged outdoors in the main square of the Venetian Ghetto, a location that not only situated the play in a particular historical context, but also allowed for a blending of the performance and the lived spaces of the Ghetto. Another distinctive feature of this production was its five Shylocks, a choice that calls attention to the multiplicity of Jewish and other 'outsider' experiences and to, in Coonrod's words, 'the myriad lightnings of Shylock: his rage, his grief, his wit' (2016a). The production includes sections in Yiddish, Judeo-Venetian, Ladino and other languages to reflect the international nature of its company and the wide-ranging implications of *Merchant*'s concerns with prejudice and bigotry.[2] And finally, the play had no backstage; actors remained in the production space throughout the performance, with all costume and scene changes completed in front of the audience. For the course, these highly visible choices provide both exemplars and objects of analysis as students prepare to stage scenes of their own.

Description

An important goal for this project was to test out the limits of teaching humanities materials on the MITx platform. This goal reflects a particular challenge facing humanities MOOCs today: as Bill Ferster notes, while 'some academic subjects have deterministic answers to problems that present easy responses [...] the difficulty comes when trying to assess more humanistic student responses' (2014: 150). To address this 'thorny problem', in Ferster's phrasing (2014: 150), we drew on the strengths of the platform, which is very effective at delivering instruction through video, and at providing students with immediate feedback on questions that have fixed solutions. Accordingly, the course includes a substantial range of video content; in fact, the diversity of this content is one way we have attempted to address some limitations of online course delivery systems for humanities teaching. There are several instructional videos of the type commonly used in MOOCs, with a single speaker explaining core concepts, but there are far more interviews and conversations, with speakers that extend well beyond faculty and Shakespeare experts to include students, actors, directors, stage managers, light and sound designers, musicians, audience members, stagehands and others.

These many voices also supported our second goal: providing a multiplicity of perspectives to form an ongoing conversation that the students themselves join. In this, we hope that our project can expand on the traditional model of MOOCs, the more 'didactic, content-centric, and instructor-driven process', as Ferster describes it, in which online courses use 'short video clips to deliver intimate but one-directional tutoring' (2014: 142). The Venice footage not only brought many different voices to this conversation, but also enabled us to share deeply contextualized explanations of key concepts. For example, an interview with Sorab Wadia, who played one of the five Shylocks, includes the actor's thoughts on how poetic stresses guide a speaker on the stage. After outlining the basics of iambic pentameter, Wadia describes how an actor can take cues from the poetry in interpreting the language of a play for performance. He says that Shakespeare's metre can assist in deciphering 'the energy, the vibe of the character, the meaning of the play', while also emphasizing the autonomy of the performer – 'you take your cues from the metre [. . .] but you don't let the metre totally rule you' (2016). Complementing this interview, the course includes a guide to scansion and reading verse, as well as a brief explanatory video and a hands-on exercise in marking out poetic feet and stressed syllables; these resources provide students with multiple pathways to understanding scansion and applying this knowledge to their own performances.

In addition to video content, online course platforms like MITx are well equipped to deliver immediate feedback on fixed response questions, such as in multiple-choice, checkbox and dropdown formats. Such questions may not seem like an obvious fit for the pedagogies of literary analysis, but the course team found that they could, in fact, be designed to open up new perspectives on course materials. We thus developed a number of 'Questions to get you thinking' with provocative, unexpected or otherwise multifaceted solutions. For example, one of the earliest questions we developed was 'Who first responds to Antonio in Act 1, Scene 1?' with possible responses of Salarino, Solanio and Salerio. This question, as with all of the course, is ungraded and offers students multiple opportunities to check their responses before presenting the answer.[3] Each correct and incorrect answer includes brief feedback, with a longer discussion after students submit their responses or select 'Show Answer' (see Figure 11.1).

What appears to be a simple reading check in fact asks students to consider the prominence of *s*-named characters in *Merchant*, the seeming interchangeability of many minor characters, the impacts of editorial decisions and the inconsistencies and elisions in early modern speaker labels. This question has two correct answers, depending on whether one consults

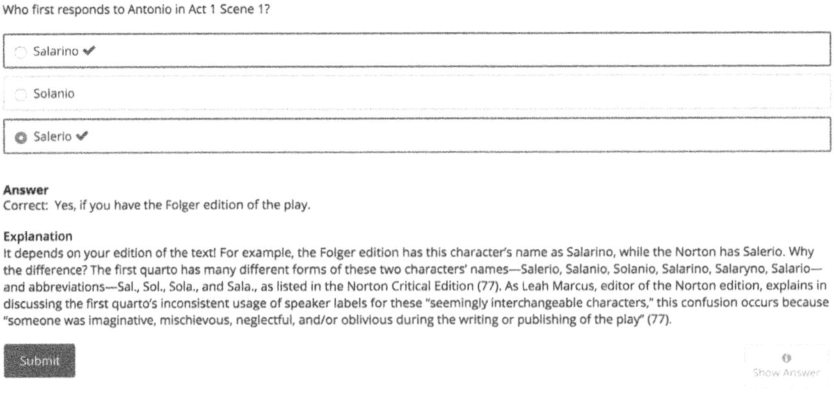

Who first responds to Antonio in Act 1 Scene 1?

○ Salarino ✔

○ Solanio

◉ Salerio ✔

Answer
Correct: Yes, if you have the Folger edition of the play.

Explanation
It depends on your edition of the text! For example, the Folger edition has this character's name as Salarino, while the Norton has Salerio. Why the difference? The first quarto has many different forms of these two characters' names—Salerio, Salanio, Solanio, Salarino, Salaryno, Salario—and abbreviations—Sal., Sol., Sola., and Sala., as listed in the Norton Critical Edition (77). As Leah Marcus, editor of the Norton edition, explains in discussing the first quarto's inconsistent usage of speaker labels for these "seemingly interchangeable characters," this confusion occurs because "someone was imaginative, mischievous, neglectful, and/or oblivious during the writing or publishing of the play" (77).

Submit   Show Answer

FIGURE 11.1 *An example question from the* Merchant *course.*

the Norton or the Folger edition, and the explanatory note that accompanies the sole incorrect response (Solanio) asks students to think about why it is so difficult to tell these two characters (with three names) apart.

Other questions along these lines include, 'What language does Portia speak?'; 'Based on the first two acts of the play, where on Antonio's body does Shylock intend to take his pound of flesh?'; and 'Who speaks the line "My daughter, O my ducats, O my daughter!"?' The course also includes more straightforward 'Comprehension check' questions such as, 'True/False? Shylock charges Antonio interest on the loan of 3,000 ducats' and 'Whose money does Bassanio spend in his efforts to win Portia?' Even these questions ask learners to think through significant aspects of the play; for instance, the answer to the latter points out that any of the possible responses – Antonio, Tubal and Shylock – could be considered correct, calling attention to the multilayered exchanges of currency within *Merchant*.

The third major focus of the course – a commitment to teaching Shakespeare through performance – was perhaps the most challenging to address on the MITx platform. Here, however, we were able to draw on the Venice production to offer perspectives from a recent and topical staging of the play. Because of its distinctive approach, there are numerous choices that this production makes visible for learners. These options are crucial because of the priority we place on asking students to articulate the thinking behind their own decisions on the final project. To make these choices and their outcomes more concrete, we have included practical advice from theatrical professionals in many different roles. For example, the unit in the fourth part on 'Rehearsing and Filming a Scene' has an interview with the Venice production's stage manager, Nerina Cocchi, while an earlier unit on production design includes Karin Coonrod speaking directly to students about how she would encourage them to approach their roles as directors. In this interview, Coonrod urges students to 'read and reread' the play, setting aside any 'romantic' idealization of its history to ask instead, 'How does it speak to us now?' (2016b). Of course, a project like this requires scaffolding that extends well beyond video guidance, particularly for independent learners. Accordingly, the course also includes exercises in which students annotate scripts with production notes, several activities that ask students to analyse production choices and outline plans for their own scenes, and ample instructions not just on staging and filming the scenes but also on technical considerations such as editing and uploading videos.

There is no doubt that the final assignment is challenging, or that it puts some pressure on what is currently possible within online course platforms such as MITx, but we felt that it was essential because it offers students an opportunity to claim expertise and authority in designing their scenes.[4] Attention to performance also contributes to the polyvocality of the course, in that some example videos are those of other students, staged and filmed during Henderson's 'Writing with Shakespeare' classes at MIT. Both performance and polyvocality have been crucial in ensuring that the course works against the sorts of learning experiences that are, as David Worster describes, 'designed to prepare students passively to receive Shakespeare in the only way they think they can: with the assistance of an expert, who serves up the difficult subject in easily digestible chunks' (2002: 368). Worster connects this type of student experience with the power relations discussed by Walker Percy in his seminal essay 'The Loss of the Creature', which shows how the 'educational package' (1975: 57) operates to distance students from any ownership they might claim over the materials they are learning. Recognizing the difficulty of disrupting the educational package model, particularly in an online course, we have nevertheless worked to position students as active creators of meaning in the course.

Like Worster, we pursue this end by adopting a teaching strategy that presents students with 'a range of editorial and interpretive approaches to the text' (Worster 2002: 369) and that draws on the insights of performance pedagogy to make space for students' constructions of their own authority.[5] We have addressed another important aspect of this goal through the platform on which learners view and post course videos, YouTube, which makes many different approaches to Shakespeare available. As Stephen O'Neill observes about *Hamlet*, 'YouTube positions us as active users, free to navigate pathways through multiple *Hamlets*, but also to create our own content' (2011: 66).[6] Ultimately, then, these three goals connect closely with each other: our attention to teaching Shakespeare through performance and offering a diversity of perspectives enables us to begin addressing some of the limitations of open online courses for humanities learning. At the same time, our digital platforms make Shakespeare available for remixing and reappropriation, linking up students' work with the many different approaches to Shakespeare collected in the course.

As befitting a project focused on polyvocality, the *Merchant* course developed out of an iterative set of collaborations among partners with a range of competencies. The course built on a long history of working with Shakespeare at MIT, including the *Shakespeare Electronic Archive* and the *Global Shakespeares Video & Performance Archive*. The project was also supported by MIT institutional resources, including MIT Open Learning, which provided grant funding and staff expertise, and the Council for the Arts at MIT, which made it possible for the team to travel to Venice. The Venice footage was shot by and featured Diana Henderson and Shankar Raman, professors of Literature at MIT, along with two MIT students: Cathleen Nalezyty and Daniel Epelbaum. The initial course development team included two members who had been in Venice – Nalezyty and Henderson – as well as MIT Postdoctoral Associate Sarah Connell; this provided continuity between the filming and development phases and ensured that the development team had key insights into the hundreds of hours of footage from Venice. Subsequent work on the course has involved MIT Research Associate Mary Erica Zimmer and MIT Research Specialist Michael

Lutz, each of whom has contributed experience in digital pedagogies and Shakespeare studies to the project. For a complex endeavour such as this one, it was necessary to bring in many different collaborators, but having a core team ensured that the project remained focused and organized throughout its multi-year development process.

Even with a dedicated group of collaborators bringing their expertise to the project, there were many challenges. For example, our commitment to ensuring that we had fully tested all of the course's components before its public release also led to an extended development phase, which itself meant that we had to migrate the course between multiple versions of the MITx platform. The initial release was developed on the 'Residential' platform, which is for internal MIT courses; we moved to a private version on the main MITx platform ('Edge') when we began piloting external partnerships; and we made the course public on MITx when releasing it as a MOOC in late March of 2020. Along the same lines we knew that annotation would be an important pedagogical component, but during initial development there was no widely available annotation tool integrated within MITx. We investigated several external tools and selected MIT's Annotation Studio, which provided the key features we needed but also required a separate login. For the public release we were able to use an integrated tool in edX that allows learners to annotate a copy of the play within the course, but this transition also required some additional reconfiguration of the pilot materials. As these examples suggest, longer-term projects such as this one often involve iterative technical updates and may also require finding a balance between desired functionalities and more seamless learner experiences.

In a sense, though, what has been most challenging about building the course is that the task itself is simply a difficult one. We have sometimes struggled with accommodating multiple use cases for the course content; while it is important for us that the course should work both for independent learners and within other courses, meeting these different needs has not always been straightforward. For example, we have included substantial text documentation for independent learners, but are aware that this may be unnecessary, and perhaps even distracting, for in-class applications. We also knew that we would need to balance our pedagogical investments in learning through discussion with the current capabilities of the platform, as well as with our own resources. We were pleased with the possibilities of using fixed-response questions to spark new insights into Shakespeare, but we cannot see these as full substitutes for the give and take of a class discussion. Discussion board fora and peer responses can offer students low-stakes spaces to articulate their ideas and exchange feedback, but there are many aspects of a synchronous class environment – such as partnered practice with reading poetry out loud – that are difficult to replicate asynchronously. Nevertheless, we want to be sure that all students are well equipped to learn about Shakespeare and complete their final projects. We therefore carefully considered these concerns in all aspects of the course's design and continue to make updates as we receive input from teachers and students. We hope that we have successfully balanced these considerations, even as new opportunities for improvement arise.

Student learning

During the pilot phase, the primary learning applications for the course were collaborations with faculty at MIT and elsewhere who were provided credentials for the course on the Edge platform; we expect, however, that learning opportunities will expand considerably now that the course has been publicly released. Our collaborations thus far have ranged widely in their scopes, from single class visits using individual components to more extended partnerships in which students have completed the final performance project. For instance, the scansion tool, which allows students to mark poetic feet and stressed syllables, has been used in partnership with upper-level Shakespeare classes at MIT and in Alexa Muse's eighth-grade English class at the International School of Boston. We have also visited Professor Erika Boeckeler's 'Introduction to Shakespeare' course at Northeastern University to share a unit on props and physical objects as part of the class's discussions about material culture. And Shankar Raman's Shakespeare classes at MIT have used the course's collection of trailers from recent productions of *Merchant* to discuss how they encapsulate the decisions made in the performances they represent.[7]

In Rhema Hokama's undergraduate 'Global Shakespeares' class at the Singapore University of Technology and Design, the *Merchant* course helps provide historical and cultural contexts for students who may be encountering Shakespeare for the first time, and also offers models of digital scholarship for students who are pursuing the university's minor in digital humanities. Rachael Deagman Simonetta at the University of Colorado, Boulder, has adapted one of the *Merchant* course's annotation assignments in her online 'Shakespeare for Non-Majors' course (see Chapter 2). In this project, students complete the 'Staging: Challenges and Considerations' unit and then annotate a scene from the play for an imagined production. Deagman Simonetta notes that this assignment, co-designed with her undergraduate Learning Assistant Seerie Clark, offers students an opportunity to think both analytically and creatively about the play, applying the close-reading skills they develop in the first part of the class to their examinations of performance.

As the project's research associate from 2017 to 2019, Erica Zimmer has taken the lead on many class collaborations, such as in her work with Kavita Mudan Finn. In Finn's Shakespeare class at MIT, students examined three variations on the 'quality of mercy' speech, comparing Linda Powell's performance as Portia in the Venice production with the 1973 Jonathan

Miller television version and the 2004 Michael Radford film. These clips are presented in a comparative framework within the course, accompanied by an exercise in which students analyse differences between stage and screen performances. Zimmer expanded on this comparison through in-class discussion, asking students to observe how the scenes were staged and videos were edited to bring out particular perspectives. The students were easily able to locate significant differences, especially in the more active role that Powell played in the Venice production; they noted that she moved more and showed more control over the physical space of the scene. Zimmer reports that students found the juxtaposition of these scenes to be effective for clarifying the choices made not just in staging performances but also in filming and editing them.

Finally, we have been introducing materials from the course into Henderson's 'Writing with Shakespeare' course since the autumn of 2016. In early iterations, students primarily experimented with the question sets and digital resources, but recent classes have more thoroughly integrated course contents and the final performance assignment. Students, for example, select scenes that connect with topics from the course and follow the exercises to annotate and prepare their scripts for production. Students perform their scenes twice, which gives them some practice in filming and uploading their videos but also (and more importantly) provides an opportunity to review their staging and editing decisions.

Feedback from Henderson's students has helped us identify several key areas of improvement for the course, particularly as it can be used within other class contexts. For instance, reflections have indicated that the abundance of information within the course was actually an impediment to students' work with it. As one wrote, 'there was just so much content, that I didn't have time to thoroughly look through most of it'; the course would be more helpful 'if a student knew exactly what they were looking for'. This sentiment was echoed by many in the class: they were aware that the course contained a great deal of potentially useful information, but they needed direction and incentive to engage with that information. To address this concern the course team added several thematic content strands, each of which focuses on a key topic related to *Merchant*: historical and contemporary contexts, gender and genre. These three strands pull materials from across the course to provide focused pathways for exploration.[8] Later iterations of Henderson's 'Writing with Shakespeare' have integrated the strands into the class, with students identifying themes that are of particular interest to them, exploring those themes through the strands and then selecting scenes for the final project that connect with their themes.

Other responses from Henderson's classes show that the technical aspects of the final performance assignment are a challenge, but enable students to, as Zimmer explains, 'consider ways staging Shakespeare remains a continual conversation: one involving collaborations with the past, yet distinguished in each case by students' evolving interests and insights' (personal communication, 23 November 2019). Some students observed that the performance aspects of the project were especially challenging, requiring them to take risks and accept some vulnerability. But reflections also show that the scaffolded activities in the course were helpful for the final projects; for example, one student wrote that these exercises 'encouraged me to be more aware of my own speaking voice'. Responses from Henderson's classes show that 'the technology dimension', as one student put it, can be a useful and effective component within Shakespeare classes, provided learners have clear direction and sufficient support for working with digital materials.

A final example can illustrate how the course's cornerstones – experimenting with the capabilities of the MITx platform for humanities instruction, teaching through performance and making a space for a range of voices in our conversations about Shakespeare – intersect in application. The Annotation Studio metadata for one student group's annotated performance playscript in Henderson's class lists two authors: 'William Shakespeare and the Consonants'. This rather playful addition of the group's name as a co-author in fact shows the depth of the students' investments in their reworking of the scene's language and the authority that they have claimed in using the course's digital tools to add their voices to Shakespeare's.

Application

As noted above, the course is designed so that instructors can integrate individual components into their classrooms.[9] Such integration might vary considerably in its scope; for example, some instructors may simply want to show the interview and performance videos or have students experiment with the tools for scansion and annotating sounds. The individual question sets can also be adapted for class activities and discussions. The thematic units within each of the module's five parts align with the subjects of diverse Shakespeare and Renaissance literature classes and might be adopted or adapted in full by those interested in more sustained integrations. For instance, the unit on props and physical objects could provide useful starting points for discussions on staging Shakespeare's plays or early modern material culture. The thematic strands also provide a set of entry points for faculty wishing to use these materials in their classes.

As shown by the diverse set of classes discussed above, the course can be used in a range of contexts; those who are interested in adapting it for their own classes will find many materials within the course site on MITx. For this chapter, one final example activity can briefly indicate some of the course's potential for application and adaptation. 'Exploring *Merchant* in Multimedia' asks students to experiment with a set of digital resources and multimedia objects on *Merchant* curated by the project team and to consider questions such as 'What passages of *Merchant* have spoken most powerfully to you so far?' and 'How does the multimedia object illuminate possibilities for your own performance?' Students are then asked to 'pick at least one (1) resource and present it through a quick (~1 minute) video clip where you narrate in the background how this resource relates to your reading of *Merchant* so far'. This activity presents an opportunity for students to become familiar with filming in a low-stakes environment as preparation for their final projects; it also encourages students to be creative in their responses as they discuss their readings of the play and helps them to discover the many other digital resources for learning about Shakespeare.

Notes

1 Centring the course on the Venice footage also served pragmatic purposes, in that it provided direct access to a range of materials from a production that was not a copyrighted film or theatrical video.
2 This multilingualism connects to the course's own framework within *Global Shakespeares*, a set of MIT initiatives that includes an online archive with performances of Shakespeare's plays from around the world. Reflecting these connections, we have designed a unit on Shakespeare in international contexts, with several multilingual productions of *Merchant* from the *Global Shakespeares Video & Performance Archive*, in addition to interviews on diversity from the Venice production.
3 While the course was designed to be ungraded, students wishing to pursue a course 'certificate' as offered by edX are 'graded' by completing units; that is, by completing the material in the course.
4 For example, it is difficult for learners in different locations to collaborate on staging scenes together, there are limited opportunities for students to receive feedback on scenes while they are in development and the technical barriers of uploading videos remain significant in many cases.
5 For some foundational work on performance pedagogy, see Riggio (1999) and the 'Teaching Shakespeare' special issue of *Shakespeare Quarterly* (Andrews 1984).
6 For more on the impacts of YouTube on Shakespeare studies, see O'Neill (2014).
7 This unit includes a 'letters supercut' with clips from each moment in the Venice production in which characters exchange documents, along with interviews with Jana Dambrogio, the Thomas F. Peterson Conservator at MIT, and Daniel Starza Smith of King's College London discussing letterlocking, an early method of folding letters such that they provide their own seals, and speaking about a letter that was created by Dambrogio and used as a prop in the Venice production.
8 The strand on gender, for example, includes commentary from Coonrod and Powell on female characters in *Merchant*, along with the exercise comparing versions of the 'quality of mercy' speech and an activity in which students consider Shakespeare's handling of minor characters.
9 See https://www.edx.org/course/global-shakespeares-the-merchant-module.

References

Andrews, J., ed. (1984), 'Special Issue: Teaching Shakespeare', *Shakespeare Quarterly* 35, no. 5: 513–656.

Coonrod, K. (2016a), 'The Merchant "in" Venice: The Staging of Shakespeare's Classic in the Jewish Ghetto', New York University, 6 October, https://www.youtube.com/watch?v=4XuyNSwaZkE&t.

Coonrod, K. (2016b), interviewed by D. Henderson, https://www.youtube.com/watch?v=dwvx2xjLE58.

Ferster, B. (2014), *Teaching Machines: Learning from the Intersection of Education and Technology*, Baltimore, MD: Johns Hopkins University Press.

Percy, W. (1975), *The Message in the Bottle: How Queer Man Is, How Queer Language Is, and What One Has to Do with the Other*, New York: Farrar, Straus, and Giroux.

O'Neill S. (2014), *Shakespeare and YouTube: New Media Forms of the Bard*, London and New York: Bloomsbury.

Riggio, M. (1999), *Teaching Shakespeare through Performance*, New York: Modern Language Association of America.

Wadia, S. (2016), interviewed by S. Raman, https://www.youtube.com/watch?v=472a3Hi1QTY.

Worster, D. (2002), 'Performance Options and Pedagogy: Macbeth', *Shakespeare Quarterly* 53, no. 3: 362–78.

12

Translating Shakespeare from Scene to Screen, and Back Again

Digital Tools for Teaching *Richard III*

Loreen Giese

Overview

Teaching Shakespeare digitally – whether in an asynchronous online course or a digital unit in a residential class – can foster a deeper engagement with and understanding of the plays by providing a platform to integrate resources and new approaches. This chapter discusses three tools – narrative summaries, study questions and a digital humanities assignment – that I developed for my asynchronous online course and also use in my face-to-face and hybrid courses. While all three tools enhance student participation and performance, the digital forms of the first two tools additionally result in four crucial developments: they 1) permit me to personalize layouts that help students find models that better suit their needs and abilities, thereby benefitting their individual involvement, comprehension and critical reading and thinking; 2) allow me to be more responsive to students' interests; 3) make the material more accessible and available to students, especially those with special needs and circumstances; and 4) create more student-centred pedagogy.

The flexibility of these tools' digital format is especially helpful when teaching a history play such as *Richard III*. Many students at my US Midwestern state university have not heard of Richard III, whether the man, the king or the play. The play's historical nature also disappointingly does not appeal to some students; those who see the play as 'non-literary' have more difficulty understanding and appreciating its artistry. The unfamiliarity of the material, its historical aspects and their complicated relationships within the play – how many Edwards hath *Richard III*? – make many students apprehensive about their ability to understand the events and relationships dramatized in the text. My digital tools also assist students who, even when familiar with the infamy of this king, the popularity of the play or the fame of Richard's opening soliloquy, still may need help overcoming their intimidation about analysing the play.

Regardless of students' familiarity with the text, these tools help students increase their understanding of, engage more deeply with and strengthen their ability to analyse this engrossing play and see that literature and history can be in dialogue. These benefits generate more textured discussions and more complicated paper topics regarding the play's historical and theoretical contexts. For example, after considering how we describe and construct Richard's character as a dramatic and historical figure, we probe the interpretative consequences of a reductive essentialism rooted in binary oppositions around the discourses of morality and immorality. We also explore how the kinds of texts by which historians gain access to information about a person or period influence our interpretations.

Description

When I began teaching online in 1999, faculty at my university lacked IT, design, pedagogical or financial support for developing and teaching an online class. Learning platforms such as Blackboard and Moodle and the technology for synchronous virtual meetings did not exist: my course, for example, had to be hand coded. Faced with the prospect of developing a course using new technology that then offered very few features, and thus lacking guidance or cautionary tales from colleagues' experiences, I was unsure how to make the most of this medium, especially when teaching Shakespeare. The first possibility was to transfer my pedagogy and content from my residential courses to my online one. In all my classes, I want – in the words of Marjorie Garber – to 'slow down the move to context' by 'redirecting attention to the language of the plays, scene by scene, act by act, moment by moment, word by word' (2010: 151). Since I teach my residential classes through close reading and discussion, I realized that online teaching would not allow me to transfer the in-class method. In fact, it would exacerbate the difficulties students experienced following a play's plot, understanding its language or overcoming the intimidation of Shakespeare's iconic status, since students would be working individually and almost always at different times of the day; they thus would lack an immediate, collaborative, audible and visual academic community with its weekly meetings of free-flowing discussions and individualized attention and support. I also grappled with how to offset the missed residential class time so that online courses could have parity with residential ones.

Wanting to embrace the opportunities of teaching Shakespeare online, I realized that creating this course required a *translation* rather than a transfer of content, approach and instructor's role. I needed to reimagine my pedagogy: my role would be as a mentor or guide with a more conversational tone, and my approach would be to design digital tools and assignments that help students understand plot and close-read content on their own. My decisions from the beginning not to include recorded lectures and later not to use VoiceThread further disrupted the face-to-face course dynamic. The tools I designed for the course – narrative summaries (detailed scene-by-scene breakdowns of what happens) and study questions (about specific speeches, events or interpretative issues in each scene) – aimed to help students connect more deeply with texts, particularly with plays in genres unfamiliar to them or whose content they find more difficult, and to strengthen their critical reading and thinking. When I started using narrative summaries and study questions in 1999, their original placement was not as helpful for all students as they are now. Originally, I placed the narrative summary before the study questions for the respective scene. When students complained about having to scroll through the sometimes lengthy summaries to reach the study questions, I made the summaries a separate link in the course website menu with a separate file for each play. Since then, while my university's learning platform, Blackboard, does not allow students to customize the tools' forms, I personalize them to some extent by offering two different models for each play. I found that students using these tools while reading on their own more than compensated for residential class participation while utilizing only two main tools prevented student distraction that can result from too many different online resources. These tools have provided further unexpected gains: they made online courses of more equitable pedagogical value to residential courses and they encouraged a different kind of engagement from both myself and students. The course required students to be more active learners and caused us all to focus entirely on the texts themselves: the plays, performances and written assignments.

Compared to when I started teaching, technological advances (such as the availability of synchronous meetings) have diminished the once large differences between online and face-to-face courses. Likewise, the tools in my online and face-to-face courses are now more similar. The positive feedback from students who used these tools in online courses, the declining levels of student preparedness for residential college courses and the increased difficulties in student comprehension when reading on their own caused me for the last decade to use these same tools in a digital format in my hybrid and face-to-face courses. Jim Casey's argument for the need of 'pre-digital close reading and analysis' for 'digital Shakespeares [to] work best' assumes that the supplemental aspect of these digital sources drives students 'farther away from Shakespeare's text' (2019: 2). The digital tools I designed are meant to guide a reader *into* the text to strengthen close reading and analysis, and the ability to personalize them allows for an even closer connection to a play. Online tools work hand in hand with the required printed editions in my online and residential courses; the printed texts as opposed to e-texts make students slow down their reading, drawing them into rather than their swiping over a text. A distinct further advantage is that *these* digital tools, unlike many such resources, will not suddenly become inactive.

Narrative summaries

Because many undergraduates struggle to grasp what happens in plays, narrative summaries help them both understand the plot and concentrate on more aspects of the texts. Furthermore, students who already comprehend the events in a scene can focus more on language, character and staging and possibly become engrossed in a text more quickly. Since I recommend that students read the play in sections that are manageable for them, whether it be one to two scenes or an act at a time, a scene-by-scene design is most helpful for my students. A detailed, narrative summary is especially necessary for a history play, especially one as long and with as many speaking parts as *Richard III*. In 1999, digital summaries were not easily accessible. Although now many are available in print or online, the existing synopses and summaries of plays differ greatly in their comprehensiveness and usefulness, and many of them are not very helpful due to their form or sparse content. These summaries usually outline a play's entire plot in one long paragraph or act by act; neither form helps students easily understand the action in a specific scene. Some greatly condense a complicated scene into a sentence, a reduction and simplification that, by missing key elements, does not help a struggling student's comprehension. For example, David and Ben Crystal's popular online site *ShakespearesWords.com* includes the following summary of Act 3, Scene 4 of *Richard III*: 'At the Council meeting, Richard reports a plot against him and arraigns Hastings, who is promptly executed' (2018).[1] In contrast, my more detailed precis of this scene helps students understand more of the plot and key elements such as the relationships among the dramatic figures, Richard's mercurial character and the representation of women – specifically, Richard's continued misogyny and Hastings being another man who acknowledges the veracity of Margaret's curses only when he heads to his execution:[2]

3.4   Hastings, Buckingham, Stanley, Bishop of Ely, Richard and others meet to discuss the day of coronation ostensibly to make Prince Edward king. The bishop suggests the next day. Buckingham asks if anyone knows what Richard thinks about it. The bishop comments that Buckingham should know best Richard's thoughts on the matter, and Buckingham responds how they 'know each other's faces' but not their hearts (10).

> Hastings recommends that the lords present pick the day and offers to speak on Richard's behalf. After Richard arrives, Buckingham tells him of Hastings' proposal to speak for him.
>
> Richard cheerfully asks the bishop to send for strawberries from his garden in Holborn.
>
> Richard privately tells Buckingham that Catesby 'hath sounded Hastings' (36) to find that Hastings would rather die than see Richard king, and then Richard and Buckingham withdraw.
>
> While Richard and Buckingham are offstage, Hastings comments on Richard's good humour and identifies Richard as the only man in Christendom who cannot 'hide his love or hate' (52) for someone (Hastings is clueless!).
>
> Richard returns in a dark mood, asking what someone deserves who uses 'devilish plots' and 'damned witchcraft' to plan his death and 'hellish charms' on his body (58–61). Hastings says, given his love for Richard, she or he deserves death.
>
> Richard reveals his withered arm and blames Queen Elizabeth and Mistress Shore for his deformity. Richard cuts off Hastings' response when he questions their guilt, calls him a 'traitor' (74) and orders his beheading.
>
> On his way to his beheading, Hastings worries for England and calls himself a fool. He re-examines his responses (Act 3, Scene 2) and points out the accuracy of Margaret's curses. He too prophesizes: 1) a wretched time for England; and 2) they that smile at him now will soon die.

Moreover, even if one assigns an edition that includes narrative summaries before each scene (Folger) or provides thorough summaries of each scene in an appendix (Modern Library), students sometimes do not use the assigned edition. Thus, my course websites include my summaries which differ in detail based on a play's difficulty. In residential courses, which are otherwise tech-free zones, the online format allows me to project the narrative summaries to help contextualize our discussions.

Study questions

Study questions help students overcome their feelings of intimidation in studying Shakespeare, assist their comprehension, encourage their engagement and strengthen their critical reading, thinking and writing skills. An added advantage is that, regardless of the mode of course delivery, they help students prepare for discussions and assignments. I encourage students to write out their responses to help develop their thinking and record their reflections. Whether I teach face-to-face, hybrid or online courses, having these questions digitally available provides many benefits in terms of my responsiveness to students' needs and class content. This format allows me to scaffold questions based on class discussions; sequence questions to build higher order thinking; synthesize different aspects of and class discussions about a play; offer a new resource; and expand discussion to continue to a subsequent scene. These questions also make the course more student-centred; their variety and specificity encourage students to take ownership of their learning by close-reading content on their own. Moreover, using study questions helps create a community, especially in online courses, between the instructor and the students and among students.

Digital humanities assignment

My most pedagogically effective digital humanities assignment is now the first assignment in all my Shakespeare courses: students rewrite a complicated, longer speech as a private Instagram story. The aim of this assignment, in part, is to avoid what Russ McDonald, Nicholas D. Nance and Travis D. Williams would call 'an overriding devotion to context and an impulse to leap from the text to a reading or interpretation' which 'is likely to omit or at least elide the process of reading' (2012: xxx). The form and timing of this assignment are beneficial. Having students translate a speech into their own language and symbols requires them to read closely and helps them overcome their initial phobia and anxiety about reading Shakespeare's language, especially since the assignment requires they take ownership of the language. This translation, coupled with peer responses and subsequent discussions of students, choices regarding what they kept, cut and changed, makes the course more student-centred from the start. Moreover, this assignment increases their involvement and strengthens their ability to produce more analytical work throughout the course. Encouraging usage of the *Oxford English Dictionary* (*OED*) is an additional advantage since this useful resource is unknown to most of my students: it helps them expand their vocabulary and gain a more nuanced understanding of a play's language, which they then can apply to the language in their Instagram stories. When studying *Richard III*, students are asked to read closely the opening soliloquy using the narrative summary and study questions before we start discussing the play. In our first class, we discuss and contextualize their findings within the first scene. Students then complete this digital assignment, the timing of which is particularly advantageous since the soliloquy's location in the text allows a due date for the second or third class; students thus engage more deeply with Richard's mercurial character and ability to manipulate through language from the start. Another advantage of the assignment's timing is that students can swiftly overcome their Shakespeare phobia and history play anxiety. Regardless of the assigned speech, many students identify this assignment as the one that most increased their confidence to understand language and characters and think critically.

Student learning

These tools benefit student learning in multiple ways. As substantiated by overwhelmingly positive student feedback, livelier classes, more analytical discussions and assignments, the content, design and availability of these tools have significant advantages: namely, they greatly strengthen student comprehension and engagement with Shakespeare plays, allow more students to enrol in a Shakespeare course and help many students perform to their highest capacity. Another benefit is that discussions in face-to-face and online classes spend less time explaining or clarifying plot. Instead, we focus more attention on textual, historical and theoretical analysis; we explicate passages, examine character and dramatic form and interpret the play's language using questions students have answered, considered or generated before class discussions. This foundation allows us then to discuss staging, investigate historical sources and examine differing theoretical approaches and critical readings. In addition, the digital humanities assignment invites students to see the ways rhetorical tools and literary devices in Shakespeare's plays exist in everyday communication. In writing their Instagram stories, they can experiment with these strategies in their own writing.

Application

Narrative summary and study questions

Under each link for the scenes that comprise the reading due that week, I offer the two designs below. Because some students' abilities to comprehend Shakespeare strengthen as the course progresses and others find certain plays like *King Lear* or different genres like the histories more difficult, they can choose the format that best suits their needs and abilities regarding the different plays and scenes. For example, while one student used the first format when reading Act 1 of *Richard III*, she switched to the second option when reading Act 3 because she was 'completely lost'.

Separate

The format I have used the longest is to have two separate links: one to the narrative summaries and one to the study questions. Students who do not struggle with understanding a play's plot usually choose this option. With the narrative summary under a separate link, many students find this format beneficial as a way to test their comprehension of the plot when they read the plays on their own.

> *Richard III* Act 1, Scene 1 – Separate
>   Narrative Summary

> 1.1   After a long civil war between the York and Lancaster families (commonly known as the War of the Roses), Richard, Earl of Gloucester, gives a soliloquy in which he explains his opinions on the present king (his eldest brother, Edward IV) as well as his own desires and motivations.
>
> Richard also makes Edward IV believe a prophesy that a family member with the initial 'G' will murder his heirs. Edward IV jails George, Duke of Clarence (Edward IV's younger and Richard's older brother) and accuses him of treason.
>
> Richard encounters Clarence on the way to the Tower. He blames the Queen, Lady Elizabeth Grey, as being behind the plot against Clarence. While he promises Clarence that he will 'deliver' (115) him from his imprisonment, he immediately reveals in a soliloquy what he means by 'deliver': he plans to have Clarence killed.
>
> In yet another soliloquy, he expresses his hopes that Edward IV will soon die and reveals his plan to marry Lady Anne, whose husband, Edward, and father-in-law, the previous king, Henry VI, Richard killed in battle.

Richard III Act 1, Scene 1 – Separate
Study Questions

This Shakespeare play is unusual because of the opening's number, placement and speaker of soliloquies. Richard opens the play with a gripping soliloquy in which he comments on current events, his appearance, his character and his plans, and offers two more soliloquies in this scene. Most titular characters enter later in opening scenes (Titus, King Lear) or in later scenes (Henry V, Hamlet). Since the play starts with the main character's connecting with the audience, the study questions for this scene mainly focus on these three soliloquies.

Read Richard's opening soliloquy carefully line by line.

- What specific language does he use (metaphors, imagery, puns, related word clusters)?
- What kinds and how many patterns of contrast occur? (personal/political; winter/summer; love/war; etc.)
- Since the soliloquy opens with a discussion of the past, what is the effect of starting with the word 'Now'?
- How many times does the first-person pronoun, I, occur?
- What roles will he assume?
- Pay special attention to the line 'I am determined to prove a villain' (1.1.30). Is this line in passive or active voice? Is he saying 'dissembling Nature' (1.1.19) made him – 'determined' him – to be a

villain through his physical deformities? Or, is he saying that he made up his mind to be a villain? If you cannot decide, what are the effects of leaving it ambiguous?
- What is the effect of the play's opening with Richard's perspective first?
- Synthesizing all these questions, how do you interpret his soliloquy?
- What is Clarence's understanding of the cause of the King's actions? What does that indicate about Richard's abilities to play a role and manipulate others, even his brothers?
- Who and what does Richard cite as the cause of the King's actions? How do you interpret Richard's citing this cause?
- How does Richard's second, short soliloquy relate to the first? What is the effect of having these two soliloquies frame this interchange with Clarence?
- What is the closing soliloquy's content?
- How do the roles he mentions compare to those in the opening soliloquy? How does his confidence in wooing women change? How do you interpret this difference?
- What language does he use to describe his activity, and what does it reveal about his attitude towards his plan?
- How does the content of the closing soliloquy relate to that in the prior two?
- How do these three soliloquies shape your understanding and interpretation of Richard? What do you learn about the disparity between Richard's genuine and feigned identities?
- What does this scene reveal about the political undercurrents at court?

Blended

The second option weaves the study questions through the narrative summary. This format offers the most guidance in terms of plot and content. Students who feel the most intimidated or least prepared often choose this design when starting the course. When they move to the other not-as-plot-centred format, they gain confidence in their abilities to understand the plays. This format allows students to check their grasp of what happens in the play as well as concentrate on key moments as they work through a scene.

Richard III Act 1, Scene 1 – Blended
After a long civil war between the York and Lancaster families (commonly known as the War of the Roses), Richard, Earl of Gloucester,

gives a soliloquy in which he explains his opinions on the present king (his eldest brother, Edward IV) as well as his own desires and motivations. Richard also makes Edward IV believe a prophesy that a family member with the initial 'G' will murder his heirs. Edward IV jails George, Duke of Clarence (Edward IV's younger and Richard's older brother) and accuses him of treason.

This Shakespeare play is unusual because of the opening's number, placement and speaker of soliloquies. Richard opens the play with a gripping soliloquy in which he comments on current events, his appearance, his character and his plans, and offers two more soliloquies in this scene. Most titular characters enter later in opening scenes (Titus, King Lear) or in later scenes (Henry V, Hamlet). Since the play starts with the main character's connecting with the audience, the study questions for this scene mainly focus on these three soliloquies.

Read Richard's opening soliloquy carefully line by line.

- What specific language does he use (metaphors, imagery, puns, related word clusters)?
- What kinds and how many patterns of contrast occur? (personal/political; winter/summer; love/war; etc.)
- Since the soliloquy opens with a discussion of the past, what is the effect of starting with the word 'Now'?
- How many times does the first-person pronoun, I, occur?
- What roles will he assume?
- Pay special attention to the line 'I am determined to prove a villain' (1.1.30). Is this line in passive or active voice? Is he saying 'dissembling Nature' (1.1.19) made him – 'determined' him – to be a villain through his physical deformities? Or, is he saying that he made up his mind to be a villain? If you cannot decide, what are the effects of leaving it ambiguous?
- What is the effect of the play's opening with Richard's perspective first?
- Synthesizing all these questions, how do you interpret his soliloquy?

Richard encounters Clarence on the way to the Tower. He blames the Queen, Lady Elizabeth Grey, as being behind the plot against Clarence. While he promises Clarence that he will 'deliver' (115) him from his imprisonment, he immediately reveals in a soliloquy what he means by 'deliver': he plans to have Clarence killed.

- What is Clarence's understanding of the cause of the King's actions? What does that indicate about Richard's abilities to play a role and manipulate others, even his brothers?

- Who and what does Richard cite as the cause of the King's actions? How do you interpret Richard's citing this cause?
- How does Richard's second, short soliloquy relate to the first? What is the effect of having these two soliloquies frame this interchange with Clarence?

In yet another soliloquy, he expresses his hopes that Edward IV will soon die and reveals his plan to marry Lady Anne, whose husband, Edward, and father-in-law, the previous king, Henry VI, Richard killed in battle.

- What is the closing soliloquy's content?
- How do the roles he mentions compare to those in the opening soliloquy? How does his confidence in wooing women change? How do you interpret this difference?
- What language does he use to describe his activity, and what does it reveal about his attitude towards his plan?
- How does the content of the closing soliloquy relate to that in the prior two?
- How do these three soliloquies shape your understanding and interpretation of Richard? What do you learn about the disparity between Richard's genuine and feigned identities?
- What does this scene reveal about the political undercurrents at court?

Having these tools available digitally offers multiple advantages: they 1) allow me to personalize them with different formats; 2) permit me to be more responsive by updating them quickly, based on class discussions and student interests; 3) make the materials more accessible to students with various disabilities, medical issues or special circumstances; 4) enable students to choose designs that best suit their needs and abilities; 5) give students the ability to customize the order in which they use them; 6) provide students with easy access to these tools through their phones or tablets, no matter their location, without carrying around or misplacing handouts; 7) encourage students to flip quickly and seamlessly between the printed texts and tools; and 8) cause less environmental damage and financial outlay in printing and copying.

Digital humanities assignment

As we discussed, Shakespeare's *Richard III* is unusual in that it opens with a soliloquy; even more so since it is a captivating and dazzling one from the titular character. Richard gives his account of the current state of England and himself, specifically identifying his motives and how others have treated him. Because the play starts with this soliloquy, you enter the play through Richard's perspective. But how accurate is he? Does his self-justification at this point in the play convince you? Does his confiding in you about his self-created role as an actor and author of a script and his gloating over his energy, wit, and ability to manipulate make you a co-conspirator? Is he manipulating and seducing readers and viewers as he details how he will manipulate and seduce other characters?

1   Please write a summary of each line of the soliloquy in your own language.
2   If a word or phrase is unclear, please consult the footnotes in your text or look it up using the *Oxford English Dictionary* online resource that is available through our library webpage under the Database tab.
3   Once you have a working paraphrase of this soliloquy – because of Richard's performative self-awareness in and the selectivity of his audience (readers and viewers and not other characters) – please rewrite it as a private Instagram story.

Questions to consider include:

- what points to emphasize,
- how to translate them into twenty-first-century language, and what punctuation to use to stress your points.

You are welcome to include emojis as appropriate, including designing your own. If you use emojis, at least 50 per cent of the paper still must be written language.

Depending on course delivery, I use two different kinds of peer responses. In face-to-face classes, after attaining student permission, I circulate anonymous handouts of the strongest two or three texts to discuss how their language and symbols best translate the soliloquy into modern language, condense it into the fewest symbols or words and aid our understanding of it and Richard as a dramatic and historical figure. After discussion, the digital format allows me to project these versions for the class to facilitate a collaborative rewriting of this soliloquy using sections students select from the distributed examples. The digital format also allows quick *OED* consultations during discussion. In online courses, the twenty-five students read all the posted papers and write replies discussing the same aspects as above in two students' papers. The written replies encourage students to think through this material even more deeply and increase their confidence to understand and analyse a Shakespeare play, especially a history play. In addition, students' written replies to others' interpretations comprise a collaborative learning experience uncommon in some face-to-face Shakespeare courses. Furthermore, for students who feel uncomfortable critically evaluating classmates' written work, the online format, without the audible and visual immediacy of a face-to-face class, empowers them to speak more openly and honestly.

As these examples indicate, new technologies provide opportunities to design tools that enhance and further an instructor's pedagogical goals, enable student textual and historical comprehension and create new spaces of inquiry so that students can take their understanding and interpretations of Shakespeare's plays in a new direction.

Notes

1 https://www.shakespeareswords.com/Public/Play.aspx?Content=Synopsis&WorkId=6.
2 All references to *Richard III* in the tools are from the Signet edition (Penguin, 1998).

References

Casey, J. (2019), 'Digital Shakespeare is neither Good nor Bad, But Teaching Makes it so', *Humanities* 8, no. 2: 112, https://doi.org/10.3390/h8020112.
Crystal, D. and B. Crystal (2018), *ShakespearesWords.com*, https://www.shakespeareswords.com/.
Garber, M. (2010), 'Shakespeare in Slow Motion', in R. G. Feal (ed.), *Profession*, 151–64, New York: Modern Language Association of America.
McDonald, R., N. D. Nance and T. D. Williams (2012), 'Introduction', in R. McDonald, N. D. Nance and T. D. Williams (eds), *Shakespeare Up Close: Reading Early Modern Texts*, xix–xxxv, London: Arden.
Shakespeare, W. (1597/1998), *Richard III*, New York: Penguin.
Shakespeare, W. (1597/2008), *Richard III*, New York: Modern Library.
Shakespeare, W. (1597/2018), *Richard III*, New York: Simon and Schuster.

13

Dividing the Kingdoms

Interdisciplinary Methods for Teaching Shakespeare to Undergraduates

Jaime Goodrich, with Sarah Noble

Overview

Across the United States, Shakespeare is a staple of General Education programmes, which seek to familiarize undergraduate students with a wide range of human knowledge through introductory courses in the arts and sciences. Since the transmission of cultural heritage plays an important role in most General Education curricula, Shakespeare courses at this level are frequently taught as a survey of Shakespeare's greatest works. While there is much to recommend this traditional approach, a Bard-centred framework suppresses the diversity of methodologies – including those of film, literature and theatre – that inform Shakespearean criticism. We set out to address this issue with our teaching support site, 'Dividing the Kingdoms: Interdisciplinary Methods for Teaching Shakespeare to Undergraduates' (https://guides.lib.wayne.edu/folgerkinglear). Produced by an interdisciplinary team of scholars at Wayne State University with the express purpose of surveying multiple ways to approach Shakespeare at university level, 'Dividing the Kingdoms' attempts to answer one guiding question: what would it look like to teach Shakespeare through more than one modality? By focusing on methodology itself as core content, 'Dividing the Kingdoms' offers an alternative model for college Shakespeare courses.

Aiming to reshape the teaching of Shakespeare in Detroit and beyond, 'Dividing the Kingdoms' conveys the research expertise of specific faculty members at Wayne State, incorporates local Shakespearean resources and connects the university with the surrounding community through service learning in local K-12 school systems. This resource reflects institutional priorities at Wayne State, a public urban research university located in Detroit, Michigan. Wayne State's mission is to 'create and advance knowledge, prepare a diverse student body to thrive, and positively impact local and global communities'.[1] Because of his cultural and literary importance, Shakespeare is an excellent starting point for pursuing the university's goal of combining excellence in research and teaching with community outreach. Indeed, 'Dividing the Kingdoms' originated in Wayne State's successful bid to bring the First Folio to Detroit in 2016 as part of the Folger Shakespeare Library's traveling exhibit 'First Folio! The Book that Gave Us Shakespeare'. Partnering with the Detroit Institute of Arts and the Detroit Public Library, Wayne State organized a series of Folio-related events that attracted 18,249 visitors to the exhibition. Faculty members involved in the First Folio visit then extended this collaboration by undertaking a follow-up grant awarded through the Folger's 'Teaching Shakespeare to Undergraduates' programme in 2016–17. Guided by three principle strategies (fostering interdisciplinary collaboration, fulfilling the university's mission and enhancing student learning), the grant team produced a digital suite of resources that allows undergraduate students to experiment with different methodologies (adaptation, cultural studies, digital humanities, performance, philosophy and text) for reading six of Shakespeare's most frequently taught plays (*Hamlet, 1 Henry IV, King Lear, Othello, Romeo and Juliet, Taming of the Shrew*). Our multi-modal approach resulted from a collaborative design process that involved a variety of community members and resources, providing a model for how other institutions of higher education might benefit from adopting a pedagogy rooted in communal exchange.

Description

Interdisciplinary collaboration was essential to 'Dividing the Kingdoms' from the start, guiding both the initial selection of the faculty and staff involved as well as the conception of the project itself. Although Wayne State's academic divisions generally operate in isolation, the multi-disciplinary steering committee for the First Folio project generated robust programming about Shakespeare that demonstrated the value of collaboration across departments, colleges and other units. Intending to replicate this experience, I convened a core team representing stakeholders across the university (English, Film, Libraries, Office for Teaching and Learning, and Theatre).[2] At a brainstorming meeting, the interdisciplinary nature of this group quickly led to a productive discussion of the ways we approached Shakespeare. While each team member had succeeded in teaching Shakespeare through one particular methodology, we realized that these different lenses could complement one another by offering divergent perspectives. Making interdisciplinarity one of the guiding principles of our enterprise, we agreed to create a digital resource for college instructors that showcased a variety of methods for reading one play at the undergraduate level.

King Lear seemed a natural choice for our central text, sufficiently complex to repay scrutiny through multiple modalities. Furthermore, the Wayne State Libraries and Detroit Public Library owned relevant texts that we could digitize, allowing us to incorporate the digital humanities into our resource and to extend the institutional collaboration of the First Folio project. We also decided to align this new endeavour with the university's mission by involving graduate and undergraduate students in the creation of our website and by including a service-learning component that would benefit K-12 students in the Detroit area. While our immediate goal was to enhance Shakespeare instruction at Wayne State, we believed that bespoke pedagogical materials featuring Detroit's rich cultural resources would contribute to broader conversations about best practices in college-level instruction of Shakespeare.

'Dividing the Kingdoms' thus began as five modules illustrating different ways to teach *Lear*: Adaptation, which covers medium specificity and the process of adaptation; Cultural Studies, which discusses gender roles and disability; Performance, which introduces scansion and operative words; Philosophy, which examines the concepts of certainty and selfhood; and Text, which compares the Quarto and Folio.[3] Each module is a capsule unit that can be taught on its own or combined with other modules from the site. All five of these modules feature lesson plans for three or four in-class activities, which undergraduate instructors can use or adapt. For assessment purposes, the modules contain two assignments (a traditional paper and a more creative assignment) for out-of-class work that ask students to practise skills introduced during the in-class activities. A service-learning activity then enables students to share insights from the module with local middle or high schoolers. These five core modules are accompanied by a three-minute video clip of the creator introducing key concepts in engaging, jargon-free terms intended to appeal to undergraduates. A series of complementary exercises involving the digitized texts ultimately became a sixth module on Digital Humanities, consisting of a bibliographical assignment and four in-class activities on topics such as annotation, data mining and data visualization.[4]

The site provides a wealth of supplemental material in support of these modules. The Wayne State Libraries digitized early printings of the play (the 1608 Quarto and the Detroit Public Library's copy of the 1685 Fourth Folio), Shakespeare's sources (*The True Chronicle History of Leir*, 1605;

Raphael Holinshed's *Chronicles of England*, 1587; Philip Sidney's *Arcadia*, 1593; and Edmund Spenser's *Faerie Queene*, 1611 edition) and Nahum Tate's 1681 adaptation of the play (1736 edition). The Performance module contains a series of videos shot at Wayne State with well-known Chicago actor Larry Yando, who had recently performed as Lear. Yando discusses the challenges of Shakespearean acting, and coaches Wayne State Theatre students as they realize an emotionally grounded performance of selected lines from the play. 'Dividing the Kingdoms' also features examples of student work produced when we piloted selected assignments from the modules in several classes during winter 2017. Finally, sample syllabi show how one or more modules can be incorporated into the survey of British literature to 1700 as well as introductory and advanced Shakespeare courses.

Each of the five main modules also features a secondary module entitled 'Going beyond *Lear*', which demonstrates how that methodology could be applied to another Shakespearean play. Created by Wayne State graduate students and revised by me, the supplementary modules are complete units in their own right, each consisting of three to four in-class exercises, two out-of-class assignments and a service-learning activity. These additional materials offer fresh takes on the five core methodologies: Adaptation and *1 Henry IV*, which covers art, film and Shakespeare's sources; Cultural Studies and *Othello*, which focuses on early modern race, racialization and material culture; Performance and *The Taming of the Shrew*, which considers non-verbal communication, costume and gender performativity; Philosophy and *Hamlet*, which introduces students to stoicism and explores the concepts of human nature and universal truth; and Text and *Romeo and Juliet*, which discusses paratexts, stage directions and textual differences.[5] In essence, each methodology now contains two modules: one for *Lear* and one for a second play. When utilized in a course with the *Lear*-centred modules, these additional exercises offer students the opportunity to investigate a particular methodology more deeply, while also giving professors the option to create methods-based syllabi that go beyond *Lear*.

Student learning

During the development phase of the project, we formed a number of partnerships that allowed students to join faculty as they sought to fulfil the first plank of Wayne State's mission statement by 'creat[ing] and advanc[ing] knowledge'. As we began initial work on the site's pedagogical materials, we convened a focus group of four top undergraduates majoring in relevant disciplines: Education, English and Film. Hand-picked by individual faculty team members for both their outstanding intellects and their academic career aspirations, these students enrolled in a one-credit directed study during autumn 2016. The course was led by a doctoral student in English as part of a separate directed study at the graduate level that focused on

Shakespearean pedagogy. Over the first five weeks the focus group read the play, discussing one act per week. The students then spent three weeks taking field trips to see Shakespearean artwork at the Detroit Institute of Arts, physical copies of texts digitized for the project at the Detroit Public Library and Wayne State's Special Collections, and Wayne State's digitization lab. The final five weeks of the semester were devoted to working through the site's core methodologies, one week at a time. The faculty member responsible for developing that module visited the focus group to lead a discussion about their approach, sharing relevant articles and draft exercises with them. In these conversations and a final reflective paper, the students provided vital assistance as we developed materials for our modules. Our team members had rarely discussed pedagogy with undergraduate students before, and these discussions not only supplied immediate feedback on specific activities but also allowed us to identify aspects of the methodologies that were especially confusing or exciting for our student population.

Other pedagogical materials resulted from student partnerships that combined professional development with an even deeper immersion in faculty research. During winter 2017, I undertook another directed study with Sarah Noble, a Vocal Music Education major and a member of the focus group who produced the service-learning assignments accompanying the *Lear* modules. In developing these 60-minute lesson plans for K-12 students, Noble kept in mind the many non-Education majors who would utilize the materials, which meant avoiding jargon and including questions the presenter should ask, the thought process they should guide their audience through and even possible answers that children might give. One of the challenges of this process was creating a stand-alone plan that included opportunities for small-group and full-group discussion as well as activities or group projects with kinaesthetic, social and visual elements. For example, the service-learning exercise for the Philosophy unit draws on the module's discussion of selfhood by introducing students to a philosophical consideration of schoolyard stereotypes. While Noble worked toward her own career goals by generating these materials, her engagement with the faculty research behind these modules also provided a basis for the university's outreach to the local community. As a result, Noble's development of the service-learning activities facilitated Wayne State's broader mission in multiple ways, both 'creat[ing] and advanc[ing] knowledge' while also aiming to 'positively impact local [. . .] communities'.

After the *Lear* micro-grant concluded, I extended the collaborative model of 'Dividing the Kingdoms' by asking MA and PhD students in English to generate new material for the 'Going beyond *Lear*' modules. This assignment was the final project in an experimental graduate course on Shakespeare and teaching (ENG 7015) which initially focused on pedagogical approaches to five of Shakespeare's most frequently taught plays: *Hamlet, 1 Henry IV, Othello, Romeo and Juliet* and *Taming of the Shrew*. After analysing the

Modern Language Association's *Approaches* volumes on these plays, the class read *Lear* and scholarship related to each of the five major critical lenses while also familiarizing themselves with the exercises from 'Dividing the Kingdoms'. The students then worked in groups to create their own modules for the plays read earlier in the semester, basing their activities and assignments on Shakespearean pedagogy and scholarship. In the process, students were able to examine the relationship between criticism and pedagogy while they explored their own pedagogical styles. As Kelly Plante, Connor Newton and Sean Renkert commented in the reflective paper that accompanied their module on *Hamlet* and Philosophy, 'the process of constructing this philosophical module allowed us, as creators, to critically consider the play anew, as well as to better prepare ourselves for our own pedagogical practices'. Finally, I revised the modules to bring them in line with the site's original content and to enhance their pedagogical effectiveness. This partnership with our graduate students facilitated their professional development as teachers even as it provided an unusual means of deepening their engagement with Shakespeare and critical theory.

At the same time, the creation of 'Dividing the Kingdoms' generated opportunities for students outside of Education and English to engage with faculty research while gaining professional and technical knowledge. For example, the Wayne State Libraries hired a student worker to digitize the texts for our site, allowing the student to hone the expertise necessary for their eventual career as a digitization technician. Working around twenty-five hours a week, the student scanned the books at high resolution and processed the images through the ABBYY software programme, which converts scanned pages to text and ultimately produces versions of it in PDF, HTML, ALTOXML and TXT. This output was then checked by hand for errors, a labour-intensive process due to the lack of fixed spelling and the idiosyncrasies of early modern print (such as the long 's'). We also employed two undergraduate students from Communication as our camera operators and editors for the site's video content. In addition to producing the video introductions to the core modules, these students filmed ten videos featuring Yando and Wayne State students. Meanwhile, two undergraduate students from Music composed a theme song that would accompany the title and closing credits for all the site's videos. In line with the university's mission to prepare students 'to thrive', the students from Communication and Music benefited professionally as they practised key skills for their intended careers (video production and scoring) and reflected on how to support the research at the heart of our project.

Once we finished the development phase, the team's members began to pilot aspects of 'Dividing the Kingdoms' in their classrooms in order to refine the site's pedagogical materials and to serve the university's mission of teaching excellence. This stage of the project was informed by a third and final principle: to enhance student learning. As we state on the website, the learning objectives for 'Dividing the Kingdoms' are:

1 to demonstrate in-depth knowledge of Shakespeare's plays;
2 to develop an understanding of the six theoretical lenses used in the six modules;
3 to analyse performances, printed texts and/or digital editions of Shakespeare in relation to one or more theoretical lenses from the modules;
4 to articulate similarities and differences between the theoretical lenses used in the modules;
5 to identify the relevance of Shakespeare's work to modern culture and share that knowledge with the local community.

To begin, we tested out one or two learning objectives at a time. Simone Chess fulfilled the second and third learning objectives in her section of our Shakespeare class for non-majors (ENG 2200) by pairing each of the five initial modules with one of the play's acts. Meanwhile, we assessed the third learning objective more rigorously in two ways. First, Simone Chess and I combined our sections of ENG 2200 and ENG 3110 (English Literature to 1700) for a team-taught session on the Text module, taking advantage of the fact that our syllabi had one overlapping day on *Lear*. In this 80-minute session, we tested all of the module's exercises in a compressed format. Because opportunities for team-teaching are limited at Wayne State, this was a particularly exciting aspect of the project, allowing us to bring the faculty collaborations behind 'Dividing the Kingdoms' into the classroom. Second, I assigned one of the papers from the Text module to my students in ENG 3110, asking the class to create mini-editions of twenty lines from Act 1, Scene 1. In a reflective essay on her experiences in ENG 3110 that semester, Amal Shukr noted that this assignment heightened her engagement with *Lear* by illustrating editorial agency: 'Creating my own mini-edition also taught me that choosing to gloss certain words and not others, and choosing to provide a footnote for certain phrases and not others, tremendously impacts the way a reader interprets what is written, and considerably influences analysis'. Finally, four Honours students from ENG 3110 (including Noble) successfully completed a trial run of its service-learning exercise at a local middle school, demonstrating that the Text module met the fifth learning objective.

The next step of the pilot phase involved testing the site's resources as a whole in order to determine whether they would enrich student learning in courses based exclusively on 'Dividing the Kingdoms'. I designed a special section of our introductory Shakespeare course (ENG 2200) that centred on *King Lear*. Taken primarily by non-majors, this course fulfilled a new General Education requirement at Wayne State, namely Critical Inquiry, which aims to teach students 'how scholars think in different disciplines' and asks students 'to engage in inquiry themselves, using diverse disciplinary methodologies to ask questions, analyse data, and make their own evidence-based arguments'.[6]

Aligning closely with the interdisciplinary ethos of 'Dividing the Kingdoms', a Critical Inquiry course was an ideal testing ground for the site's materials. The initial five sessions of the class were devoted to discussion of the play, meeting the first learning objective. Students read one act for each class, which allowed them to hone their close-reading skills and gain familiarity with the basics of characterization, plot and theme within the play. They spent the following six weeks exploring the methodologies of 'Dividing the Kingdoms' in the following sequence: digital humanities, performance, text, cultural studies, adaptation and philosophy. During class, I tested out the exercises developed by each faculty member, tailoring them to an introductory audience. Students also completed two assignments each week. A short homework exercise allowed them to practise skills from the methodology and served as a basis for a three-page traditional paper. I also offered several out-of-class activities to enhance student learning. In addition to screening a western adaptation of *Lear* (*King of Texas*, 2002), I arranged field trips to local institutions (the Detroit Institute of Arts, the Detroit Public Library and the Wayne State Special Collections). These activities fulfilled the project's second, third and fifth learning objectives.

For the rest of the semester, students worked in groups on two final projects that allowed them to delve into one of the methodologies covered in the course, thereby achieving the second and fifth learning objectives in new ways. I divided the class into five groups, one for each approach, and these teams produced a final project of five to eight pages based on a non-traditional assignment from 'Dividing the Kingdoms'. The Cultural Studies team composed a ballad about Lear, while the Text group edited a scene from the play. The Adaptation group transformed *Lear* into a fairy tale, and the Philosophy team used Shakespeare's play and its sources to write a version of the Lear story that explored philosophical concepts such as selfhood. Finally, the Performance group acted out a scene and produced a reflective paper about their experiences. At the same time, these groups prepared to visit a local middle school where they completed service-learning activities related to their assigned methodologies. For example, the Performance group taught sixth graders to scan poetry, while the Cultural Studies team introduced eighth graders to high and low culture through the genres of the tragedy and ballad. The semester concluded with group presentations summarizing what students learned through these final assignments. Each student also turned in a portfolio of their papers from the semester, capped by a reflective essay about the class. The portfolio and reflective paper provided one last chance for students to fulfil all of the site's learning objectives by capturing the sum total of their experiences in the course.

The experiential nature of the materials from 'Dividing the Kingdoms' fostered in-class community. Some students were apprehensive about reading a single play for the whole semester, but the reflective papers demonstrated that they enjoyed seeing the play through different lenses and felt many prior concerns about reading Shakespeare fall away. As Natalie Harshman observed in her reflective paper, 'thinking about the play from multiple angles helped me to better understand the content of the play itself as well as [be] able to better relate it to the real world and my own life'. Through the process of reading and rereading *Lear* over the semester, students also developed a tight bond with one another, which I facilitated by running the course as a Learning Community (at Wayne State, a Learning Community creates an enhanced classroom experience based on shared intellectual inquiry). Learning Community funding allowed me to hold special extracurricular events, such as meals with the class after or during field trips. More typical of a liberal arts college than a research university, these events helped me develop a personal connection with students that enhanced in-class interactions.

I also used the Learning Community budget to employ Amal Shukr as a peer mentor. In many ways, this Shakespeare class was more difficult than General Education courses in literature at Wayne State, which usually focus less on writing and more on reading representative literary works. While students only read one play over the entire semester, they produced five short papers (fifteen pages) as well as a group paper (five to eight pages). Shukr kept office hours to help students with the reading and their papers, and she attended class sessions to assist with final projects and service-learning assignments. As Scout Riddle noted in her reflective paper, she appreciated the resulting classroom dynamic: 'The classroom was a great learning environment and you were never alone. Not only did I have my Professor, but I also had my classmates and a Peer Mentor that I could email or talk to in class. Everyone worked as a large group with each other, so everyone would be on the same page and no one would be left behind'. While the 'Dividing the Kingdoms' team did not explicitly aim to create community, our pedagogical approach resulted in a unique learning experience that encouraged intellectual fellowship and thereby succeeded in enhancing student learning.

In winter 2019, I piloted the material from 'Going beyond *Lear*' in my section of ENG 5150 (Shakespeare), an advanced class for English majors. The five core methodologies of 'Dividing the Kingdoms' were as much the subject matter of this experimental course as Shakespeare himself. On the first day of the semester, I used Sonnet 130 as a showcase for reading Shakespeare through the lenses of adaptation, cultural studies, performance, philosophy and text. Students then spent six sessions on *King Lear*, which introduced these frameworks in more detail through condensed versions of the modules I had developed for ENG 2200. At the end of this unit, students produced a short paper that required independent primary research into *Lear*'s metre, editions, sources or adaptations. For example, students who were interested in the Performance module wrote a paper that analysed their scansion of thirty lines from the play as well as how those lines were performed in filmed versions available on YouTube. The class then explored each methodology more intensively by testing the modules from 'Going beyond *Lear*'. In addition to working through revised versions of the exercises produced in ENG 7015, students read criticism exemplifying that approach in order to gain a better understanding of the theories behind these in-class activities. A second short paper on a methodology of their choice helped students strengthen their engagement with a particular approach. As in ENG 2200, students felt that they benefited from exposure to different methodologies. Jalen Erickson commented in her reflective paper that:

> the most important takeaway from this class for me is that all of these approaches can be used to look at not only Shakespeare's works, but other works of art and literature. By not simply looking at texts from exclusively a historical or contextual perspective, we can better understand their complexity and reflect on their work as cultural pieces.

This in-class work met the first, second and third learning objectives of 'Dividing the Kingdoms' even as it enriched student learning by allowing students to broaden their knowledge of Shakespeare and learn transferable skills.

At the end of the semester, students spent two weeks working in teams to prepare final projects and service-learning assignments based on the 'Going beyond *Lear*' modules, thereby fulfilling the project's fifth learning objective. In doing so, students heightened their own knowledge of one particular play, and they found that these assignments required a deeper engagement with the material than did traditional forms of assessment. As Hamad Ali observed, 'To test our knowledge of Shakespeare, we taught younger students through a collaborative project, which is more engaging than an exam'. At the same time, these projects helped students realize Shakespeare's contemporary relevance. Inspired by the service-learning activity in ENG 5150, Paige Bottorff expressed interest in finding more opportunities to interact with the community: 'I hope to be able to spread awareness of how vital Shakespearean works can be, not only within an English major's education but also with just how much they can impact the community'. Through these final exercises, students reinforced their own newfound knowledge on the topic, learned about its broader significance and enjoyed an enriched classroom experience.

The only learning objective that went unmet in either class was the fourth: to 'articulate similarities and differences between the theoretical lenses used in the modules'. No single assignment asked students to compare and contrast the different lenses, although the final presentations and reflective papers implicitly offered a basis for this sort of reflection. If desired, the final reflective papers could be modified to include an analytical comparison of two or more methodologies.

Application

The website for this project (https://guides.lib.wayne.edu/folgerkinglear) contains a number of 'useable' pedagogical components. The videos may be directly assigned to an undergraduate audience or screened within the classroom to introduce a module or illustrate the fundamentals of performance. Each module has a variety of lesson plans and assignments that instructors can adapt according to their particular student population and learning objectives. Likewise, a series of syllabi offers concrete plans for incorporating these modules into courses of different kinds and levels. The digitized texts can be used by instructors in the classroom or by students on their own as part of the assignments offered elsewhere in 'Dividing the Kingdoms'. The Analysis button offers access to digital humanities tools such as annotation, data mining and data visualization. The Mirador reader permits side-by-side comparison of texts (an especially useful feature for the Text module), while the BookReader option allows text-searching and clipping of images. Finally, users can download a PDF of the text for offline reading.

Notes

1 Wayne State University, 'Our Mission', https://wayne.edu/about/mission.
2 The initial team members were Judith Arnold, Tom Aulino, Simone Chess, Matt Ouellette, Chera Kee and Ken Jackson.
3 These modules were created by the following faculty members: Chera Kee (Adaptation), Cultural Studies (Simone Chess), Performance (Tom Aulino), Philosophy (Ken Jackson) and Text (Jaime Goodrich).
4 The Digital Humanities module was created by Judith Arnold.
5 These modules were created by the following teams of graduate students in the English Department at Wayne State and then revised by Jaime Goodrich: Erika Carbonara, Carolyn Hall and Matthew Jewell (Adaptation); DeAnna Miller, Diane Washington and Megan Webster (Cultural Studies); Sarah Chapman, Lynn Losh and Lindsay Ragle-Miller (Performance); Connor Newton, Kelly Plante and Sean Renkert (Philosophy); Livingston Garland and Joseph Martinez (Text).
6 Wayne State University, 'Group Requirements (Inquiry Courses)', https://bulletins.wayne.edu/undergraduate/general-information/general-education/group-requirements/.

PART FIVE

Teaching in Web 3.0

14

Mapping the Global Absent in Shakespeare

Lessons Learned from a Student–Faculty Collaboration

John S. Garrison, with Ahon Gooptu

Overview

This collaboration between a faculty member and an undergraduate student led to the creation of a digital mapping tool ((https://absentshakespeare.sites.grinnell.edu/) which renders visible 'absent' figures, places and objects in Shakespeare's plays (e.g., the Indian boy in *A Midsummer Night's Dream*; Antonio's ships bound for the Indies, Mexico, England and Tripoli in *The Merchant of Venice*; the university in Wittenberg in *Hamlet*). By tracing such elements, the map aims to not only provide students with a lens through which to close-read texts but also help them understand how much of the *action* on stage relies on playgoers' imaginations to fill in what is not overtly shown or dramatized. The tool pinpoints elements of their (sometimes shifting) geographic locations in relation to the action of the play and provides textual references to these elements. Inspired by scholarship on the global imagination of Renaissance writers, the map serves as a model project not only for those courses focusing on Shakespeare but also for those exploring the history and culture of the globalizing early modern world.[1]

Although we describe below the map's functionality and potential uses, we primarily focus on our collaborative process and what we learned from it, articulating lessons that can inform efforts within different types of institutions or campuses, classrooms and partnerships. We outline the project's growth from one student's personal interest and early research questions in an introductory course.² We then describe the leadership role that the student assumed during the project development, how he built partnerships across campus and how the tool was subsequently utilized in the classroom.

The effort involved an undergraduate project leader, who designed the user flow and determined the technology solution with input from faculty and staff as well as fellow students. Indeed, our core idea came from the student's own experience as an international student from Kolkata, India. Ahon Gooptu (co-author of this chapter and student lead for this project) brought a unique perspective on how Shakespeare is taught in a global context and what a non-Western reader might notice is missing from the text. Throughout the work, he integrated his prior knowledge of interpreting Shakespeare's work for academic and theatrical purposes, both in India and the United States.

We had three overall goals for the digital tool. We wanted it to be interactive, so that users would actively engage with it rather than passively receive content. We wanted the tool to be visual in such a way as to differ from viewing a text, and we felt that a world map (especially with its nod to Shakespeare's 'Globe') would provide this new way of looking at the playwright's corpus. Finally, we wanted the tool to not simply deliver information but also model a mode of analysis that could apply more broadly to any literary study.

Description

Several key principles guided our design process, all of which we would try to duplicate in future endeavours. As noted above, the project stemmed from a student discovery, which both empowered him to take ownership of the digital work and suggested that the tool would appeal to other undergraduates. We also learned to rely on collaboration across the organization for desired expertise and resources. Finally, we strived to stay open to serendipity, as surprise discoveries both improved the final product and added a sense of joy to the project overall.

The appeal of the absent

Ahon initially became interested in absent elements within Shakespeare's work when reading *King Lear*. He noted the figure of the absent mother, who goes largely unmentioned in the play yet still seems to exert force upon the narrative. This interest led him to write a paper for Dr Garrison's 'Introduction to Shakespeare' course, in which he traced people, places or objects unseen on stage yet still influencing plays' plots and thus playing a part of the action.

Ahon found a particularly intriguing example in the Indian, or 'changeling', boy in *A Midsummer Night's Dream* (2.1.23). Titania and Oberon feud over this boy, who is mentioned repeatedly in the play but has no speaking part and is not listed among the characters. However, as Madhavi Menon observes, 'the boy's present yet non-materialized body performs a crucial theatrical function' (2013: 330).[3] At times, the dialogue implies the boy to be present on stage and productions have variously reacted to the question of how or if to depict him in any way. Ahon noted Emma Rice's Bollywood-inspired *A Midsummer Night's Dream* produced at London's Globe Theatre in 2016.[4] That production evocatively stages the boy as a puppet in traditional Indian dress and infuses the performance itself with Bollywood-like elements such as song and dance.

This early inquiry sparked Ahon's larger interest in how the absent-present boy echoed early modern fascination with India and other points east in a speech where Titania invokes the rich sensorium ('spicèd Indian air') and goods ('trifles') that, through trade with the east, were becoming known to Shakespeare and his audiences (2.1.128, 138). We also hear the means by which these elements were reaching England's shores ('embarkèd traders', 'a voyage, rich with merchandise'; 2.1.131, 139). Examples such as these in Ahon's paper struck both of us that tracing absent-present elements would expand understandings of not only *where* the plays took place but also show the breadth of Shakespeare's global imagination. It also made us acutely aware of how 'absent-presence' might describe a reading practice. That is, the more we discussed what we individually noticed as missing or where we found ourselves filling in the blanks, the more we became aware of the individual perspectives we bring to texts. In turn, we wanted to find a way to leverage the potential of absent-presence as a category that might help students become more aware of their own processes as readers and viewers of plays.

An interactive map seemed the natural tool to employ for displaying the locations or origins of such elements. And the first step in the project would be to seek institutional support for both financial resources and technical knowledge.

Institutional and other support

It is important to note at the outset that many readers will not have access to the types of resources that drove this project. As we are all too painfully aware, we all operate in an era when colleges and universities, especially the humanities departments within those institutions, are asked to do more with less. While some resources described below have significant monetary cost (as some digital humanities projects do), many do not. Thus, we describe the resources here with a twofold goal: to allow readers to think about how they might scale their project based on available resources and also to think about equivalent resources at their institution that might be tapped.

Ahon's work was supported during the summer of 2018 by a Mellon-funded partnership between the University of Iowa and Grinnell College and then later through an internal programme called Vivero, which trains under-represented students in the possibilities of the digital liberal arts and, in turn, hires these undergraduates as 'consultants' to help faculty with projects. Ahon had previously taken an introductory course in the digital humanities, which offered him a foundation in destructuring text, organizing information, and data visualization. He still, however, had limited experience with technology and with the knowledge to go about such an ambitious project without mentorship and guidance. Thus, he incorporated the help of a dedicated librarian at Grinnell who specializes in digital humanities. He also worked with representatives from Grinnell's Digital Liberal Arts Collaboratory to understand user interface design and with our Data Analysis and Social Inquiry Lab to think about options for mining data.

Imagining our users

Before formally assessing possible technologies, we developed what we thought at the time to be likely 'user scenarios'. These short vignettes imagined possible users of the tool and pictured situations in which they might encounter it. The goal was to help us think about what level of expertise users might possess and how the tool might serve multiple ends. We imagined people in various stages of life, each with a different background and occupation, to cast a wide net of possible users who might employ our mapping tool for their respective scholarly, pedagogical, theatrical or recreational purposes. We tried to make them as concrete as possible, giving each of them names and a particular moment when they might encounter the tool. These user scenarios would ultimately prove aspirational, as the initial launch of the tool would target students in particular classes on our campus. Still, this ideation helped us to imagine a broad, often more advanced, user base in order to challenge ourselves to see the tool for what it might grow into and to ensure that our basic architecture could support such future uses. Here are three, abbreviated examples:

- Noah, twenty-six, is pursuing a PhD in English at the University of Iowa and intends to explore the role of family in Shakespeare. Our tool presents Noah with an overview of missing parents in Shakespeare's plays and provides him a database-of-sorts as a starting point.
- Rajiv, thirty-eight, is a globetrotter interested in traveling to places of interest in and around Italy. When he visits Italy, he uses our tool to trace the routes and locations of some of these missing elements, which allows him to visualize Shakespeare's characters playing out their respective stories before his eyes.

- Aisha, fifty-one, is writing a play in which many of Shakespeare's characters come together from their respective plays with their own set of problems. However, she struggles to find avenues/reasons to bring them together. Our tool gives Aisha opportunities to decide when these characters may go off their destined path and end up in the premise of her play.

Ultimately, in the first phase of the project, these scenarios proved beyond our scope as we narrowed our attention to those with whom we had front-line access: students at our home campus. However, each of these scenarios, we realized later, embodies the type of lifelong reader, researcher or theatregoer whom we hope English classes will inspire.

Choosing the platform

The initial aim of our project was to use digital mapping software to display elements that play crucial roles in Shakespeare's plots but do not appear on stage. With limited experience in different mapping software, we met with the Humanities and Digital Scholarship Librarian at Grinnell College who pointed us towards sample projects across various fields. We distilled from those examples a shortlist of possible tools to utilize. Because specific applications and platforms (especially free ones) come and go, we list these to give a sense of the range of options that we faced. We quickly realized that the largest differentiator was functionality, and we decided to prioritize ranking the tools based on that before addressing issues of price or steepness of developer learning curve. The mapping software options are listed below in increasing order of our preferred functionality.

- Google MyMaps: an easily customizable feature under Google Maps, on which users can add points and shapes, along with notes and images for sharing information regarding various locations on a map. It is free, as long as you have a Google account.
- Leaflet: uses open source JavaScript library to custom-build mapping applications. It is slick but requires a prior knowledge of coding. The online tutorials are very helpful and can be used for self-teaching.
- Carto: a strong platform for engaging with spatial data or for visualizing data analysis. A subscription needs to be purchased after the fourteen-day free trial.
- Neatline: a 'geotemporal exhibit-builder' that uses Omeka, a free open-source web-publishing platform, to narrate stories or histories through maps and timelines. A host of demos and samples are available for users to peruse and sample.
- Tableau: similar to Carto with regard to functionality, it is powerful software for spatial data representation and data visualization, requiring a subscription plan after the fourteen-day free trial.

- QGIS: possesses the combined functionalities of Neatline and Carto/Tableau.
- ArcGIS: a more specialized and customizable version of QGIS, which does not rely on any open-source library. Both the online and desktop versions (the latter is only available to Windows devices, not to Mac) require a purchased subscription after a twenty-one-day free trial.

Matching the function to the users' needs

With the user scenarios in mind, we took the next logical step familiar to those who have worked in software development by articulating a 'functional specification'. This consisted of a bullet-pointed list of the desired functionalities (e.g., search by play, see a map of present vs. absent elements in a particular play). It also addressed which modality (e.g., drop down menu, search field) might work best for each functionality. We then assessed each of the technologies using these criteria:

- Integrating an early modern map.
- Evaluating the user interface and customizability to filter users' search for absent elements.
- Displaying textual information for each element, preferably along with a pictorial representation of it.
- Including a time feature to depict the chronology of plays.
- Offering easy editing/updating data, as needed.

Additionally, we placed higher value on those platforms for which a prerequisite knowledge of coding was not essential for a developer or end-user to interact smoothly with the software. We also took into account which software programmes were free to use and which ones the college subscribed to for development purposes. A basic requirement was that any user could use the tool on the front-end. Ahon had used Carto for mapping text and data in his digital humanities class, but the focus of our project was not on representing spatial data or visualizing data. Thus, neither Carto nor Tableau seemed to be the right fit. MyMaps allowed us to share textual information along with pictures, but the filtering did not support how we envisioned students searching for information.

We wanted our users to be able to categorize their searches in ways familiar to them in other digital environs. For example, if a customer were looking for men's jeans on the Amazon website, they would be able to filter their search in the men's department with clothing, type of garment, brand, size and colour. We wanted our user looking for absent fathers in Shakespeare's comedies, for example, to detail their search in a similar manner and then view the results (see Figure 14.1).

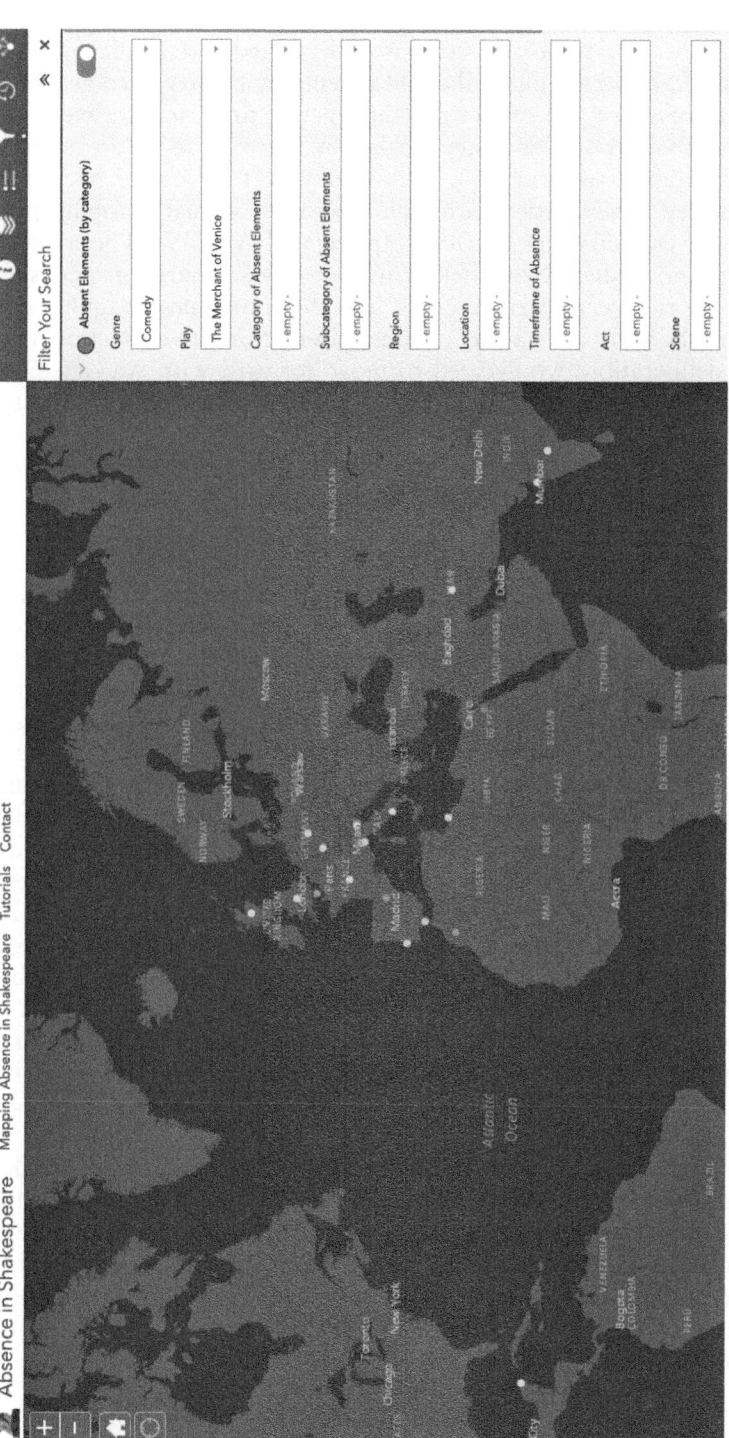

FIGURE 14.1 *Filtering a search for absent elements in* The Merchant of Venice *on the mapping tool. Each dot on the map represents a different element. Different colours represent different categories of absent elements: persons, places, objects and other.*

After studying some projects that were created with Leaflet and Neatline, we realized our mapping tool could potentially be presented as a history or timeline of plays, essentially playing up the 'time' feature we wanted to include. QGIS took this a step further by allowing us to do so with maps and geographic information, a crucial aspect of our desired tool. We experienced serendipity in stumbling across a virtual mapping project, a StoryMap created using ArcGIS. Mapping with ArcGIS did not require prior coding knowledge. Nonetheless it demanded hours of persistence to overcome the steep learning curve into the sometimes-opaque vocabulary used by the software and its at-times counter-intuitive functionality. After much deliberation, we decided to move forward with ArcGIS due to the potential it held in very specific customization on the creators' part, which would in turn enhance the user experience.

Ahon used small datasets of just three or four absent elements to conduct initial trial runs. This was his first time dealing with ArcGIS and he subsequently experienced several failed trials until he adjusted the representation of the raw CSV (Comma Separated Values) file. A key breakthrough regarding visual presentation occurred in Chicago, where we studied rare materials at the Newberry Library. Ahon looked at maps of England and Europe from the sixteenth and seventeenth centuries, which were helpful in understanding the level of cartographical knowledge people in England had at that time. Nonetheless, we concluded that using a map from Shakespeare's time as our interface would not be the best idea, considering the illegibility of the names of the locations depicted. During the research trip, Ahon continued compiling his list of elements that represented the global absent. We met weekly to assemble and to fact-check the data set.

While we hoped the map would help students understand Shakespeare's global imagination and consider the implications of absent elements, our goal was not to present students with a massive archive of secondary research on those topics. The primary users of the tool, we quickly began to see, were first-year students with a mix of majors and those with a general interest in Shakespeare. While we might introduce a key article or two at some point alongside an assignment using the map, our goal was to stimulate student reading and viewing practices rather than to use the tool as an entry point into an extensive research project.

By July 2018, a sizeable portion of data had been collected and the focus shifted primarily to the mapping. Dr Katherine Walden, the Digital Liberal Arts Specialist at Grinnell College who had substantial experience working in ArcGIS, became a primary point of contact regarding navigating and overcoming major obstacles on the mapping software. She would become a co-lead on the project, and her assistance reassured us that our goals could be realized using ArcGIS:

- Using a time slider feature to display 'absent' elements in relationship to the chronology of Shakespeare's plays.

- Using a customizable filter feature that would allow users to select absent elements by different categories (e.g., genre, play, categories and subcategories of absent elements, location).
- Providing media representations of the absent elements, either in the form of seventeenth-century maps or in images of people, places, events or objects closely related to the element.

After several weeks, we completed the first phase of our project – mapping absent elements from twelve of Shakespeare's plays, including the six that Dr Garrison would be teaching in his autumn 2018 courses. This version of the map included the informational pop-ups for every pinpoint, embedded with a media representation and link to the original source page, the filter feature and the time slider. Furthermore, all the primary locations for each of these plays were also mapped under a different set. For example, for *The Merchant of Venice*, Venice is mapped as the central site of action in the play. We also mapped the fictional Belmont by drawing on suggestive hints in Shakespeare's text itself. In our narrative description of the map on the website that houses it, we describe our process of estimation and make clear that at times locations reflect what an audience might imagine based on described directions or travel time.[5] This framing website also contains a link to the map, basic information about the overall project, and additional resources, both textual and digital.

As of the writing of this chapter, the tool is publicly available and is being used in both 100-level and 300-level courses on Shakespeare. It also serves as a model project for collaborative development involving faculty, staff and a student. Dr Walden, currently a co-PI of the Vivero Digital Scholarship Fellows programme, is a core member of the project and remains accessible to us. The next phase of the project will involve expanding the references inventoried in the tool and including more multimedia, including links to excerpts from recent adaptations of the plays.

Student learning

This project enabled two levels of student learning. On one level, Ahon received an in-depth experience in which he gained increased knowledge of Shakespeare, new skills in technical project management, professional skills in cross-campus networking and exposure to a range of scholars at a major conference. On another level, students on our campus utilized the tool to stimulate new thinking and new writing about Shakespeare's plays while also gaining the sense that they contributed to the tool's development.

All of Ahon's experiences during the project constitute important student learning as he developed project management skills and knowledge of technology. At the same time, his role was to ensure that the tool would be of use to a wide range of students. In an attempt to facilitate the user experience, Ahon scripted and narrated a series of video tutorials to guide a first-time user through the mapping tool. These tutorials are short and concise yet very detailed, thus catering to the demographic that is not well versed with technology or is unfamiliar with the digital humanities.

As an initial test of the usefulness of the tool, students in Dr Garrison's 'Introduction to Shakespeare' course were asked to experiment with the digital map – guided by the video tutorials – and to write short essays that considered the implications of an absent element in one of the plays. While we knew that the tool would be used in classrooms on campus, these users were not the aspirational ones described in the user scenarios above. One of the lessons learned concerned our anticipation that a variety of users would discover and use our digital resource towards diverse ends. However, our most obvious audience was right in front of us, and we could offer them a guided experience of the map. Thus these twenty students (of different class years and majors) became one of the project's first focus groups, providing fresh eyes on the tool and offering valuable feedback as representatives of what we were now beginning to see as the map's primary target audience: Grinnell's own students.

The feedback would afford an opportunity to reflect on the usability of the map, especially its offerings, display functionalities and instructions. While some requests made sense for an individual user but did not take into account technical feasibility, others were incredibly helpful: for example, having more specific regions to filter with (e.g., the Middle East, Southern Europe, North Africa) instead of whole continents, zooming in on the locations of the results after filtering a search, and making it clearer that one should watch the video tutorials if unsure how to navigate the map or use specific features. We helped users understand that some choices for the tool were governed by the needs of users with low vision or another disability. For instance, students suggested that dramatic colour coding be used throughout the site, which would automatically create challenges for the colour-blind.

After implementing some of the student feedback, we had the opportunity to share our work with different audiences on the college campus: students in an upper-level Shakespeare seminar, who suggested we include information about how contemporary adaptations of the plays have handled the inventoried absent elements; people interested in the digital humanities at the college's annual Technology Fair; and a larger audience, non-specific to either Shakespeare or the digital humanities, at the annual Student Research Symposium. These helped us condense the project's core mission to focus primarily on student users on our home campus and promote the need for investigating the global through digital methods.

By April 2019, the data had been updated from just twelve to thirty plays, comprising all the tragedies and comedies (inclusive of the 'problem plays'), with *King John* as the only history play. Unfortunately, the spreadsheet with the remaining data for the history plays was accidentally deleted and could not be retrieved in time for our presentation at the Digital Exhibits session as part of that year's Shakespeare Association of America (SAA) conference. Sharing the work with Shakespeare enthusiasts there was perhaps the climax of our project. This was Ahon's first time at a conference and provided him with unrivalled exposure to professional networking with Shakespeare scholars from around the world. In fact, a faculty member from a major R1 university approached him about partnering so that participants in a graduate seminar in the digital humanities might contribute their efforts towards completing the data for the remaining plays.

Application

Having successfully launched and utilized this digital tool (https://absentshakespeare.sites.grinnell.edu/) in pedagogical environments, we offer these lessons learned that might be adopted by readers.

Be flexible

Do not be discouraged if your organization does not have access to a particular piece of software. Be open to working with different platforms. Consider looking for partners at local colleges and universities that may have digital learning specialists who might be of assistance. A modest version of your envisioned project can garner additional collaborators or funding resources, either from within your campus or an external source, such as an NEH grant.

Consider multiple focus groups

Different users will have different needs. Those needs will change over time and as the digital tool evolves. For our project, we received feedback about the tool from third- and fourth-year undergraduates involved in a summer research team, a class populated by mostly first- and second-year students, and graduate students and faculty attending the SAA conference. Crucial to this user testing was that we did not do it all at once. We improved the tool iteratively, responding to one group's feedback before soliciting more reactions. As we had come to realize that our original user scenarios were aspirational in nature, it was helpful to hear from real-life scholars about whether they would use the map in their teaching or in their research.

Maximize student involvement

Involving a student on the development team offers a variety of payoffs, not the least of which is a collaborator with a different point of view. The student receives valuable work experience and obtains a marketable app or URL that can be shown to potential employers. The inclusion of a student and focus on students as end-users can open doors to increased funding across campus and can excite partners from different units on campus, while simultaneously serving the needs of the faculty member's research. Our project went beyond benefitting just one student, as we included other students in focus groups whose feedback shaped successive versions of the digital tool.

Promote, promote, promote

Faculty and staff may have the best of intentions, but do not always want to consider a new tool when existing habits or tools work just fine. Accept invitations whenever feasible to share the work and seek out opportunities to present both at local and broader venues. Many academic conferences welcome presentations that showcase digital projects rather than a traditional scholarly paper.

Work across the organization

Rarely, if ever, will a needed resource be solely located in one department. To design, launch and sustain your project, your allies may be other students, information technology specialists or librarians. Know that there will be no 'one-stop shop' for solutions. Key partners will change as the project moves from idea to reality.

Notes

1 While the map is driven by the categories *absent* and *global*, our goal was to highlight new ways of reading and visualizing Shakespeare's texts rather than to introduce students to the broad body of scholarship on these categories. Nonetheless, our own thinking about the global category was informed by C. H. Parker (2010), A. Gerritsen and G. Riello (2015), A. Dickson (2015) and A. Ramachandran (2015). Our thinking about the category of absence was informed by theoretical considerations such as Jacques Derrida's thinking about hauntology. We were also inspired by fruitful studies of the absent figure such as those by C. Kahn (1986) and S. Orgel (1986). While works such as these did not play a role in the use of the digital tool in the 'Introduction to Shakespeare' course, they did offer starting points for students writing seminar papers in the upper-level course.

2 The fact that one of us is a Shakespeare scholar and one of us is an undergraduate student – and that neither of us brought significant technological skills – would limit the project in terms of shared and needed expertise. At the same time, these limitations strengthened the project, as we approached its

development from a position many of its student users would occupy: that of newcomers to the content or novices in the use of interactive mapping.
3 Menon's essay instantiates an enduring interest in this particular figure. See, for example, the earlier discussion of the figure in the final chapter of S. Raman (2002).
4 The production can be viewed online via the Globe Player at https://globeplayer.tv/videos/a-midsummer-night-s-dream-english-2016.
5 A future iteration of the map might allow users to add new absent elements or suggest alternative locations for ones we have mapped based on evidence in the text. While this is not in our immediate plans for the tool, we see this as very much in the spirit of our focus on encouraging new reading practices.

References

Dickson, A. (2015), *Worlds Elsewhere: Journeys Around Shakespeare's Globe*, London: Bodley Head.
Gerritsen, A. and G. Riello, eds (2015), *The Global Lives of Things: The Material Culture of Connections in the Early Modern World*, New York: Routledge.
Kahn, C. (1986), 'The Absent Mother in King Lear', in M. W. Ferguson, M. Quilligan and N. J. Vickers (eds), *Rewriting the Renaissance: The Discourses of Sexual Difference in Early Modern Europe*, 33–49, Chicago: University of Chicago Press.
Menon, M. (2013), 'Desire', in H. S. Turner (ed.), *Early Modern Theatricality*, 327–45, Oxford: Oxford University Press.
Orgel, S. (1986), 'Prospero's Wife', in M. W. Ferguson, M. Quilligan and N. J. Vickers (eds), *Rewriting the Renaissance: The Discourses of Sexual Difference in Early Modern Europe*, 50–64, Chicago: University of Chicago Press.
Parker, C. H. (2010), *Global Interactions in the Early Modern Age, 1400–1800*, London: Cambridge University Press.
Ramachandran, A. (2015), *The Worldmakers: Global Imagining in Early Modern Europe*, Chicago: University of Chicago Press.
Raman, S. (2002), *Framing 'India': The Colonial Imaginary in Early Modern Culture*, Palo Alto, CA: Stanford University Press.
Shakespeare, W. ([1600] 2004), *A Midsummer Night's Dream*, eds. B. Mowat and P. Werstine, New York: Simon and Schuster.

15

Shakespeare Reloaded's *Shakeserendipity* Game

Pedagogy at the Edge of Chaos

Liam E. Semler

Overview

Shakeserendipity is a gamified, blended-learning approach to the teaching of Shakespearean drama. Its three online modules focus on *Julius Caesar*, *The Tempest* and *Richard III*, because these plays are widely taught within the Australian high-school English curriculum and the project is based in Sydney. Each module uses a digital flipcard mechanism to present the user with a diverse array of resources as prompts for face-to-face discussion of the plays. The resources are open-access content reached through hyperlinks which are activated by clicking on digital playing cards. As the name suggests, *Shakeserendipity* explicitly builds serendipity into the learning process by facilitating students' open-ended exploration of unexpected resources and ideas in the Shakespeare classroom. I have argued elsewhere that this constitutes an example of an educational 'ardenspace', which is to say, a temporary and refreshing educational space characterized by a high degree of experiential (and indeed experimental) innovation (Semler 2016). Students find the activity engaging not just because flipping digital playing cards can be fun (especially in class), but also because many of the resources bring contemporary issues to bear on Shakespeare's plays. As an 'ardenspace', *Shakeserendipity* does not pursue specific, content-focused learning outcomes, but rather creates a context of exploratory thinking and discussion in which students interrogate, connect and synthesize ideas, experience meta-learning and build complex arguments about the plays. *Shakeserendipity* can, therefore, help make Shakespeare pedagogy more relevant and engaging for students while also extending their higher order cognition skills.

At the start of the game the user is presented with the backs of nine playing cards: seven are identical in appearance and two have labels (one labelled 'Wild Card', the other 'Tame Card'; see Figure 15.1). When a card's back is clicked it 'flips over' to reveal a short, tantalizing title for the resource (for example, from the *Richard III* game, 'The Remains of Richard' and 'Horrible Olivier Mashup'), an indicator of its medium ('video', 'image' or 'text') and the link to 'Access this item'. Up to four cards may be flipped in any one session and the player may email the web addresses of the content to a personal email address for later viewing or reviewing. The content 'behind' the cards shuffles each time the page is refreshed so the player does not know which resource lies behind which card until it is flipped by clicking. The exception is that the resources behind the Wild Card and Tame Card do not change. For each Shakespeare play, the Tame Card will connect through to a resource that is straightforwardly connected to the play (such as an extract from the playtext itself), while the Wild Card will have a more cryptic relevance (for instance, *Richard III*'s Wild Card is a pop-science essay exploring whether a spider's web may be considered part of its mind). The other cards lead to an array of articles, videos and images that have direct, yet various, bearing on the play.

The three-stage core of the game amounts to the selection of cards to flip (which can be a fun classroom activity conducted via voting, in groups or individually), the engagement with the resources behind the cards (which is done individually by participants outside class time) and the discussion of ideas arising in response to the resources (which is managed collaboratively within a later class). Extension activities, creative work, learning tasks and assessable assignments can be developed easily on this foundation based on whatever resources or ideas students find most interesting.

Although *Shakeserendipity* has proven effective in the classroom, it was not initially designed for student use. It was in fact created to facilitate professional learning workshops that treat English teachers as mature professionals seeking collaborative participation in content-rich and open-ended discussions of the texts they teach. The impetus was the project team's awareness that teachers were yearning for more time with each other to share and grow their expertise, because such professional co-development opportunities had been limited in New South Wales by the need to service an overly crowded curriculum, prepare senior students for a high-stakes final examination system, and respond to burdensome tasks imposed by an overly compliance-based management system. These structural constraints that simultaneously drive and hobble teachers and students are part of a sector-wide condition of managerialism and performativity that blends objectives-based learning models with managerial audit cultures and is underwritten by a neoliberal privileging of market economies.[1] Getting the balance right between imposed structures and allowed freedoms is, of course, a challenging task, whether one is thinking of the curriculum, pedagogy or staff management, and success varies from jurisdiction to jurisdiction around the world. In New South Wales, teachers widely reported a perfect storm of structural constraints which I have described elsewhere as 'SysEd' (Semler 2016), a pejorative moniker designed to highlight the over-systematization of the sector which is having a negative impact on teacher effectiveness, wellbeing and retention, and on student learning.[2]

Shakeserendipity was well received by teachers because it spoke directly to their desire for more liberated and inspiring professional experiences not tied to managerialist outcomes. This can be seen in the anonymous feedback provided by teachers who participated in the pilot of *Shakeserendipity*. One teacher wrote that *Shakeserendipity* was a 'wonderful opportunity to discuss fantastic resources and contemplate in new ways how they can connect with the stodgy parameters of the curriculum'. A similar, yet fuller, response was this: 'It does open up ways of thinking – creates a sense to trust student responses more and follow unusual directions. It also gives a chance to dream how education could be better if there was more room, more time and more freedom'.[3]

Although *Shakeserendipity* was created for and piloted by teachers, they immediately brought it back to their high-school classrooms where they used it to facilitate deep and divergent discussions of the plays with their students. One teacher took it into her Year 11 English class which was being observed by teachers from other schools. She found that the 'kids lapped it up and learned lots' and the 'visiting teachers loved it too and said they'd do the same lesson tomorrow'.[4] The novelty of the online game structure combines with the intellectual challenge of open-ended exploration of unexpected content to deliver a refreshing teaching and learning experience for both teachers and students. One would not use the game every day in class, but it certainly offers a revitalizing break from normal business or overly driven educational processes. The online mechanism is simple to use and the Wild and Tame Cards give an additional range of possibility for the facilitator or teacher when running the game.

Description

Shakeserendipity was designed and created by Better Strangers, a collaborative educational research project involving academics from three Australian universities and teachers from our partner high school Barker College in Sydney.[5] The project commenced in 2008 and launched its open-access website, Shakespeare Reloaded (shakespearereloaded.edu.au), in

2014. Since 2013, among various other project activities, the Better Strangers team has been running an annual professional learning event called the 'Imaginarium'. This is basically a shell workshop structure within which the project team can trial innovative professional learning ideas each year. It takes the form of a series of two-hour workshops that are run in the evenings over two to four weeks during the school year. It is a free series hosted by Barker College and attended by teachers from there and other schools in Sydney. In 2013 it commenced with the 'Shakespeare Imaginarium' that paired the study of some plays with the exploration of specific educational ideas (such as *Hamlet* with educational potential and *The Tempest* with empathic learning). In 2015 *Shakeserendipity* was piloted as a series of three two-hour workshops attended by nineteen teachers from eight schools.

When the 'Imaginarium' structure was launched in 2013 the team created a set of principles to guide its approach to these annual workshop series. The principles are (1) to stimulate fresh thinking about subject content *and* pedagogy; (2) to be aware of professional constraints such as set curricula, but not to foreground them; (3) to include teachers from differing institutions to maximize the freshness of ideas; (4) to have a theme and some structure, but to be actively open to novelty; and (5) to value imagination and creativity highly, but remain aware of the complicating role of systemic structures. *Shakeserendipity* was designed according to these principles and piloted as a series of face-to-face workshops supported primarily by hard-copy handouts of resources. It was only after the success of the pilot in 2015 that the activity was translated to digital format on the Shakespeare Reloaded website in 2016. This development trajectory illustrates how the pedagogical concept was created and successfully piloted in a purely face-to-face mode, yet as the Better Strangers project began developing its new website the team reconsidered how best to share our innovations globally via the internet. Thus, as the team became more comfortable with the possibilities of online pedagogy, the activity morphed into its current, and richer, blended-learning form.

Shakeserendipity is not about creating educational chaos: it is underpinned by a coherent theoretical paradigm known as complexity theory. The Better Strangers project has from its inception been inspired by complexity theory, which accounts for the way novel structures and insights may arise from systems that have enough positive feedback or energy within them to move their internal routines from relatively inert or predictable processes to far more dynamic states of interactivity, approaching (but not fully plunging into) chaos. Complexity theorists refer to this fertile system-state by various terms including 'the edge of chaos', and cite examples in disparate fields of how genuinely new paradigms may emerge from systems experiencing such high, but not crippling, levels of disequilibrium (Waldrop 1992/1993: 222–35, 292–9; and Stacey, Griffin and Shaw 2000/2006: 146–50). The breakthrough phenomenon whereby new paradigms, structures and insights appear in complex systems is called 'emergence'.

There is a large and growing body of work exploring the theoretical and practical implications of complexity theory for education.[6] The Better Strangers project has been exploring how emergence might be imagined as an alternative and more fertile methodology to the often heavy-handed implementation of 'constructive alignment' and predetermined 'outcomes' within formal learning systems. In other words, educational scenarios – including a mix of teachers, students, subject content and much else – are thought of as complex systems that have the potential to generate extraordinary forms of learning if they are pushed out of their comfort zone and into 'the edge of chaos', which is conceptualized not as a mere boundary line *between* order and disorder, but as an invigorating domain partaking of both order *and* disorder. The key point about this, whether one is thinking about student learning or teacher training, is that the new insights that emerge are not predetermined outcomes or the result of a single guiding force, but are genuinely novel and unpredicted insights produced by the local interactivity of the entities comprising the complex system.

Shakeserendipity is an educational game designed to operationalize 'the edge of chaos' in the classroom by setting aside transmission-style forms of instruction and pursuit of intended learning outcomes. Instead, it ramps up the unpredictability in the classroom by putting into play diverse, yet equally valid, participant responses to an uneven array of unexpected resources. Rather than transmitting the 'right' information about the Shakespearean play in a unidirectional way from teacher to student, the game promotes the turbulent circulation of disparate ideas and the 'watchful anticipation' (Seel 2006: 7) by all participants of the emergence of novel insights and approaches. While this loosens up rigid or content-focused educational expectations, it delivers on an array of higher-order, transferrable learning goals relating to conceptualizing, critiquing, synthesizing and arguing.

The project team sought to put into practice the possibilities of pedagogy at 'the edge of chaos' during both stages (non-digital and blended) of the development of *Shakeserendipity*. This is exemplified by the workshop on *Richard III*. The team randomly sorted the registered participants into five equal groups and assigned each group two resources with which all its members had to engage. Only five resources in total were required for the workshop because every resource was used in two groups, yet no two groups had the same pair of resources. Each group had a unique pairing of resources, but they knew that their two resources were being considered separately by two other groups. The following table from the *Richard III Shakeserendipity* workshop pilot (2015) tabulates the structure.

Group 1	Group 2	Group 3	Group 4	Group 5
Resource 1 The real body of King Richard	**Resource 2** Teaching *Richard III*	**Resource 3** Disabled, deformed, dismodern	**Resource 4** Props and relics	**Resource 5** *Richard III* on film
Richard III: The New Evidence. Documentary about a young British man with scoliosis.	Martine van Elk, '"Determined to prove a Villain": Criticism, Pedagogy, and *Richard III*', *College Literature* 34.4 (2007): 1–21.	Katharine Schaap Williams, 'Enabling Richard: The Rhetoric of Disability in *Richard III*', *Disability Studies Quarterly* 29:4 (2009).	Philip Schwyzer, 'Trophies, Traces, Relics, and Props: The Untimely Objects of *Richard III*', *Shakespeare Quarterly* 63.3 (2012): 297–327.	Various *House of Cards* clips (US version) on YouTube.
Resource 2 Teaching *Richard III*	**Resource 3** Disabled, deformed, dismodern	**Resource 4** Props and relics	**Resource 5** *Richard III* on film	**Resource 1** The real body of King Richard
Martine van Elk, '"Determined to prove a Villain": Criticism, Pedagogy, and *Richard III*', *College Literature* 34.4 (2007): 1–21.	Katharine Schaap Williams, 'Enabling Richard: The Rhetoric of Disability in *Richard III*', *Disability Studies Quarterly* 29:4 (2009).	Philip Schwyzer, 'Trophies, Traces, Relics, and Props: The Untimely Objects of *Richard III*', *Shakespeare Quarterly* 63.3 (2012): 297–327.	Various *House of Cards* clips (US version) on YouTube.	*Richard III: The New Evidence.* Documentary about a young British man with scoliosis.

This is a 'flipped classroom' model because each participant engages with their group's two provided resources before the workshop. They must individually consider how each of their resources provokes fresh thinking about teaching *Richard III*, and they must give some thought to conceptually colliding or blending ideas from the two resources to see what novel hybrids might emerge in their understanding of the play. Each participant then brings their ideas to the workshop where they share their responses with their cohort before the group shares its freshest ideas with the entire workshop. At that point, the person running the workshop facilitates the exchange of ideas between all the groups to see what other insights might emerge.

For example, Group 3 combined its two academic resources on 'disability studies' and 'props and relics' to come up with some adventurous thinking regarding Richard's social capital and challenges, as well as classroom dynamics in respect of students with special needs or special claims of all kinds. The group explored how ability and disability were variously perceived in classroom contexts and in the play. They considered how objects, tools and rhetorics were used as props and relics in *Richard III* and by teachers and students (with or without visible disabilities). In the classroom, certain things and behaviours (wheelchairs, mobile phones, talkativeness or silence, teacher stasis or mobility, hard-copy handouts of texts) were considered to function as props or relics with special powers to affect the educational dynamics.

In contrast, Group 4 juxtaposed the academic 'props and relics' article with clips from the popular US television series *House of Cards* and came up with new definitions of what constitute the props and relics of modern political power. These very words, 'props' and 'relics', raised nuanced ideas about inherited power structures (rituals, legacies, families, traditions, hegemonies) and current power dynamics (entrepreneurship, social capital, marketing, messaging) of governance.[7]

The group structure meant there was a mixture of knowledge throughout the workshop: all participants knew two resources, but not the other three. Consequently, when it came to sharing ideas with the whole workshop there was a degree of intellectual focus and agility required (as participants heard about resources they had not encountered) alongside elements of common knowledge to help moderate the cognitive load. Since all resources collided conceptually with two other resources, there was great potential for each resource to spark fresh ideas among diverse groups. The Better Strangers team found that this arrangement genuinely actualized 'the edge of chaos' as a pedagogical experience and delivered a high degree of engagement and discovery for participants.

The team had three objectives in translating *Shakeserendipity* to an online format: (1) to ensure that all the resources were open-access on reliable websites (the non-digital pilot had used some subscriber-only content in hard-copy form); (2) to preserve the focus on serendipitous learning (in a context where the team could no longer manually sort participants into groups with carefully controlled resources to explore); and (3) to start exploring the possibilities of the gamification of learning, feeling that building a digital version of *Shakeserendipity* was an ideal opportunity for this. The reasons for these objectives were, respectively, (1) to make sure the tool would work for anyone with internet access without unnecessary problems caused by paywalls and short-lived websites (thus promoting the value of open-access resources and avoiding laboursome attendance to broken weblinks); (2) to preserve the benefits of the insights of complexity theory especially in relation to operating at 'the edge of chaos'; and (3) to begin to learn, via practical experimentation, how gamified educational tools may or may not enrich engagement and learning.

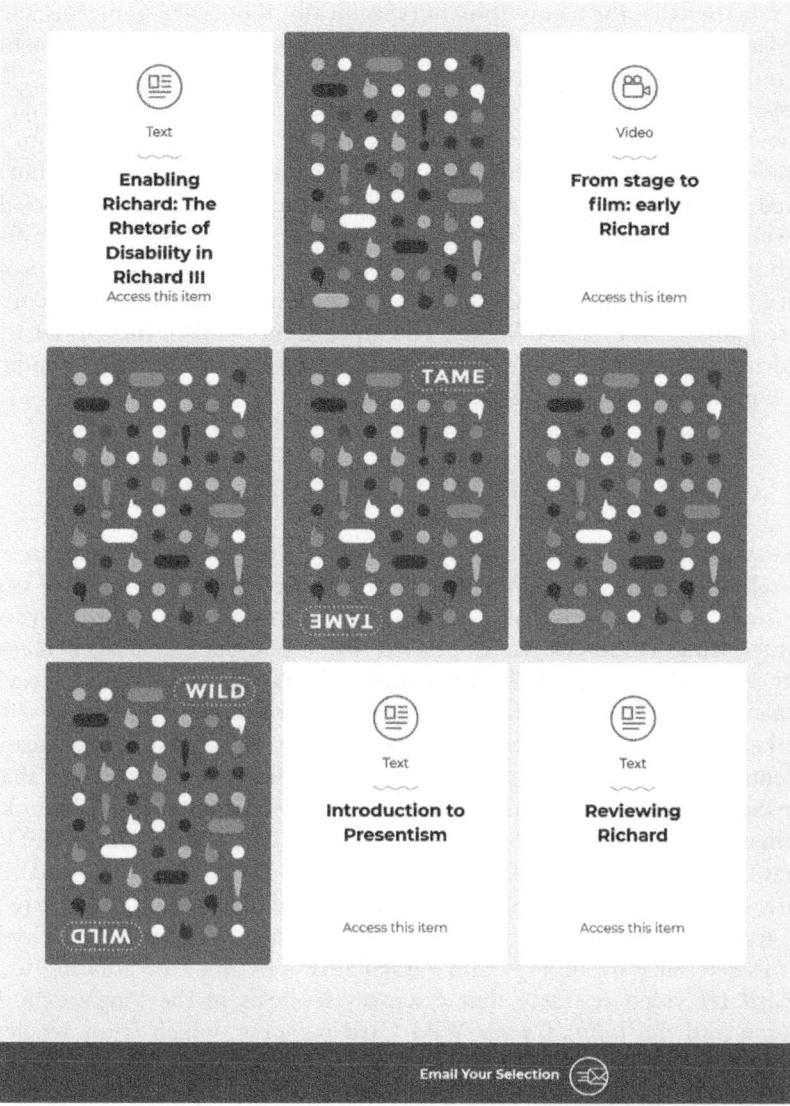

FIGURE 15.1 *Screenshot of* Shakeserendipity *online game page for* Richard III *with four flipped cards.*

The team set about assembling an array of suitable, open-access resources for each play and discussed what might be a simple game mechanic that would be able to deliver on the serendipity remit relatively autonomously. In discussion with the website development company Digital Garden (which had built the Shakespeare Reloaded site), we arrived at the idea of digital flipcards (see Figure 15.1).[8]

It was then that the team – thinking specifically about card-game mechanics – devised the idea of having Wild and Tame cards to add an extra element of fun and to widen the possibilities for variations in play and pedagogy. This process of ideating, developing and building a new educational activity for our website followed what has become a standard process for the team. The team devises a new idea, trials it in face-to-face workshops (often within the annual Imaginarium structure) at Barker College, then brings a proposal to the web development company for discussion of the possibilities in terms of functionality and design. Once the activity's structure is built, the project team can add or revise modules thanks to the technical skills of our members Claire Hansen and Lauren Weber. The flipcard mechanism turned out to be the ideal online actualization of the team's interest in gamification, serendipity and exploratory teaching and learning.

Student learning

Shakeserendipity has been used by high-school students, university students and school teachers in professional development workshops. In all cases, the simplicity and novelty of the flipcard game mechanism and the diversity of interesting resources were praised by the users. A sixteen-year-old South Australian student, Dylan Carpinelli, wrote an unsolicited review of the activity in an Australian newspaper for young people in 2016: '[Shakeserendipity] promotes thinking outside the square' and 'teaches students about Shakespeare in a more exciting way' (14). He added that it 'helps teach players about topics such as biology and surveillance by linking the themes with sections of Shakespeare's plays' (14). What is important here is that the game actually does not do the linking to that degree of specificity: it offers a resource to a user exploring a particular play, but leaves it to the user to make whatever connections they feel are interesting or valuable. Dylan's reference to 'biology and surveillance' (14) may be alluding to the *Richard III* video resource that discusses scoliosis in the king's exhumed skeleton and the *Julius Caesar* Wild Card resource, which is an article on surveillance in smart cities. It is interesting that he feels the game teaches both ways – about the Shakespearean play and about the topics addressed in the resources. His concluding paragraph is worth quoting in full:

> The game is a bit confusing to work out at first, and needs a few people to get it up and running. But it turns the learning experience into an enjoyable one that encourages interaction and discussion. We need more activities that are as interactive and innovative as this.
>
> 14

This is an illuminating response that confirms how the game works best in groups where it can facilitate enjoyable learning grounded in interactive discussion of ideas. It also implies that the game is probably not ideal for junior high-school students or entirely individual use: its value comes out powerfully when used by older high-school students working in groups led by a teacher and in professional learning workshops.

A superb example of *Shakeserendipity* in action is provided by Australian teacher Nathan Compton, who works at the Oatley Senior Campus of Georges River College in Sydney. Nathan used *Shakeserendipity* with his Year 12 English students in 2018. The students were doing a final-year module called 'Intertextual Perspectives' that required them to compare *Julius Caesar* and Machiavelli's *The Prince*. He reported that *Shakeserendipity* helped him boost the students' associative and comparative thinking, and deepen the sorts of arguments they might make about the play. He explains:

> In the module we analysed key scenes in *Julius Caesar* then played *Shakeserendipity*. Students needed to flip two cards, read and develop an argument which they would then share. They 'flipped' the cards in the lesson and read the articles for homework over the weekend. The next lesson, students wrote down the arguments on large A3 paper, and the rest of the lesson, students read each other's and added in supporting textual evidence and hypothetical links to *The Prince* which we would start soon after (they had read *The Prince*, but we had not explored it in great detail).[9]

Nathan explains that this individual and collaborative exercise helped his students develop more complex 'arguments' or theses about the play, more authoritative voices as critics and skills in connection-making:

> The need to create and find connections is an important skill, especially between texts and features that can seem disparate. *Shakeserendipity* helped develop this skill as students had to navigate and build a bridge between the concepts which we then transferred to the comparative analysis with *The Prince*. The students also needed to develop more conceptual arguments that went beyond simplistic 'themes.' The idea of finding a 'novel' argument helped some students develop a more confident voice.[10]

What is particularly notable about Nathan's account is that *Shakeserendipity* does not take over his teaching and reduce him to a supernumerary figure in the room. On the contrary, he uses his professional expertise and curiosity to integrate the game into his teaching of the curriculum. He leverages the affordances of the game in a learning task that blends digital and face-to-face activities, is authentically collaborative and exploratory, and successfully facilitates student acquisition of both content knowledge and disciplinary methods. SysEd has not held him back and his innovative teaching has given his students a vivid and positive experience that gels with the set curriculum.

In Nathan's hands, *Shakeserendipity* has achieved its aim of facilitating pedagogy at 'the edge of chaos'.

In sum, *Shakeserendipity* is a gamified digital interface that offers students and teachers a stimulating way to engage with evocative resources. It makes the relevance case for Shakespeare because most of the resources connect with modern ideas and consequently students can start their approach to Shakespeare from that familiar (if unexpected) territory. It also helps teachers who may not be tech-savvy to easily incorporate an engaging digital component into their teaching, boosting students' capacities in thinking, collaboration and argumentation. Finally, it values teacher expertise and autonomy by leaving game activities and additional learning or assessment tasks up to the teacher.

Application

Shakeserendipity is an open-access, blended-learning module that is available on the Shakespeare Reloaded website (shakespearereloaded.edu.au). The website includes information on the pilot of the game and how to play the online version. *Shakeserendipity* is put in a broader theoretical context in my open-access article 'Prosperous Teaching and the Thing of Darkness' (2016).

Notes

1 See, for example, S. J. Ball (2003), M. W. Apple (2005), R. Connell (2009), G. J. J. Biesta (2010) and S. C. Ward (2012).
2 For two vivid accounts of the problem in Australia, see G. Stroud (2018) and S. McGrath-Champ, R. Wilson, M. Stacey and S. Fitzgerald (2018).
3 Responses from the anonymous survey of teachers participating in the *Shakeserendipity* pilot in 2015.
4 Anonymous teacher's response in survey of pilot participants (2015).
5 The project team comprises Liam Semler (project lead), Penny Gay, Jackie Manuel and Lauren Weber (all associated with the University of Sydney); Will Christie and Kate Flaherty (both Australian National University); Claire Hansen (James Cook University); and school lead Andrew Hood (Head of English, Barker College).
6 On 'the edge of chaos' and 'emergence' in education, see P. Tosey (2006/2007: 29–42), B. Davis and D. Sumara (2006), W. Doll Jr, M. Jayne Fleener, D. Trueit and J. St. Julien (2005/2008) and K. Morrison (2002). See also *Complicity: An International Journal of Complexity and Education* (2020).
7 When *Shakeserendipity* was launched online in 2016 the *House of Cards* clips were used unproblematically as a resource. This was before allegations of sexual assault against the show's male lead Kevin Spacey emerged in 2017. The *House*

of Cards resource has been replaced by a new resource because the project team want teachers to feel confident that the *Shakeserendipity* resources will not be problematic in the classroom.

8 See https://www.digitalgarden.com.au/.
9 I quote personal email communication (with permission) on 11 February 2019.
10 Personal email communication (with permission) on 11 February 2019.

References

Apple, M. W. (2005), 'Education, Markets and an Audit Culture', *Critical Quarterly* 47: 11–29.
Ball, S. J. (2003), 'The Teacher's Soul and the Terrors of Performativity', *Journal of Education Policy* 18, no. 2: 215–28.
Biesta, G. J. J. (2000), *Good Education in an Age of Measurement: Ethics, Politics, Democracy*, Boulder, CO: Paradigm.
Carpinelli, D. (2016), 'The Ultimate Bard Game', *Crinkling News*, 3 May, 14.
Complicity: An International Journal of Complexity and Education, https://journals.library.ualberta.ca/complicity/index.php/complicity.
Connell, R. (2009), 'Good Teachers on Dangerous Ground: Towards a New View of Teacher Quality and Professionalism', *Critical Studies in Education* 50: 213–29.
Davis, B. and D. Sumara (2006), *Complexity and Education: Inquiries into Learning, Teaching and Research*, Mahwah, NJ: Lawrence Erlbaum Associates.
Doll Jr, W., M. Jayne Fleener, D. Trueit and J. St. Julien, eds (2005/2008), *Chaos, Complexity, Curriculum and Culture: A Conversation*, New York: Peter Lang.
McGrath-Champ, S., R. Wilson, M. Stacey and S. Fitzgerald (2018), *Understanding Work in Schools: The Foundation for Teaching and Learning*, University of Sydney and Curtin University: Report to the NSW Teachers Federation, https://news.nswtf.org.au/application/files/7315/3110/0204/Understanding-Work-In-Schools.pdf.
Morrison, K. (2002), *School Leadership and Complexity Theory*, London and New York: Routledge Falmer.
Seel, R. (2006), 'Emergence in Organisations', http://doingbetterthings.pbworks.com/f/RICHARD+SEEL+Emergence+in+Organisations.pdf.
Semler, L. E. (2016), 'Prosperous Teaching and the Thing of Darkness: Raising a *Tempest* in the Classroom', *Cogent Arts & Humanities* 3, no. 1: 1–10, https://doi.org/10.1080/23311983.2016.1235862.
Stacey, R. D., D. Griffin and P. Shaw (2000/2006), *Complexity and Management: Fad or Radical Challenge to Systems Thinking?*, London and New York: Routledge.
Stroud, G. (2018), *Teacher: One Woman's Struggle to Keep the Heart in Teaching*, Sydney: Allen and Unwin.
Tosey, P. (2006/2007), 'Interfering with the Interference: An Emergent Perspective on Creativity in Higher Education', in N. Jackson, M. Oliver, M. Shaw and

J. Wisdom (eds), *Developing Creativity in Higher Education: An Imaginative Curriculum*, 29–42, New York: Routledge.

Waldrop, M. Mitchell (1992/1993), *Complexity: The Emerging Science at the Edge of Order and Chaos*, New York: Touchstone.

Ward, S. C. (2012), *Neoliberalism and the Global Restructuring of Knowledge and Education*, New York: Routledge.

A Closing Note

Diana E. Henderson and Kyle Sebastian Vitale

For teachers and learners alike, we hope your journey through these chapters has been productive, inspiring you to try an application or two, or even to initiate a collaboration of your own. The collaborations we present and invite in these pages affirm that, as a field, we would benefit from more coordination among our tools and projects. In leaving these pages, our next steps might include not only sharing and adapting their insights but also exploring how we can embrace what Liam Semler calls 'serendipity' while building greater coordination amongst ourselves – the latter move not to please 'SysEd' but rather to use our finite energy and resources in as effective and satisfying a way as possible. We welcome our readers' thoughts and suggestions for how we might build on the great work represented here to move forward together, serving our students' needs as well as our own while keeping the field of Shakespeare studies vital through thoughtful attention to the diverse possibilities and meanings of digital pedagogy.

INDEX

African American(s) 80
  literature 52–4, 57
  Shakespearean performance 82, 85–6
African-Caribbean Shakespeare
    practitioners 78, 79, 80,
    81, 85–6
antiracism/antiracist 52–4, 58–9
Anzaldúa, Gloria 63–6, 73
ArcGIS 66, 67, 70, 72, 190, 192 (*see also* StoryMaps; vApps)
archive(s) 3, 4, 29, 83, 192
  pedagogical applications 31–3,
    99–101, 126–30
    preservation of class discussion
      109, 110
    student-created 7, 133–41
      project description 141–2
  performance 79, 89–99 (*see also*
    A|S|I|A; BBASPD; Global
    Shakespeares)
  visual art 120–6
  (*see also* database; EEBO; VISA)
Asian(s) 53, 57, 78, 87n2, 89, 134
  Shakespearean performance 79–87,
    90–96
    challenges in translation 91, 93
Asian Intercultural Digital Archives 94,
  102n5
Asian Shakespeare Intercultural
    Archive (A|S|I|A) 89–92
  description 92–9
  pedagogical application 99–101
asynchronous 25, 26, 27, 42, 153,
  159
Australia 3, 198, 200, 206, 207

Basecamp (platform) 107–12
  COVID-19, impact of 115–17
  sample course on *Henriad* 112–13
  sample course on *Hamlet* 113–14
  scaffolded essay assignment 118
Better Strangers project 200–2, 204
  (*see also* Imaginarium;
    Shakeserendipity;
    Shakespeare Reloaded)
Blackness 44, 51, 55, 56, 57
British Black and Asian Shakespeare
    Performance Database
    (BBASPD) 78–9
  description 79–81
  pedagogical applications 81–7

chaos 33, 55
  educational 201–5, 208
CoLab (platform) 25–7
  pedagogical applications 27–9
    EEBO exercise 30–3
    etymology exercise 29–30
    textual encoding 33–6
collaboration 1, 117, 155, 186, 208, 211
  across institutions 8, 39–40, 154
  interdisciplinary 80, 81, 92, 152,
    173–4, 178
  tools for 16, 67–8, 91, 116
  with/between students 14, 17,
    18–19, 68, 133–4, 185
    assessment 23, 139
Comedy of Errors, The 18, 140, 141–2
complexity theory 201–2, 204
computer 2, 34, 36, 42, 99, 135
  laptop 15
COVID-19 2, 26, 112, 115, 116, 117
critical digital pedagogy 52–3, 54, 58–9

data 6, 28, 69, 71, 86, 124, 178, 182,
    188, 189–90
  collection 13, 26, 133, 137, 174,
    192, 194–5

organization 18, 80–1, 83,
    A|S|I|A 90, 91, 92, 93, 94–100
database 4, 27, 29, 42, 90, 170, 188
    A|S|I|A 93–5
    BBASPD 78–87
    (*see also* archive)
Detroit (MI, USA) 173, 174, 176, 179
digital edition(s) 26, 27, 28, 29, 40,
    Folger Shakespeare Editions 14,
        150–1
    student-created 25, 29, 33–6, 178
        (*see also CoLab*)
digital facsimile(s) 39, 41, 42, 43, 44, 45
digital humanities 1, 15, 41, 133, 135,
        173
    classroom applications 29, 33, 154,
        179, 195
        assignments 159, 164, 165,
            169–71
        project description 71–6
    tools 26, 182, 190, 194
    institutional support for 40, 78,
        174, 187–8
Digital Scribes project 14, 16, 18–19
    assignment 21–3

Early English Books Online (EEBO)
        30–3, 35–6, 42, 43
England 3, 45, 67, 163, 169, 185, 187,
        192
etymology 27, 29–30, 31, 35, 42

Global Shakespeares 5, 89, 90, 91, 92
Global Shakespeares Projects (MIT)
        134, 136, 157n2
    Merchant of Venice module 147,
        148, 152, 154
Google Books 41
Google Docs 14, 16, 17, 42, 45

Hamlet 30, 72, 86, 107, 115, 136, 152,
        173, 176
    character 81, 83, 87n4, 166, 168
    pedagogical strategies for 31–4,
        113–14, 139, 141, 171,
        175
Henry V 20, 79
    Henry V (character) 86, 166, 168
    sample syllabus 112–13

hybrid teaching 3, 4, 15, 29, 159, 161,
        163–4, 203

Imaginarium 201, 206 (*see also* Better
        Strangers; Shakespeare
        Reloaded)
Instagram 56, 67, 164, 165, 170
intercultural(ity) 4, 39, 89–101
        (*see also* A|S|I|A)
intertextuality 29, 33, 39, 44, 207

K-12 (US) 173, 174, 176
keyword(ed) 26, 29, 33, 93, 94–5,
        123–4, 126, 140
    assignment 30–2, 35–6
King Lear 93, 165, 173, 174, 178–80,
        186
    Lear (character) 83, 166, 168

lecture 6, 7, 19, 41
    documentation of 14–5, 20
        assignment 21–3 (*see also*
            Digital Scribes Project)
    recorded 111, 161

Macbeth 31, 47n1, 79, 82–3
mapping 2, 94, 186
    tools 66, 72, 185, 188–93
metadata 92, 94, 124, 125, 140, 156
meme 14, 17, 20, 22
Merchant of Venice, The 27, 63, 65–7,
        185, 191, 193
    Global Shakespeares (MITx course)
        147–57
    syllabus 73–4
mestizaje 63–5
Midsummer Night's Dream, A 31,
        44, 79, 93, 125, 185,
        187
    assignment 98, 99
MITx 27, 147, 149, 150, 151, 153,
        156
Montemayor, Jorge de
    Siete libros de la Diana (1542) 40,
        43
    translation by Bartholomew
        Yong (1598) 41, 45
Multicultural Shakespeare Project 78,
        79, 80

National Theatre (UK) 82
note-taking 14, 15, 18, 19, 20, 21

open source 31, 64, 65, 69, 189–90
optical character recognition (OCR) 42, 45
Othello 79, 82–3, 173, 175, 176
   performance history exercise 85–7
Oxford English Dictionary (OED) 29, 30, 42, 164, 170

performance studies 29, 99, 126
   pedagogy 132, 152
phone 107, 169, 204
printing 41, 46, 122, 169, 174
   3D 64, 68
professional learning 199, 201, 206, 207

racism/racist 41, 43, 44, 56–8, 86
rhetoric 53, 107, 115, 133, 137, 204
Richard III 159, 162–3, 165
   game in *Shakeserendipity* 198, 199, 202–206
   Richard III (character) 160, 164
   sample study questions 166–70
Romeo and Juliet 44, 93, 97, 173, 175, 176–7
   Romeo (character) 83
   Romeo + Juliet (1995 film) 54
Royal Shakespeare Company (UK) 79, 82, 86

Shakeserendipity (online game) 198–208
Shakespeare Reloaded (website) 200–1, 205, 208 (*see also* Better Strangers; *Shakeserendipity*)
Shakespeare's Globe Theatre 82, 85, 186, 187
Singapore 3, 90, 93, 154
soliloquy 43, 160, 164
   classroom exercise 166–70
sonic color line 51–2, 53, 56
StoryMaps 66, 68, 69, 70–1, 72

tablet 15, 19, 169
Tempest, The 79, 125, 127, 141, 198, 201
   assignments 83–5
text encoding 3, 7, 26, 46
   Text Encoding Initiative (TEI) 29, 33–5, 42
textual editing 3, 7, 28–9, 30, 36
Titus Andronicus 55–6, 57, 63, 67
   assignments 166, 168
   syllabus 73–4
translation 5, 39, 45, 91, 96, 161, 164
   student activity 40–1, 43, 45–6 (*see also* Yong, Bartholomew)
transcription 28
   student activity 41–3, 45–6
Twelfth Night 17–18, 19, 25, 40
   assignments 84, 128
Twitter 21, 56
Two Gentlemen of Verona, The 40, 42–4, 47n3, 84

vApps 64, 67, 69–70
Venice 147–9, 151, 152, 154–5, 193
Victorian Illustrated Shakespeare Archive (VISA) 120–3
   description 123–6
   pedagogical applications 126–8
   lesson plan 128–30
Voyant (digital corpus linguistics tool) 52, 54, 60n5, 65–6, 69
   how to use 71–2
   Titus Andronicus assignment 55–6

whiteness 51, 53, 55, 57–8, 59
   as theatrical default 79, 81

Yong, Bartholomew (translator) 40–1, 43, 45
YouTube 5, 152
   classroom use 54, 56, 89, 180, 203
      Basecamp 114
      TouchCast 65
   performance medium 18, 133